Moral
Principles

BLOOMSBURY ETHICS SERIES

Bloomsbury Ethics is a series of books written to help students explore, engage with and master key topics in contemporary ethics and moral philosophy.

Autonomy, Andrew Sneddon
Intuitionism, David Kaspar
Moral Realism, Kevin DeLapp
Reasons, Eric Wiland
Virtue Ethics, Nafsika Athanassoulis
Ethics Without Intention, Ezio Di Nucci

Forthcoming in the series:

Climate Ethics, Sarah Kenehan
Moral Skepticism, Basil Smith
Moral Psychology, Jay R. Elliott
Trust, Ethics and Human Reason, Olli Lagerspetz
Value Theory, Francesco Orsi

Series Editors:

Thom Brooks is Reader in Law at Durham Law School. He is the founding editor of the *Journal of Moral Philosophy* and runs a popular Political Philosophy blog called The Brooks Blog.

Simon Kirchin is Senior Lecturer in Philosophy at the University of Kent, UK. He is President of the British Society for Ethical Theory and co-editor of *Arguing About Metaethics* (Routledge, 2006).

Moral Principles

MAIKE ALBERTZART

BLOOMSBURY

LONDON • NEW DELHI • NEW YORK • SYDNEY

Bloomsbury Academic

An imprint of Bloomsbury Publishing Plc

50 Bedford Square	1385 Broadway
London	New York
WC1B 3DP	NY 10018
UK	USA

www.bloomsbury.com

Bloomsbury is a registered trademark of Bloomsbury Publishing Plc

First published 2014

British Library Cataloguing-in-Publication Data
A catalogue record for this book is available from the British Library.

ISBN: HB: 978-1-4725-7420-6
PB: 978-1-4725-7419-0
ePDF: 978-1-4725-7421-3
ePub: 978-1-4725-7422-0

Library of Congress Cataloging-in-Publication Data
Albertzart, Maike.
Moral principles / Maike Albertzart.
pages cm.– (Bloomsbury ethics)
ISBN 978-1-4725-7419-0 (paperback)– ISBN 978-1-4725-7420-6 (hardback)– ISBN 978-1-4725-7422-0 (epub) 1. Ethics. I. Title.
BJ37.A36 2014
170–dc23
2014013102

Typeset by Fakenham Prepress Solutions, Fakenham, Norfolk NR21 8NN
Printed and bound in India

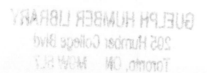

CONTENTS

ACKNOWLEDGEMENTS

This book started as a PhD thesis submitted to the University of Cambridge in 2010. I am deeply grateful to my supervisors Onora O'Neill and Hallvard Lillehammer for their constructive criticism, advice and support. I have been extremely fortunate to be supervised by them.

While the Cambridge Philosophy Faculty was the perfect place to start this project, the Humboldt-Universität zu Berlin offered me an ideal environment to finish it. Once again, I have been very fortunate with my colleagues and students. Special thanks are due to Kirsten Meyer for her encouragement to turn the thesis into a book.

In writing the book I have been helped by the comments of various people. I would like to thank in particular Simon Blackburn, Cristian Constantinescu, Mark Hanin, Philip Stratton-Lake and Christine Tiefensee. I am also very grateful to Thom Brooks and Simon Kirchin, the series editors of Bloomsbury Ethics.

Parts of Chapter One, 'The Current Particularism/Generalism Debate', are based on my article 'Missing the Target: Jonathan Dancy's Conception of a Principled Ethics' published in *The Journal of Value Inquiry* 45 (2011), pp. 49–58. Parts of Chapter Three, 'Moral Principles and the Activity of Judgement', draws on my article 'Principle-based Moral Judgement' published in *Ethical Theory and Moral Practice* 16 (2013), pp. 339–54. I would like to express my thanks to the Editorial Boards of these journals and to Springer for their permission to reproduce this material here.

Finally, I would like to thank my parents for their unconditional support and for teaching me, among many other important things, what it means to be a person of principle.

INTRODUCTION

The history of normative ethics has largely been a history of attempts to identify, articulate and defend moral principles which explain when and why certain actions, institutions and characters count as right or wrong, just or unjust, virtuous or vicious. From Plato to Epicureans and Stoics, from medieval natural law theorists to consequentialists like John Stuart Mill and deontologists like Immanuel Kant, moral and political philosophy has been dominated by principles. While moral and political philosophers have argued – and continue to argue – about which principles are the correct ones, there has been a tacit agreement that morality can and should be understood in terms of moral principles. Alan Donagan, for instance, defines morality as 'a system of laws or precepts'.[1] Bernard Gert even claims that trying to do moral philosophy without referring to moral rules or principles 'is to give up moral philosophy'.[2] And the idea that morality has to be understood in terms of principles is by no means an invention of moral philosophers. Rules and principles play a dominant role in all major religions as well as in our everyday life. Prominent examples are the Ten Commandments and the Golden Rule.

However, what justifies this predominance of moral principles? The fact that normative ethics is dominated by principled approaches itself is no proof that principles are indispensable or even useful for understanding morality. For a long time the assumption that morality can and should be understood in terms of principles has received no defence, at least no defence independent of the defence of particular moral theories. Why should – and how can – morality be principled? These are the two leading questions of this book. The aim of the book is to offer a defence of the importance of moral principles. In contrast to many traditional normative ethicists, I will be concerned with the nature and roles of moral principles, rather than their content. I wish to defend the importance of moral principles independently of the defence of any particular moral or political theory. The book works towards a general account of the nature and roles of moral principles in moral thought and action. By choosing this foundational or metaethical approach to the defence of moral principles, I do not mean to imply that traditional principled ethics is necessarily wrong or inadequate. Some first-order moral theories might turn out to have the resources that are needed to illuminate and defend moral principles. However, at least so far the proponents of these theories have not spent enough time on thinking about the nature and roles of moral principles. Moreover, I hope that approaching the question of how morality can, and why it should, be principled without any prior first-order theoretical commitments will make the following enquiry more flexible and open-minded.

Despite the hegemony of principles in moral and political philosophy, there have also always been critical voices. How can the complexity and diversity of moral and political life be captured in a finite set of principles? Is there not a danger that by focusing on general moral principles, we overlook the details of the particular situations with which we are confronted? Do principles and rules not prescribe uniform action where we need to distinguish between the particular needs of particular individuals? Some principled ethics can seem 'tyrannical and disproportioned'.[3] Is the good moral person not a person of empathy, sensibility, judgement and virtue, rather than a person of principle? There are numerous examples of cases where people have made bad and even disastrous moral decisions because they followed rules or principles blindly. The twentieth century's history is full of such cases. Rule-fetishism is not only responsible for a good deal of the frustrating inefficiency and inflexibility of bureaucratic institutions with which most of us are familiar. Many of the most horrible crimes of the twentieth century are the result of people blindly following the rules and commands they were given. In the *Dialectic of Enlightenment*, Max Horkheimer and Theodor W. Adorno go so far as to claim that philosophers' preoccupation with rules and principles, their quest for '[a] moral system, with axioms, corollaries, and iron logic, and reliable application to every moral dilemma',[4] prefigured the organized system of terror and mass murder of fascism. According to Adorno and Horkheimer, the 'architectonic structure of the Kantian system, like [...] the formalised principles of early bourgeois freemasonry, […] prefigures the organisation, devoid of any substantial goals, which was to encompass the whole life'.[5] Bearing in mind the history of the twentieth century, scepticism towards principles and rules is understandable, and to some extent even appropriate. Defenders of principled ethics have to show that rather than being an inevitable by-product of following principles, rule-fetishism is the result of the misuse and misunderstanding of moral principles. Defenders of principled ethics need to clarify the nature and roles of moral principles.

Over the last three decades, the scepticism and uneasiness about moral principles has grown into what is now a well-established position in moral philosophy. So-called moral particularists have forcefully argued against giving moral principles the prominence they have so long enjoyed. Particularists like Jonathan Dancy claim that 'morality can get along perfectly well without principles'.[6] According to David McNaughton, 'moral principles are at best useless, and at worst a hindrance, in trying to find out which is the right action'.[7] John McDowell claims that 'one knows what to do, if one does, not by applying universal principles, but by being a certain kind of person: one who sees situations in a certain distinctive way'.[8] For particularists the traditional link between morality and principles is little more than an unjustified prejudice. The rise of particularism has made the need to justify the importance of moral principles more pressing than ever. Particularism poses a serious challenge to the tradition of principle-based ethics.

However, defining the particularist challenge proves difficult. Doing so will be the task of the first chapter of this book. There are many different forms of, and arguments for, moral particularism. Some particularists deny that there are any true moral principles, while others claim that there are no good reasons to believe there are any, and again others argue that even if there were moral principles we ought not to rely on them. Arguments in favour of particularism emerge from diverse areas of philosophical enquiry including first-order moral theory, metaethics, theories of practical reasoning, and anti-theory.[9] I will focus on Dancy's version of moral particularism. Dancy not only presents a distinct and strong form of particularism, he is also the most prominent contemporary defender of the doctrine. His theory has dominated and shaped debates about particularism for over 20 years. But Dancy's theory is also highly problematic, and the current debate between moral particularists and so-called moral generalists notoriously obscure. I will identify the most serious problems and misunderstandings of the debate. Since the questions addressed in the debate are of great importance, sorting out its problems and misunderstandings is worth the struggle. I argue that, suitably rephrased, particularism poses a challenge that defenders of principled ethics should not ignore.

The second chapter of the book discusses three recent attempts to answer the particularist challenge: Sean McKeever and Michael Ridge's 'generalism as a regulative ideal', Pekka Väyrynen's theory of hedged moral principles, and Mark Lance and Margaret Little's theory of defeasible generalizations. This selection of authors needs justification. Why not discuss some better-known and influential utilitarian or Kantian accounts of moral principles? What distinguishes these recent authors from other defenders of principled ethics is their attempt to defend moral principles independently of any particular first-order moral theory. They set out to develop a defence of moral principles, but 'not a defence of any specific moral principle'.[10] This metaethical approach makes their theories especially interesting and worth discussing. While I share this metaethical approach, I do not agree with the proposed theories of moral principles. The purpose of the second chapter of the book is twofold. First, it provides a survey of the most recent attempts to fend off the particularists' attack. Secondly, the discussion of the problems of these current generalists will help to clarify the desiderata of a theory of moral principles. It thus prepares the ground for the third chapter of the book.

The third chapter answers the particularist challenge formulated in the first chapter of the book by offering an account of the nature and roles of moral principles. I will define moral principles in terms of what I take to be their two essential features and point out why moral principles so defined are necessary for moral thought and action.

Although this book will say little about the content of moral principles and remain relatively neutral with regard to first-order moral issues, the question of whether morality can and should be principle-based has important practical implications. If the predominance of moral principles in normative theory and our everyday life were to turn out to be no more than an unjustified prejudice in favour of principles, hospital ethics committees, for example, would have to reconsider seriously the methods by which they reach and justify their decisions. If the traditional predominance of moral principles were unjustifiable this would not only undermine most first-order moral theories, but also subvert large parts of our private and public moral discourse. In order to make sure that we are not mistaken to talk and reason in terms of – and act in accordance with – moral principles, it is crucial that we become clear about their nature and roles.

Notes

1 Alan Donagan, *The Theory of Morality* (Chicago: University of Chicago Press, 1977), p. 7.

2 Bernard Gert, *The Moral Rules. A New Rational Foundation For Morality* (New York: Harper & Row, 1973), p. 6. In this book I will not distinguish between moral principles and moral rules. For an author who draws such a distinction see, for example, Ronald Dworkin, *Taking Rights Seriously* (Cambridge, MA: Harvard University Press, 1977), pp. 22–31.

3 Stephen Toulmin, 'The tyranny of principles', *The Hasting Center Report* 11 (1981), pp. 31–9, p. 38.

4 Max Horkheimer and Theodor W. Adorno, *Dialectic of Enlightenment. Philosophical Fragments*, Gunzelin Schmid Noerr (ed.), trans. Edmund Jephcott (Stanford: Stanford University Press, 2002), p. 197.

5 Ibid., p. 69.

6 Jonathan Dancy, *Ethics Without Principles* (Oxford: Oxford University Press, 2004), p. 2.

7 David McNaughton, *Moral Vision. An Introduction to Ethics* (Oxford: Wiley-Blackwell, 1988), p. 190. McNaughton's view has considerably changed. See McNaughton, 'An unconnected heap of duties?', *The Philosophical Quarterly* 46 (1996), pp. 433–47; McNaughton and Piers Rawling, 'Unprincipled ethics', in Brad Hooker and Margaret Olivia Little (eds), *Moral Particularism* (Oxford: Oxford University Press, 2000), pp. 256–75.

8 John McDowell, 'Virtue and reason', in John McDowell, *Mind, Value, and Reality* (Cambridge, MA: Harvard University Press, 1998), pp. 50–73, p. 73.

9 For arguments from anti-theory see Annette Baier, 'Doing without moral theory?', in Annette Baier, *Postures of the Mind. Essays on Mind and Morals* (London: Taylor and Francis, 1985), pp. 228–45. For an argument based on a specific understanding of practical reasoning see Dancy, *Ethics Without Principles*, pp. 101–8, where he stresses that practical reasoning is non-inferential. I will say more about other types of arguments for particularism shortly.

10 Sean McKeever and Michael Ridge, *Principled Ethics. Generalism as a Regulative Ideal* (Oxford: Clarendon Press, 2006), p. 3.

CHAPTER ONE

Moral Particularism

From scepticism about moral principles to particularism

Moral particularism comes in various different forms and degrees. What unifies particularists is their scepticism about moral principles. They challenge the hegemony of principles in moral and political philosophy. The purpose of this first chapter is to understand and formulate the particularist challenge.

Particularists challenge traditional consequentialist and deontological theories. They distinguish themselves from other critics of traditional moral theories by their optimism. In contrast to moral sceptics or moral error theorists, particularists are sceptical about moral principles, but not about morality itself. Moral sceptics and error theorists will view the ongoing disagreements between, for example, Kantians and utilitarians as evidence for their claim that there are no nontrivial moral truths or knowledge to be found. They are pessimistic about the very possibility of normative ethics. Particularists offer a more optimistic analysis of the problems of traditional moral theories. According to particularists, it is the focus on principles that lies at the heart of these problems and which obscures moral knowledge. Particularists like Dancy argue that abandoning the link between morality and principles is the route to a defence of morality rather than an attack on it.[1] They purport to offer an alternative for those who are discontent with traditional, principle-based ethics, but who want to avoid the rather distressing consequences of moral scepticism. Many of the issues posed by contemporary particularists have concerned philosophers since at least Aristotle. Indeed, many contemporary particularists see Aristotle as a close ally. In this first section I will offer a short historical survey of the different forms and degrees of scepticism toward principle-based ethics. Far from claiming completeness, the aim of the following remarks is to give an impression of the historical inspirations of contemporary particularists and to situate their concerns within a broader context.

At the beginning of the *Nicomachean Ethics*, Aristotle points out that the variability of fine, just and good things makes it impossible to find necessary and universal principles.[2] In any field of enquiry we can ask only for so much exactness and necessity as our object of enquiry allows. Aristotle emphasizes that the practical nature of ethics makes it inappropriate to demand mathematical exactness or formal necessity. According to Aristotle, the practical nature of ethics also means that its body of principles can never be systematic in the way abstract theoretical principles such as the principles of geometry are. We must thus not demand too much exactness in moral theory and instead 'be satisfied to indicate the truth roughly and in outline'.[3] Particularists have interpreted these passages as expressing a sceptical view about moral principles and their capacity to guide our moral decisions.[4] A further reason why one might ascribe particularist tendencies to Aristotle is his emphasis on the importance of perception. Aristotle points out that although we can try to give an agent more and more detailed moral advice, particular cases have to be decided by the agent herself and in doing so she has to bridge an inevitable gap between the general advice and the particular action. According to Aristotle, this gap between the general and the particular can only be filled by 'perception'.[5] Perception also plays a role in Aristotle's account of prudence or practical wisdom (*phronesis*). Prudence is concerned with 'what action we must or must not do'.[6] Since 'all the things achievable in action are particular'[7] and since particulars are the province of perception, prudence has to include a perceptual element in order to enable us to make particular moral judgements. Since the moral demands that arise in particular situations depend on the varied and detailed circumstances of that particular case, ethics cannot rest on strict universal generalizations. One might take these remarks to imply that particular perceptual judgements are the foundation of moral virtue, and that they do not need any backing up by general moral principles. On this picture, moral principles are no more than incomplete summaries of the correct moral judgements of virtuous agents.[8] Yet this reading of Aristotle is controversial. For example, one might argue that Aristotle's reason for emphasizing the exception-ladenness of moral principles is not to warn us against taking them too seriously, but rather to warn us that we ought not be deterred from taking them seriously.[9] On this interpretation, moral principles are important despite, and even because of, their exception-ladenness. For Aristotle, moral theory is essentially practical and one might argue that this focus on practice explains why we ought to be satisfied with principles that are stated only roughly. To try to spell out all the exceptions of moral principles would be as misguided as a carpenter's seeking absolute geometrical precision about right angles.[10]

Furthermore, it is worth pointing out that Aristotle is also committed to exceptionless moral generalizations. For example, he believes that we ought never to make fun of people simply to raise a laugh, without any regard for what is fine and expedient.[11] Even Aristotle's remarks on perception can be read in a way that is far less critical of moral principles than contemporary particularists would like us believe. In this context Terence Irwin argues that Aristotle thinks of perception as a means of applying general principles to particular cases, so that we recognize all the relevant aspects of a particular situation to which our principles apply.[12] Thus understood, perception supports, but does not replace moral principles. Finally, it is important to note that when it comes to moral education, Aristotle takes moral principles to be essential.[13] So while it is safe to say that Aristotle anticipated many of the concerns of contemporary particularists, it is far from clear that particularists can claim monopoly on his ideas.

A further historical source of potential inspiration for particularists is casuistry. The term 'casuistry' is derived from *casus* (Latin for case) and refers to the study of morally problematic cases.[14] Casuistry was developed in the Middle Ages as a method of bringing abstract and universal religious precepts to bear on particular moral situations. It begins in the early decades of the Christian era and reaches its peak in the century between 1550–1650, followed by a slow decline.[15] Casuistry is often described as the natural outgrowth of Aristotle's *Nicomachean Ethics*.[16] Like Aristotle, casuists believe that it is impossible to secure theoretical exactness in ethics. Casuists hesitated to universalize their judgements and instead of, for example, saying that something is never the case, they preferred to say 'well, hardly ever' or 'never, in any circumstances we have yet considered'.[17] Moreover, like Aristotle, casuists emphasize the importance of practical wisdom for right conduct. According to casuists, the person of practical wisdom has to exercise circumspection, that is, the awareness of circumstances.[18] If casuists would have to put the essence of their approach in the form of a slogan, it would probably be the proverb 'circumstances alter cases'. In this context, Thomas Aquinas, one of the most important precursors of medieval casuistry, remarks that 'the human act ought to vary according to diverse conditions of persons, time and other circumstances: this is the entire matter of morality'.[19]

In their seminal monograph on the history of casuistry, *The Abuse of Casuistry*, Albert R. Jonsen and Stephen Toulmin identify Cicero's *On Duties* (*De Officiis*) as the cradle of casuistry. Casuistry can be seen as an answer to the moral problems explicated by Cicero. His discussion of particular moral cases leads Cicero to the conclusion that 'there are many actions which appear honourable by nature, but which cease to be honourable in certain contingencies'.[20] For example, Cicero denies that deposits should always be returned. He argues that '[i]f a person left a sword with you when he was of sound mind, and asked for it back when he had gone mad, it would be a sin to give it back, and your obligation would be not to do so'.[21] Similarly, promises on occasion should not be kept and agreements not be observed.[22] As we shall see later, this belief in the context-sensitivity and variability of morally relevant considerations is one of the main motivations behind current particularism. However, in contrast to current particularists, Cicero and medieval casuists used the discussion of individual moral cases as a way of bringing general moral principles to bear on particular moral situations, rather than as a way of discrediting these principles.

Since they did not formulate an explicit methodology, the casuists' method can be inferred only from their practice.[23] Medieval casuists ordered their cases into an taxonomy such as the Ten Commandments or the Seven Deadly Sins. They usually started with a general statement about these principles. For example, they might have started by explaining the general meaning of the fifth commandment, 'Though shalt not kill', and offered a definition of the key terms, such as 'killing'. This general statement about the principle is then followed by particular cases that exemplify the principle in particular circumstances. In doing so, casuists moved from obvious cases to cases in which the circumstances make the application of the principle increasingly less clear.[24] For example, in discussing the fifth commandment, one might start with a case of a direct unprovoked attack resulting in the death of another. Cases of progressive difficulty are then construed by adding complicating circumstances to one's paradigm cases. For example, one might discuss a case of homicide in the course of defence against an unjust aggressor.[25] In analysing the moral status of more complicated cases, casuists used reasoning based on analogies with paradigm cases as well as so-called moral maxims. These maxims were used to determine the morally relevant features of the cases at hand. Arguments about self-defence, for example, often turned on the maxims 'force may be repulsed by force' and 'defence measured to the need of the occasion'.[26] Such arguments were then accumulated and finally let to the practical resolution of a particular problematic case. In light of this method, Jonsen and Toulmin define casuistry as follows:

> [Casuistry is] the analysis of moral issues, using procedures or reasoning based on paradigms and analogies, leading to the formulation of expert opinions about the existence and stringency of particular moral obligations, framed in terms of rules and maxims that are general but not universal or invariable, since they hold good with certainty only in the typical conditions of the agent and circumstances of action.[27]

Given this understanding of casuistry, it is a method of moral reasoning which presupposes the existence of moral principles. It does so for the classification of particular cases as well as the determination of their morally relevant features. However, at the same time medieval casuists' insistence on the context-sensitivity and variability of morally relevant considerations, their scepticism toward strictly universal moral principles and their believe in the importance of practical judgement will receive the full approval and praise of current particularists.

The term 'moral particularism' itself was first introduced by R. M. Hare in his *Freedom and Reason*.[28] It was not until the

1980s, however, that particularism established itself as a position in moral and political philosophy. Many sceptics of moral principles challenge only certain types of principles. Communitarians, for instance, have argued against the universal and abstract principles of justice that liberals like John Rawls have defended. Michael Sandel, for instance, claims that 'the ideal of a society governed by neutral principles is liberalism's false promise'.[29] According to communitarians, universal and abstract principles cannot account for the fact that standards of justice are inseparably bound up with the forms of life and traditions of particular societies, and can hence vary from context to context.[30] Alasdair MacIntyre suggests that the very fact that liberal political philosophers are unable to agree on the correct principle(s) of justice even among themselves should make us wary of their project:

> [I]f those who claim to be able to formulate principles on which rational moral agents ought to agree cannot secure agreement on the formulation of those principles from their colleagues who share their basic philosophical purpose and method, there is […] prima facie evidence that their project has failed.[31]

MacIntyre's answer to the alleged shortcomings of contemporary moral and political philosophy is a form of virtue ethics. According to MacIntyre, 'the ordering of evaluative concepts has been misconceived by the spokesmen of modernity and more particularly of liberalism': at the beginning of our normative enquiries ought to stand certain virtues rather than principles.[32]

Liberal theories of justice are not the only normative theories which have been criticized for their reliance on moral principles in recent years. In bioethics, the so-called 'principlist' approach – most famously defended by Tom Beauchamp and James Childress – has met with increasing opposition. In their highly influential book *Principles of Biomedical Ethics*, Beauchamp and Childress advanced a set of moral principles intended to serve as a framework for biomedical ethics. The principles in this framework are grouped under four general categories: respect for autonomy, nonmaleficence, beneficence and justice.[33] Especially so-called 'new casuists' have argued that this principle-based approach has proven useless and even harmful in clinical decision-making and public debates about bioethical questions. With regard to the abortion debate,

Jonsen and Toulmin – the main defenders of the new casuists movement in bioethics – allege the following:

> [T]he public rhetoric of the abortion controversy has increasingly come, in recent years, to turn on 'matters of principle'. The more this has happened, the less temperate, less discriminating, and above all less resoluble the debate has been. […] Those who insist on arguing out the abortion issue on the level of high theory and general principle thus guarantee that on the practical level the only possible outcome is deadlock.[34]

According to Jonsen and Toulmin, the attempt to resolve the ethical and legal issues surrounding abortion on the basis of moral principles has resulted in 'pure head-butting'[35] with the 'pro-life' action league defending an embryo's unqualified and unconditional 'right to life' on one side and the 'pro-choice' advocates on the other. Inspired by the methods of medieval casuists, Jonsen and Toulmin argue that bioethicists and health professionals should use paradigm cases, instead of moral principles, as their final objects of reference in moral arguments.[36] However, it is important to note that Jonsen and Toulmin do not reject moral principles altogether. They acknowledge that 'no sound casuistry can dispense with principles'.[37] Jonsen and Toulmin stress the importance of moral judgement and point out that the real-life application of moral principles always calls 'for the exercise of human perceptiveness and discernment'.[38] But this is an insight principlists are fully aware of. According to Beauchamp and Childress, moral principles need to be specified and balanced when put to use; and this requires judgement. Beauchamp and Childress recommend thinking through moral problems 'by creatively using principles', rather than by trying to apply principles mechanically to particular cases.[39] Beauchamp and Childress are even prepared to acknowledge that we sometimes have more reason to trust our responses to specific cases than a general principle.[40] In light of this considerable agreement between principlists and new casuists, one might view the latter not so much as a rival to principle-based theories in bioethics, but rather as its necessary complement.[41]

While communitarians and new casuists have been primarily concerned with the alleged flaws of specific forms of, or arguments for, moral principles, other sceptics of principle-based ethics focus more on the aspects of morality that we seem to miss out if we focus solely on principles. For instance, some feminists have complained that moral philosophy's fixation on principles masks the importance of care and commitment.[42] In this context Nel Noddings argues that 'our inclination toward and interest in morality derives from caring'.[43] She explicates that when we care 'we accept the natural impulse to act on behalf of the present other'.[44] Moreover, Noddings claims that 'we do not say with any conviction that a person cares if that person acts routinely according to some fixed rule'.[45] Accordingly, morality should depend 'not upon rules, or at least not wholly on rules [...] but upon a constellation of conditions that is viewed through the eyes of the one-caring and the eyes of the cared-for'.[46] Noddings is especially concerned that principle-based ethics cannot account for the different responses that we ought to have in different kinds of relationships. Under normal circumstances, what one must do for a colleague, for example, is different from what one must do for one's child. Noddings believes that by relying on principles in our moral decisions we risk to 'become detached from the very heart of morality: the sensibility that calls forth caring'.[47]

A similar concern about the ability of principle-based morality to account for the moral significance of personal relationships can be found in Bernard Williams' work. Williams argues that morality cannot be adequately captured in a system of principles of general obligations and rights. According to Williams, the moral principles brought forward by Kantians and consequentialists take no account of the special relationships between individuals which are essential for character, integrity and flourishing in a human life.[48]

A number of virtue ethicists have claimed that due to their preoccupation with principles, consequentialists and Kantians have missed the importance of virtue, moral judgement and sensibility.[49] For example, Martha Nussbaum claims that a person armed only with moral principles 'would, even if she managed to apply them to the concrete case, be insufficiently equipped by them to act rightly in it'.[50] Nussbaum points out that we are responsible for getting the details of the context of our actions right: 'for feeling fully, for getting the tone right'.[51] According to Nussbaum, obtuseness is a moral failing and she believes that, trusted for and in themselves, moral principles 'are a recipe for obtuseness'.[52]

In contrast to these critics of moral principles, current particularists attack traditional principle-based morality at a more fundamental level. According to Dancy, 'to accept particularism is to accept a change at the very centre of one's conception of the moral'.[53] While the objections of communitarians, feminists, anti-principlists and virtue ethicists against traditional principled ethics arise from specific first-order moral concerns or are framed by specific first-order moral theories, current particularists base their criticism on metaethical considerations. These metaethical considerations range from epistemological considerations inspired by certain forms of moral intuitionism,[54] metaphysical arguments about the so-called shapelessness of moral properties with respect to the non-moral,[55] arguments from semantics,[56] Wittgensteinian considerations about rule-following,[57] to specific views about normative reasons.[58] Particularists like Dancy not only argue against some specific moral principles or against some moral theories, but rather they purport to challenge the whole generalist tradition in moral philosophy. They believe that there is something wrong at the very basis of principle-based morality. However, particularists differ in their diagnosis of what exactly *is* wrong with a principled approach to morality, and they also vary widely in the negative claims they make about moral principles. Some deny that there are any true moral principles.[59] Others deny that there are any true moral principles which carry us from non-moral concepts to moral concepts, but affirm the possibility of intra-moral principles.[60] That is, they deny that there are any true moral principles with a descriptive antecedent such as 'causing pain' and a thin moral concept such as 'wrong' in the consequence, but they believe in the possibility of moral principles with so-called thick moral concepts such as virtuous or cruel in the antecedent and thin or thick moral concepts in the consequence. Yet other particularists argue that there are no good reasons to think that there are any true moral principles. They purport to show that none of the reasons given for thinking there are true moral principles is sound, and that particularism presents a coherent alternative.[61] A further form of particularism claims that we ought not to rely on moral principles. In the introduction, I have already quoted McNaughton, according to whom 'moral principles are at best useless, and at worst a hindrance, in trying to find out which is the right action'.[62] Proponents of this form of particularism do not need to deny that there are moral principles.

The reasons that particularists bring forward for being sceptical about moral principles are manifold. They challenge principled ethics on many different levels and to various degrees. Since principles have dominated morality and moral philosophy in diverse ways and for different reasons, this is not surprising. The problem is that this variety of different forms of particularism renders the task of identifying and formulating *the* particularist challenge extremely difficult.

This is one reason why I will focus primarily on Dancy's version of moral particularism. According to Dancy, particularism is the view that 'the possibility of moral thought and judgement does not depend on the provision of a suitable supply of moral principles'.[63] However, even with this restricted focus on one specific form of particularism, it proves difficult to state what exactly it is that is supposed to be wrong with principled ethics. Dancy's particularism has changed in considerable ways over the years, emphasizing different metaethical considerations. In *Ethics without Principles* Dancy points out, for example, that while he 'used to think that particularism was a position in moral epistemology',[64] he now thinks that it is a view about moral metaphysics. Given such remarks, it is not surprising that many philosophers refuse to take particularism seriously. But this reaction is premature. In the next section I will argue that although particularism suffers from various inconsistencies, it poses a challenge that defenders of principled ethics need to take seriously.

The current particularist/generalist debate

In what follows I will offer a more detailed diagnosis of why it is so difficult to define the challenge that particularists pose to the generalist tradition. I will show that particularists fail to specify sufficiently, and often misconstrue, their target. Many of their arguments are based on a misconception of the tradition of principled ethics. Dancy's particularism is targeted against the whole tradition of principle-based ethics. Dancy denies that there is 'any essential link between morality and principles'.[65] He suggests that all forms of principled ethics are guilty of the same error or errors. In order for this to be true, principle-based theories as diverse as Mill's *Utilitarianism*, Kant's *Groundwork*, Rawls' *Theory of Justice* and, say, Tom Beauchamp and James Childress' *Principles of Biomedical Ethics* would need to have something in common. However, particularists in general, and Dancy in particular, do not make clear what exactly this common feature is supposed to be. This has earned recent debates about moral particularism the reputation of being notoriously obscure. I will identify two main sources of confusion: first, the failure of particularists to specify their understanding of moral principles and principled ethics, and secondly, the conflation of the debate about the nature and roles of moral principles with a debate about the nature of moral reasons.

'The particularist challenge' (pp. 31–52) will then explain why, despite these serious deficiencies of particularism, generalists should not ignore it. I will present what I take to be the central challenge that particularism poses for principled ethics. It is not my aim to give an explanation of why individual moral philosophers are actually attracted to particularism. Nor do I expect that all particularists will agree with my formulation of the particularist challenge. What I want to show is that the most plausible and charitable reading of particularism is as a challenge to the tradition of principled ethics, rather than a conclusive argument against it. My aim is to offer a formulation of the particularist challenge and to show why generalists must respond to it.

Particularists' understanding of moral principles

Whether one thinks that morality can, should or needs to be principle-based depends crucially on one's understanding of moral principles. It is, therefore, unfortunate that particularists tend to leave their understanding of moral principles and principled ethics rather vague. In order to make sure that particularists and generalists are not talking at cross-purposes it is essential to clarify the conceptions of moral principles and principled ethics used in the debate.

A look at the recent literature on particularism reveals three main understandings of moral principles. Moral principles are understood as standards, guides or algorithms. Before I set out these three understandings of moral principles, two preliminary points are in order. First, it is widely agreed that not just any generalization which employs a moral concept counts as a moral principle. For instance, 'Any action is either morally required, or not' is a true generalization which employs a moral concept, but there is a wide consensus that it does not qualify as a moral principle.[66] The same holds true for generalizations that make empirical statements about people's moral beliefs and attitudes such as 'Incest is seen as wrong in most societies'. Even the most radical particularists do not deny such generalizations. In order to qualify as principles, moral generalizations have to fulfil certain functions. What one takes these functions to be will depend on whether one understands moral principles as standards, guides or algorithms.

The second preliminary point concerns supervenience-functions. According to supervenience there can be no moral difference without non-moral difference. Supervenience entails the existence of generalizations which link moral evaluations to non-moral descriptions of the world. The antecedents of these generalizations contain a description of the entire non-moral world in which a given object of evaluation satisfies the moral concept in question. Any complete specification of the descriptive nature of a possible world necessarily determines whether or not, say, a certain action is right in that world. Particularists like Dancy want to allow for such supervenience-functions.[67] However, they deny that supervenience-functions are moral principles. Supervenience generates generalizations of a size and detail that ensures that there is effectively no chance that they can recur. Dancy rightly points out that a principle that has only one instance is useless. Furthermore, supervenience-functions will contain all sorts of irrelevancies.[68] Even so-called local supervenience tells us only that if one act is right then another act that is just like it must also be right. But many facts about a right act are irrelevant to whether it is right.[69] For these reasons there is a wide consensus among generalists and particularists that supervenience-functions do not qualify as principles.[70]

With these preliminary remarks out of the way, let me set out the three conceptions of moral principles prevalent in the recent debates about particularism. Dancy and some of his generalist interlocutors conceive of moral principles as standards. According to these authors, moral principles have to articulate correct sufficient conditions for the application of a moral concept.[71] There is disagreement about whether and to what extent these standards can include exceptions. Particularists tend to insist that moral principles have to provide *strictly* sufficient conditions for the application of moral concepts. Dancy, for instance, seems to think that exception-laden moral principles 'are not principles at all, in any real sense'.[72] Some of Dancy's generalist critics, by contrast, present the application conditions that moral standards purport to formulate as some sort of *ceteris paribus* conditions.[73] Moral standards are thus thought of as exceptionless or as hedged by exception clauses.

To qualify as a standard, a moral generalization has to be explanatory. That is, a moral standard has to do more than provide the application conditions for a moral concept; it has to do so in a way that can help explain why that concept applies when it does.[74] Dancy demands that moral principles tell us why a given action has the moral status it has.[75] McKeever and Ridge accept this demand and argue for moral principles which articulate 'true application conditions for a given moral concept by referring to those features of the world which explain why the concept applies when it does'.[76] According to Väyrynen, a moral principle is a 'proposition that identifies conditions or properties in virtue of which something has a given moral property such as rightness, and which are thus explanatory of why it is right'.[77] For Lance and Little moral principles are 'explanatory, interrelated moral generalizations that are capable of serving key epistemic functions'.[78] The explanatory value of moral standards is supposed to distinguish them from mere generalizations and supervenience-functions.[79] The traditional example that is usually cited as a moral standard is the principle of utility. A principle according to which an action is right if and only if it maximizes the overall utility, provides us with sufficient application conditions for the concept 'right'. The principle of utility is also explanatory in the sense that it explains why an action is right or wrong. Moral standards thus seem to have a place in the history of principled ethics. However, as moral agents we not only need to decide whether a given action is right or wrong, we also need to act morally. Many utilitarians believe that the principle of utility is too complex to guide action. They distinguish between the principle of utility as a standard of rightness and other principles which fulfil an action-guiding role.

This leads us to the second prominent conception of moral principles that can be found in the current particularists' writings: moral principles as guides. McKeever and Ridge point out that unlike standards, guides need not provide entirely accurate application conditions for moral concepts. They might not cover all cases and might even have some false implications.[80] Understood as moral guides, principles are vindicated by their value in guiding our moral thought and action.[81] While some particularists want to make room for moral guides, understood as rules of thumb, others oppose moral guides as well as moral standards. In this context McNaughton acknowledges the usefulness of principles in the moral education of children. However, he also emphasizes that mature moral agents do not need moral principles. McNaughton claims that if the principles are not dispensed with at some point of a person's moral development, they encourage serious vices, such as inflexibility and rigidity in one's moral thinking.[82]

Many authors hold that moral principles, if there were any, would have to be capable of functioning as guides as well as standards. That is, they conceive of moral principles as action-guiding standards.[83] According to Dancy, for example, moral principles do not only have to provide a criterion of rightness and wrongness, but also 'be capable of functioning as a guide to action in a new case'.[84]

According to the third conception of principles prevalent in current particularists' writings, moral principles are algorithms, where an algorithm is understood as a purely mechanical decision-procedure that can be applied without any insight, imagination or judgement. McNaughton, for instance, assumes that the aim of traditional principled ethics is to find 'a set of rules which could be applied by anyone, whatever their sensitivity or experience, to discover the right answer'.[85] He then argues that moral judgement 'cannot be replicated by the use of a decision procedure which could be grasped by someone who had no appreciation of what was at stake'.[86] Similarly, John McDowell points out that there are cases 'in which a mechanical application of the rules would strike one as wrong'[87] and Dancy emphasizes that '[t]here is no possibility of computing'.[88] But these are things no sensible generalist would deny. Neither utilitarians nor Kantians, for example, think of moral principles as algorithms. Utilitarians generally acknowledge that the principle of utility will be useless unless moral agents are able to identify options, to predict and calculate their likely consequences, and to rank them according to some decision-procedure. Similarly, Kant points out that a correct application of the categorical imperative requires 'judgement sharpened by experience, partly to distinguish in what cases [the categorical imperative is] applicable and partly to provide [it] with access to the will of the human being and efficacy for his fulfilment of [it]'.[89] Thus, if the particularists' arguments are targeted against moral algorithms they are attacking a straw man.

Given that particularists usually fail to specify their understanding of moral principles, it is not surprising that their conception of principled ethics is equally difficult to pin down. In what follows, I will discuss Dancy's conception of a principled ethics.

Dancy's conception of a principled ethics

Since Dancy is one of the most prominent defenders of moral particularism, it is important to be clear whether his characterization of the tradition of principled ethics is one which generalists would or have to accept. In *Ethics Without Principles* Dancy lays down the following four conditions for a principled ethics:

> *Coverage*: The moral status of every action must be determined by the principles, in one way or another.

> *Reasons*: Of each action that has a moral status, the principles must somehow tell us why it has that status.

> *Epistemology*: We must be able to learn the principles, either from experience in some way or from each other, i.e. by testimony.

> *Applicability*: The principles must be capable of functioning as a guide to action in a new case; having learnt them, one must be able to *follow* them, or *apply* them.[90]

It is important to do Dancy justice at this point. The fact that he remarks that 'we could probably continue this list'[91] indicates that he does not intend to give us a list of necessary and sufficient

conditions for a principled ethics. It also shows how little importance he attaches to the specification of his target. Dancy lists the
above conditions in the context of discussing Lance and Little's
notion of defeasible generalizations in order to show that a morality
built around these generalizations will not qualify as a principled
morality.[92] However, there are nevertheless good reasons not to
downplay the importance of Dancy's proposed conditions for a
principled ethics. Dancy himself notes that the four conditions are
conditions that have emerged over the course of his discussion in
Ethics Without Principles. This suggests that they are closely linked
to his overall argument and, therefore, deserve our attention.
Furthermore, most of Dancy's interlocutors tacitly accept his
four conditions. McKeever and Ridge, for instance, argue for the
possibility of a finite and manageable set of moral principles which
together codify all of morality and which thereby fulfil Dancy's first
condition of coverage.[93] They hold that moral principles provide
the truth-conditions for moral judgements by referring to those
features of the world which explain why those judgements are
true. McKeever and Ridge thus believe that moral principles are
explanatory in the sense of Dancy's second condition. Moreover,
they purport to show that moral principles can and should play
an important role in guiding action and thereby acknowledge the
two final conditions.[94] Given the influence of Dancy's conception
of principled ethics in the current particularist/generalist debate, it
is worth examining whether the above four conditions do justice
to the generalist tradition. I will consider one traditional and one
contemporary generalist theory which Dancy himself takes to be
paradigmatic examples of principled ethics.

W. D. Ross' theory of *prima facie* duties is one of Dancy's
prime examples of a principled ethics. Understood as *prima facie*
principles, moral principles identify morally relevant features and
specify whether they count in favour or against an action. *Prima
facie* principles are not decisive, that is, they do not determine
the *overall* rightness or wrongness of a particular action. A *prima
facie* principle according to which breaking promises is wrong, for
example, tells the moral agent that breaking a promise is always
a feature that counts against the action. However, other morally
relevant features which are present in a certain case, e.g. that it
was necessary to break a promise in order save someone's life,
can outweigh the moral wrongness of promise-breaking. Thus, an

act that involves breaking a promise is always *prima facie* wrong, but it might be judged as the right thing to do overall, when other features of the case are taken into account. A particular action is *overall* right if 'of all acts possible for the agent in the circumstances, it is that whose *prima facie* rightness in the respects in which it is *prima facie* right most outweighs its *prima facie* wrongness in any respects in which it is *prima facie* wrong'.[95] What is crucial is that, according to Ross, there are no further, second-order principles which tell us how to weigh the *prima facie* rightness and wrongness of the different options in a given case. There 'is no principle by which we can draw the conclusion that [an action] is on the whole right or on the whole wrong'.[96] To determine the overall rightness or wrongness of a particular action is a matter of judgement:

> [W]hat I have to do is to study the situation as fully as I can until I form the considered opinion [...] that in the circumstances one of [the *prima facie* obligations] is more incumbent than any other.[97]

Ross' ethics of *prima facie* principles thus fails to satisfy Dancy's condition of coverage according to which the moral status of every action must be determined by the principles. It also fails to satisfy the second condition since *prima facie* principles do not tell us why a particular action has the overall moral status that it has.

One contemporary generalist approach Dancy discusses is Frank Jackson, Philip Pettit and Michael Smith's constitutive generalism.[98] Jackson, Pettit and Smith defend a form of generalism according to which we need moral principles in the form of patterned connections between the descriptive ways things are and the moral ways things are. They argue that in order for us to grasp moral predicates such as 'is right', there must be a pattern that unifies all right actions, a pattern in which the purely descriptive features of 'rightness' are codified.[99] What is important for my present purpose is that Jackson, Pettit and Smith do not make any claims about the practical use or applicability of these principles:

> Although we insist that there must be a pattern and that it must be codifiable in principle, we take no position on whether it is sometimes, always or never codified, in the sense of being 'before the mind', when a moral judgement is made.[100]

Jackson, Pettit and Smith do not claim that moral agents should, or actually could, consciously apply and follow the type of moral principles they advance. They grant particularists that at least sometimes the best way to make a moral judgement in a given case is to consider the case in all its particularities and follow one's intuitive moral response.[101] At least as it stands, Jackson, Pettit and Smith's generalist approach is not designed to guide moral actions and thus fails to fulfil Dancy's fourth condition. In order to provide useful moral guidance, moral principles must not be too complicated. Jackson, Pettit and Smith argue for the existence of a principle of rightness that codifies the pattern exemplified by the various sets of descriptive features which determine rightness case by case. Such a principle is likely to be highly complex. However, assume for a moment that the pattern which unifies all right actions turns out to be rather simple and that 'X is right' means 'X maximizes happiness'. The difficulties of the application of such a utilitarian principle of rightness are well known. We are simply not able to foresee and calculate all consequences of each act for every person for all time. Most consequentialists, therefore, do not claim that a principle like, say, Bentham's principle of utility is capable of functioning as a moral guide. They distinguish moral principles as standards of moral rightness and wrongness from moral principles as guides or decision-procedures. Jackson, Pettit and Smith show that generalists can argue for the former without committing themselves to any claims about the latter. Their argument for moral generalism is based on semantic and metaphysical considerations. Understood as a view in moral metaphysics, generalism carries no commitment to the claim that people actually need, can, or do, make particular moral judgements on the basis of moral principles.[102] Thus, generalists in general, and Jackson, Pettit and Smith in particular, are not committed to Dancy's conditions of applicability. The above two examples illustrate that Dancy's four conditions fail to capture the core commitments of some of the very same generalists he explicitly targets. The criteria are thus too strong even on his own terms.

In addition to the conception of moral principles and principled ethics, the second major source of confusion in the current particularist/generalist debate is the conflation of a debate about moral principles with a debate about the nature of moral reasons. Or so I shall argue next.

Moral reasons in the current particularist/ generalist debate

The current debate between moral particularists and moral generalists is a debate about the extent to which morality can and should be understood in terms of moral principles. But it is also a debate about the nature of moral reasons. Dancy's *Ethics Without Principles* is a defence of the thesis that 'moral judgement can get along perfectly well without any appeal to principles',[103] as well as a 'book [...] about how to understand the way in which reasons work'.[104] His generalist interlocutors have followed Dancy in phrasing their claims about moral principles in terms of moral reasons. Väyrynen, for instance, understands particularism and generalism as 'doctrines about the role of moral principles regarding the status of certain facts as moral reasons'.[105] According to Väyrynen, moral principles identify moral reasons and 'the normative basis of any moral reason requires the existence of a true moral principle'.[106] Similarly, McKeever and Ridge argue that 'our knowledge about moral reasons [...] presuppose[s] the availability of a suitable stock of moral principles'.[107]

This preoccupation with reasons in the current particularist/ generalist debate is part of a general trend in moral philosophy. It is now widely believed that normativity is mainly, if not entirely, based on reasons. Joseph Raz, for instance, claims that '[t]he normativity of all that is normative consists in the way it is, or provides, or is otherwise related to reasons'.[108] Reasons are thought to be the 'building blocks'[109] of the normative realm. The term 'reason' has become a technical term that often bears little resemblance to our everyday practice of giving and asking for reasons. Philosophers talk about 'available reasons', 'potential reasons', 'putative reasons', and 'grounding reasons'.[110] There are reasons for belief and reasons for action as well as theoretical and practical reasons, and these reasons are thought to be 'ultimate',[111] 'perfect',[112] 'pro-tanto',[113] 'contributory',[114] or 'presumptive'.[115] Recently the notion of default reasons has received much attention.[116] According to some authors there are 'insistent' and 'non-insistent reasons',[117] while others believe in 'enticing reasons' and 'peremptory reasons',[118] postulate 'operative reasons',[119] or speak of 'right- and wrong-making reasons'.[120] This list could be continued. I believe this focus on the notion of reasons in contemporary moral philosophy to be problematic. The preoccupation with reasons often seems to distract moral philosophers from other important moral notions such as the notions of duties and rights. Moreover, thinking in terms of reasons often appears to obscure rather than illuminate issues. However, I will not argue for these claims here.[121] My point is of a much more limited scope. I will show why Dancy should not phrase his particularist challenge in terms of reasons for action.

According to Dancy, particularism is the view that the possibility of moral thought and judgement does not depend on the provision of a suitable supply of moral principles. He defines generalism as the view that 'the very possibility of moral thought and judgement depends on the provision of a suitable supply of moral principles'.[122] Dancy draws a close connection between these views about moral principles and certain views about moral reasons. He understands moral reasons as features of a situation which speak in favour or against an action.[123] Dancy claims that an 'undistorted view about how reasons work leads naturally to a particularist account of moral thought and judgement'[124] and that 'the errors of generalism can mostly be traced back to errors in the theory of reasons'.[125] So what exactly is the link between the generalist/particularist debate and different views about normative reasons?

Dancy assumes that 'all moral principles specify features which they suppose to constitute the same reason wherever they occur, regardless of context'.[126] He believes that moral principles need to be understood 'as claiming that a certain feature has an invariant moral relevance'.[127] According to Dancy, the 'principle that it is wrong to lie, for instance, [...] claims that mendacity is always a wrong-making feature wherever it occurs'.[128] Dancy assumes that one of the main characteristics of defenders of principled ethics is their commitment to – what he dubs – atomism in the theory of reasons. Atomism is defined as the view that 'a feature that is a reason in one case must remain a reason, and retain the same polarity, in any other'.[129] If the fact that something is a lie, for example, counts against doing an action in one situation, this fact must have this negative polarity in all situations in which it occurs. For Dancy this belief in invariant moral reasons is essential to all principled ethics.[130] Dancy opposes atomism and instead defends a holistic conception of moral reasons, i.e. the view that 'a feature that is a reason in one case may be no reason at all, or an opposite reason, in another'.[131] Dancy emphasizes that there are cases where it can be wrong to return what has been borrowed, right to inflict pain intentionally, wrong to please another, right to lie to another, and so on.[132] To say that moral reasons function holistically does not only mean that their reason-giving force may be outweighed or counterbalanced by other reasons: moral reasons can also cease to be reasons and may even change their polarity, if the context is suitable. Imagine, for instance, that I have borrowed a book from someone. In most situations, the fact that I have borrowed a book from someone gives me a reason to return it to that person. But suppose I discover that the person has stolen the book from the library. In that context, the fact that I borrowed the book gives me, according to Dancy, no reason at all to return it to that person.[133] Dancy's standard example of a moral reason that can change its polarity is the fact that something would promote pleasure. That something promotes pleasure is a reason in favour of doing it in some contexts, but not in others. In the case of a torturer who gains sadistic pleasure from the suffering of her victim the pleasure counts against the action: it makes the act of torturing even worse. A similar point can be made with regard to hunting. Many people who object to foxhunting do so because of the pleasure that the hunters get out of it. They do not object to the killing of foxes if it is necessary for the safety and survival of other species, but they believe that the slaughter ought not to be fun.[134] Holists take these and other examples as evidence for the context-sensitivity and hence variability of moral reasons.

On the face of it, the implications of holism for the particularist/generalist debate seem clear. If moral principles presuppose an atomistic conception of moral reasons, the fact that moral reasons function holistically seems to undermine the possibility of principle-based ethics. Atomism, moral principles and generalism appear to stand and fall together. Given that holism provides particularists with such a powerful argument against principled ethics, it seems only natural that large parts of Dancy's *Ethics Without Principles* are about reasons rather than principles. The debate between generalists and particularists about the proper role of moral principles seems to come down to a debate about the nature of moral reasons. Unfortunately, this turns out to be a mistake.

In *Ethics Without Principles*, Dancy himself concedes – contrary to remarks in his earlier work – that holism does not provide a direct argument for particularism. He acknowledges that holism is 'compatible with the existence of at least some principles'.[135] This is due to the fact that Dancy presents holism as a modal claim. He claims only that a feature which counts as a reason in one case *may* be no reason at all, or an opposite reason, in another. Holism 'concerns only what may happen, not what must'.[136] Holism allows for the possibility that, although every reason may alter or lose its polarity from case to case, actually in some possible worlds – including ours – no moral reason ever does change its polarity. These reasons would be contingently invariant. Accordingly, Dancy leaves open the possibility that there are some invariant moral reasons and hence moral principles defined in his sense.

Holism is also compatible with moral reasons that are necessarily invariant, that is, invariant across all possible worlds. Dancy remarks that reasons that are necessarily invariant in this sense will 'be invariant not because they are reasons but because of their specific content'.[137] A possible example of such a necessary invariant reason is inflicting gratuitous pain on unwilling victims. Another example might be causing a universal genocide, which arguably is a reason against doing the action in all possible worlds. Thus, so long as the invariance of moral reasons is either contingent or due to the specific content of the reasons, holism is compatible with the existence of invariant reasons and hence with the possibility of moral principles defined in Dancy's sense.

What is more, McKeever and Ridge have successfully shown that defenders of principled ethics do not even need to insist on the existence of invariant moral reasons in order to accommodate holism.[138] Their argument is based on the insight that holism is a claim about the variability or context-sensitivity of moral reasons, but neutral with respect to the question of whether this context-sensitivity is codifiable in terms of moral principles.[139] McKeever and Ridge point out that even strong, traditional forms of principled ethics such as utilitarianism can account for the fact that moral reasons are variant. Consider a utilitarian principle according to which the fact that an action would promote pleasure is a reason to perform the action if and only if the pleasure is non-sadistic. This principle is compatible with holism because the fact that an action would promote pleasure is a variant reason: it does not provide a reason for performing the action if the pleasure is sadistic. Whether or not the fact that an action would promote pleasure is a reason for performing the action depends on the context; in particular, it depends on whether the pleasure is sadistic.

Since it is now widely agreed that principled ethics is compatible with holism, I shall not discuss these arguments further here. Instead I will argue that not only can generalists be holists, but particularists can also be atomists. The latter point has been overlooked so far. McKeever and Ridge and a number of other generalists have shown that principle-based ethics is compatible with a holism, but they did not seem to notice that the reverse is true as well: particularism is compatible with an atomistic conception of reasons. The debate between atomists and holists in the theory of reasons is, therefore, orthogonal to the debate about whether morality can and should be understood in terms of principles. Particularists will not make any progress by talking about reasons.

In order to see how atomists can be particularists, it is helpful to start with the pleasure example I mentioned earlier. According to holists, the fact that something would be pleasant is a variant reason because there are contexts where it counts in favour of doing it and contexts where it counts against the action, as in the case of sadistic pleasure. Atomists will reply that holists are mistaken about what counts as a reason in this example. According to atomists, my reason for going to the cinema, say, is not that it gives me pleasure, but that it gives me non-sadistic pleasure. If we come across a case in which the ability of something to give non-sadistic pleasure fails to provide a reason for action, we will need to specify further this reason.[140] Atomists can be said to be 'expansionists', while holists are 'minimalists' about the content of reasons. Holists insist on a sharp distinction between features that count in favour of an action, i.e. reasons for action, and other features of the context that can affect whether something is a reason. That something would be pleasant, for instance, counts in favour of doing it. That the pleasure is non-sadistic functions as – what Dancy calls – an enabler. It is not itself a reason for taking the action but enables the first feature to count in favour of the action. In its absence, the fact that something is pleasant would not have been the reason it is. There are also considerations that intensify or attenuate the force of reasons.[141] It is important to note that, for holists, these considerations are not part of the reason. It is in virtue of the complex interplay of various enablers, disablers, intensifiers and attenuators that reasons are sensitive to the particular context in which they occur. In contrast to holists, atomists consider this complexity to be part of the reason.[142]

The crucial point for my argument is that atomists need not claim that we are in a position to specify fully these complex reasons in order to understand and act on them. Holism and atomism are views about the metaphysics rather than the epistemology of reasons. That is, they are views about what reasons are and not about what it is for a moral agent to know, understand or act on reasons. In this context Joseph Raz – an avowed atomist – argues that we can act for reasons which do not figure in our deliberation.[143] Raz holds that we act for reasons whenever we act intentionally. Actions which are embedded in automatic routines are done for reasons in this sense, but we do not deliberate about these reasons before acting. For example, a doctor who washes her hands before and after each patient contact does so for a reason, but she normally does not deliberate about this reason before washing her hands. Moreover, Raz points out that we can refer to reasons without understanding them well and even be mistaken about some of their aspects. A person who does something because he promised to do it, for example, can act for the right reason even though he might be mistaken about the precise conditions under which promises expire or in what ways and under what conditions binding promises are made.[144]

Raz is a generalist, but his conception of reasons could lead one to adopt the very opposite position and become a particularist. An atomist who shares Raz's epistemology of reasons could consistently argue that moral reasons are just too complex to be adequately captured in the form of moral principles. That is, an atomist could come to believe that, given that it is the function of moral principles to specify features as general reasons, there can be no moral principles. What is more, she could claim that since we can be guided by reasons without fully articulating and understanding them, there is no need for moral principles which do this. She could be led to think that 'the possibility of moral thought and judgement does not depend on the provision of a suitable supply of moral principles'.[145] Atomists can thus be particularists in Dancy's sense. A commitment to atomism in the theory of reasons, therefore, cannot be what is distinctive about principled ethics. Given that the debate about the proper roles and nature of moral principles cannot be settled by appealing to the debate between atomists and holists in the theory of reasons, particularists are well advised to stop talking about reasons and to start thinking about principles. So far I have shown that Dancy is not likely to make any progress by talking about reasons. In the next two sections I will argue that talking in terms of reasons actually undermines his position.

As I pointed out before, Dancy purports to challenge the very basis of traditional principle-based ethics. His particularist critique, therefore, has to do justice to the different forms of moral principles which have been argued for by the various defenders of principled ethics, otherwise it will miss its target. According to Dancy, moral principles are 'in the business of specifying features as general reasons'.[146] The problem is that traditional defenders of principle-based ethics such as John Stuart Mill, Immanuel Kant, or W. D. Ross did not phrase their claims about moral principles in terms of moral reasons. Although talk of reasons is undeniably an integral part of everyday moral thought and practice, its prominence in moral philosophy is a relatively recent phenomenon. While some traditional principle-based ethics such as Ross' theory of *prima facie* duties might be quite easily translated into the terminology of moral reasons, others resist such a move. In particular, it is mistaken to say that Kant's categorical imperative specifies features as reasons for action. The categorical imperative tells us to 'act only in accordance with that maxim through which you can at the same time will that it become a universal law'.[147] It provides a way of testing the moral permissibility of what we propose to do, i.e. the maxim of our action. However, the fact that an action is morally permissible provides no reason for action. That it is morally permissible to count the blades of grass on the lawn, for example, is no reason for doing it. Thus, the fact that an act is in accordance with a maxim which we can will to become a universal law does not provide us with any reason for action. One might object that while the categorical imperative does not provide us with reasons *for* action, it at least specifies reasons *against* doing certain actions by telling us that the maxims underlying these actions are morally impermissible. If the categorical imperative tells us that it is impermissible to get ourselves out of difficulties by a false promise, we can be said to have a very strong reason not to do so. Moreover, there are cases where the fact that our maxim does not pass the categorical imperative implies a moral requirement to do something. If the rejected maxim is one of not doing something, for example never helping other people, the veto of the categorical imperative requires us to do something, namely to at least sometimes show beneficence toward others. Finally, it is important to note that many contemporary Kantians talk in terms of reasons for action. Maxims can be understood as reasons for action, and the categorical imperative can thus be said to test reasons. Kantians can also say that moral duties provide us with reasons to do or refrain from doing a certain action.

However, all this does not show that the categorical imperative qualifies as a principle in Dancy's sense. The categorical imperative is not, as Dancy puts it, in the business of specifying features as general reasons. The categorical imperative itself does not specify duties and hence does not specify reasons. In this context Barbara Herman rightly points out that the categorical imperative 'does not set duties directly, but assesses agents' maxims of action'.[148] If at all, it is the combination of the maxim and the fact that it does or does not pass the categorical imperative that generates the duty and hence the moral reason. How general or specific the duty or the moral reason is will depend on the generality of the maxim that is tested. As an agent's subjective principle of volition, maxims are circumstance- and interest-specific. The categorical imperative therefore cannot, and is not supposed to, specify features which constitute the same reason wherever they occur, regardless of context. It is because the categorical imperative does not specify features as general reasons that Herman, for example, proposes to supplement it with her so-called rules of salience which pick out certain features of actions or situations as generally morally relevant and thus provide us with potential reasons for or against action.[149]

Dancy's conception of moral principles as principles that specify certain features as general reasons fails to capture the categorical imperative because it is restricted to a certain model of moral judgement. According to Dancy, moral principles have the function of telling us which features of situations are of general moral relevance. He views the task of moral judgement as one of finding the relevant description of a given situation or 'seeing' the morally salient features of a case.[150] Dancy can be said to defend an 'aesthetic' model of moral judgement. In a similar way as we see and describe the relevant features of a painting or a sculpture, we see and describe the morally relevant features of a given case or situation. This model of moral judgement conceives of the moral agent as a spectator whose primary task is to observe carefully the situation in which he finds himself. Dancy believes that 'one's main duty, in moral judgement, is to look really closely at the case before one'.[151] I will discuss and criticize this model of moral reasoning in more detail in Chapter Two of this book. For my present purpose it suffices to point out that the notions of moral action and practice receive little attention because Dancy assumes that once we see the situation in the right light, it will be clear what we should do, morally speaking. Kantians reject this picture of moral judgement. Their focus lies on the agent who is about to act, who is planning to do something. In contrast to Dancy, Kantians stress the fact that a good moral person is not only a careful observer, but also someone who acts morally, that is, someone who acts on the right maxims. Kant is concerned with agents who ask themselves whether the maxim on which they propose to act is morally permissible. If we ask ourselves whether, say, it would be permissible for us to escape from difficulties with a false promise, we do not agonize about which features of the situation are morally relevant.[152] In such cases the task of moral judgement is not one of finding the appropriate description of a given situation or action, but of deciding whether an action *as it is described in our maxim* is morally permissible. An agent who is planning to do something 'sees' her situation in a certain light, and she might even be convinced that she sees it in the right light, but she can nevertheless be in doubt about whether her proposed action would be morally permissible. The categorical imperative tells the agent whether the features which she has taken as relevant in determining her course of action, in fact give moral warrant to what she is planning do. A conception of moral principles as principles that specify certain features as reasons for action cannot account for this form of moral judgement. The categorical imperative does not specify reasons for action, it helps us to determine whether the reasons on which we propose to act are morally valid.[153]

Dancy's conception of moral principles as principles that specify reasons for action provides him with an unfortunate basis for his project. It is Dancy's declared aim to provide an argument against the whole generalist tradition. The fact that his notion of moral principles fails to capture the core principle of Kantian ethics is fatal for this project. More generally, the example of the categorical imperative suggests that the domain of moral principles is wider than that of moral reasons. Moral principles formulate normative requirements – prohibitions, obligations, permissions, etc. – or express recommendations and warnings. It is doubtful whether these various normative functions of moral principles can be adequately captured in terms of reasons for action.

I would like to mention one final argument against Dancy's phrasing his thesis in terms of reasons. The worry is that particularism – as defined by Dancy – is incompatible with a coherent notion of moral reasons. Selim Berker has recently brought forward an argument to this effect.[154] Although I believe that Berker's argument ultimately fails, it will nevertheless be helpful to briefly outline his criticism before I offer two alternative arguments for the incoherence of Dancy's notion of moral reasons.

Berker starts his argument by pointing out that Dancy's distinction between a contributory and an overall level presupposes a weighing model of practical deliberations. Dancy understands the overall moral status of actions – their being right or wrong, obligatory, forbidden, etc. – in terms of contributory reasons. A contributory reason is a feature whose presence in a given situation favours a certain action, but in such a way that the overall case for taking that action can be strengthened or diminished by other reasons present in the situation.[155] The overall moral status of an action must, therefore, be somehow constituted by the preponderance of contributory reasons. When an agent deliberates about what to do in a certain situation, she can choose between a variety of possible actions, and there are reasons which speak in favour or against each of these different options. Every moral reason has a metaphorical weight corresponding to how heavily it counts in favour of, or against, a given action. Each available action's overall moral status is determined by balancing the weights of the relevant reasons against each other in order to see where the overall weight of reasons lies.[156] Thus, on the weighing model the facts at the contributory level determine the facts at the overall level. According to Berker, this presupposes the existence of a function which takes as input the weight of all the reasons present in a possible situation and gives as output the rightness or wrongness of each action available in that situation.[157] The most straight-forward function would be an additive one. However, Dancy explicitly denies that 'once one has assessed the separate weight of each element, evaluative judgement consists of adding up the pros and cons to see which side is weightier'.[158] What is more, Dancy not only denies that there is an additive function, but he also denies that there is *any* finitely specifiable combinatorial function: additive, multiplicative or otherwise. Berker argues that this belief in the ultimate uncodifiability of the moral realm conflicts with the weighing model on which Dancy's notion of reasons is based. According to Berker, the coherence of the weighing model and of the corresponding notion of reasons 'depends on there being a quasi-additive combinatorial function'.[159] By denying the existence of such a function, particularists deprive themselves of a coherent notion of moral reasons. In Berker's words, 'the conjunction of the particularists' radical claims about the behaviour of reasons leaves them without a coherent notion of a reason for action'.[160]

The problem with Berker's argument is that it presupposes a cardinal reading of the weighing metaphor. That is, it presup-poses that items need to be assigned exact weights in order to be weighed or ranked against each other. However, particularists seem to conceive of the weighing of moral reasons as comparative or ordinal rather than cardinal. We can compare and rank different options – and our reasons in favour or against them – without assigning them anything like an exact weight. When we weigh our reasons for and against an option in a particular situation we do not normally seem to assign exact weights to these reasons, nor do we need a calculus to compare our different options. In weighing and comparing our options, we also appear to be well aware that something counting as a reason in one context might be no reason at all, or an opposite reason, in another. Dancy does not explain how we accomplish this everyday task of weighing reasons, but as long as we understand the notion of 'weighing reasons' in the loose, metaphorical way just sketched, his particularism does not conflict with it either. Thus, Dancy's conception of moral reasons is not incoherent in the sense Berker claims. However, it can be said to be incoherent in a different way. In order to provide a model of moral reasoning it is not enough to say that reasons lend some kind of weight to conclusions and that these weights are assembled somehow. The weighing metaphor itself does little to illuminate the process of moral reasoning, let alone provide a model of moral reasoning. It neither tells us how we come to see which options are available to us in a particular situation, nor does it give us an account of how to compare and balance these different options or reasons. Defenders of a weighing conception of moral reasoning need to unpack the metaphor of 'weighing reasons'. Dancy does not do this. Dancy's conception of moral reasons is incoherent in the sense that it advocates a certain conception of moral *reasons* without offering a corresponding model of moral *reasoning*. Thus, Berker's conclusion can be said to hold true even though the argument by which he gets there does not. In the hands of moral particularists moral reasons become 'free-floating cogs in the normative machinery'.[161] Dancy fails to embed his notion of moral reasons within a suitable model of moral reasoning.

Dancy's conception of moral reasons is incoherent in a second sense. The postulation of a structured framework of moral reasons, enablers, disablers, intensifiers and attenuators is in conflict with the particularist insistence on the uncodifiable complexity of the moral realm. According to Dancy's model of reasons, the normative landscape divides into an overall and a contributory level consisting of a set of reasons, enablers, disablers, intensifiers and attenuators, each of which have clearly defined functions. However, given the extreme complexity of the moral realm, how can Dancy be so completely confident that this realm divides neatly into a contributory and an overall level: why not four or five levels?[162] And how does Dancy know that there are no other types of morally relevant features? Recently he himself has added the notion of a default reason to his list of types of normative features, but how can we be sure that this completes the list?[163] Moreover, what makes Dancy so confident that it is possible to isolate individual normative features and assign them clearly defined functions? There is, for example, no clear difference between the function of an enabler and a disabler. As Dancy himself points out, enabling comes along with disabling because 'trivially, the absence of an enabler will disable what would otherwise be a reason'.[164] The fact that a consideration needs an enabler entails that it can be disabled and vice versa: the absence of a disabler can be under-stood as an enabler. That a promise was given under duress, for instance, is a disabler and that it was not given under duress is an enabler. The distinction between enabling and disabling ultimately collapses. Thus, contrary to what Dancy's model suggests, enablers and disablers are not two distinct types of normative features with a clearly defined function. Dancy's confidence that the moral realm can be captured in a structured and well-defined framework of reasons, enablers, disablers, intensifiers and attenuators is difficult to reconcile with his belief in the extreme complexity of this realm. His notion of moral reasons does not fit well with the spirit of particularism.

However, how should particularists phrase their claims, if not in terms of moral reasons? Given the omnipresence of reasons in current moral philosophy, the prospect of trying to reformulate the particularist challenge outside a reasons-based framework might seem daunting. Moreover, what remains of Dancy's particularism once we acknowledge that reasons-holism does not provide particularists with any argument in favour of their position? And it is not only about their conception of moral reasons that particularists need to worry. Earlier in this section I showed that Dancy's stipulated conditions for what counts as a principled ethics are unjustifiably strong. They fail to cover the positions taken by some of the very generalists he explicitly targets. Due to Dancy's narrow definition of principled ethics, his particularist critique is, contrary to his own claim, of very limited scope and, therefore, misses its target. In light of these in parts devastating deficiencies in Dancy's particularism, one is tempted not to take it seriously. But as I noted at the beginning of this section, this response is premature. In what follows I will show why.

The particularist challenge

In the previous section it became clear that Dancy's conception of moral reasons undermines his particularist project and makes it difficult to define the challenge that particularism poses to the generalist tradition. I want to avoid, therefore, Dancy's terminology of reasons. However, terms like 'moral facts',[165] 'right- or wrong-making features'[166] or 'moral properties',[167] which are sometimes used in place of the terminology of reasons in the current particularist literature, are similarly problematic because they carry with

them a strong realist connotation. Since Dancy and other particularists usually insist that their position does not presuppose moral
realism, it is desirable that the particularist challenge be phrased in
terminology that is as neutral as possible with regard to different
metaethical theories.[168]

I propose to reformulate the particularist challenge in terms of
act-descriptions. I will understand the term 'act-description' in a
very broad sense that includes descriptions of emotional responses
and attitudes, descriptions of character traits and institutions. The
particularist challenge, as I will define it, has two parts. The first
part stresses the need for context-sensitivity, while the second
concerns the need for moral judgement. I will start with the former.

Holism revisited: The need for context-sensitivity

Holism is based on the observation that an action can be correctly
described in numerous different ways. This observation has, of
course, been made before, and independently from, the advent of
holism and moral particularism. J. L. Austin points out that 'it is
in principle always open to us, along various lines, to describe or
refer to "what I did" in so many ways'.[169] According to Donald
Davidson, individual actions are concrete particulars that can be
variously described.[170] Moral generalists like Ross acknowledge
that 'any act may be correctly described in an indefinite, and in
principle infinite, number of ways'.[171] Elisabeth Anscombe illustrates this point with the following example.[172] A man is pumping
water into the cistern which supplies the drinking water of a house.
Someone has found a way of contaminating the source with a
deadly cumulative poison whose effects are unnoticeable until they
can no longer be cured. The house is regularly inhabited by a small
group of party chiefs who are engaged in exterminating the Jews
and perhaps plan to continue a world war. The man who contami-
nated the source has calculated that if these people are destroyed
some good men will get into power who will govern well, or even
institute the Kingdom of Heaven on earth and secure a good life
for all the people; he has revealed the calculation, together with
the fact about the poison, to the man who is pumping. What is
this man doing? Should we describe him as earning his wages
or as supporting his family, as making a disturbance of the air,

as sweating, operating the pump, replenishing the water supply, poisoning the inhabitants, saving the Jews, or as working toward the Kingdom of Heaven? Which description we pick will be crucial for the moral assessment of the man's action.

It is widely acknowledged that an action can be correctly described in numerous different ways and that it often matters which of these act-descriptions we choose. When we describe an action we stress certain features and omit others. Which features we stress and omit will depend on various different factors such as the purpose of the act-description and the background knowledge we expect our interlocutors to have. As good moral agents we aim not to omit features of an action which we take to be morally relevant. We stress those features of the action which we think are especially morally significant and omit aspects which appear to us to be morally irrelevant. Part of what it means to have moral knowledge is to know which descriptions are relevant and which are not.

In this context it is worth noting that in his very early papers on particularism Dancy himself did not make use of the terminology of reasons. Instead, his focus lies on the notion of moral relevance.[173] He understands the question of 'how moral principles are (or in the case of the particularist, are not) related to particular cases'[174] as a question about 'the relation between general relevance and relevance in a particular case'.[175] Moreover, he presents the process of moral justification as a process of describing an action or situation.[176] According to Dancy, moral justification consists in a kind of narrative which stresses the relevant features of the situation. The persuasiveness of the moral justification is the persuasiveness of the narrative, that is, an internal coherence in the account which compels assent.[177] A good narrative is a narrative which 'sounds good'.[178] Dancy asks us to think about the moral description of a situation by analogy to the aesthetic description of a building:

> Suppose that I want to explain to someone how I see a particular building [...]. No description worth the name would simply start from the left, as it were, and work its way along until it reached the last feature on the right. [O]ne might start with that feature which one takes to be central to the building's architectural structure [...]. Perhaps the building should be seen

as basically flat rectangle, against which certain other features stand but to which they are complementary. [...] There are going to be plenty of features of the building that do not get in to this description at all, and a lot more that only play the sort of secondary role referred to above.[179]

Dancy emphasizes that the relevance or salience of a description is a matter of context: 'alter the context and what was salient may cease to be so or begin to play a different role in the story'.[180] That a building can be described as a flat rectangle, for instance, might be relevant in assessing the aesthetic value of one building, but not another. The same holds true in the moral case. Particularists emphasize that a description we take to be morally relevant with regard to one particular action might be irrelevant, although applicable, with regard to another. Assume, for example, that we describe a particular action as 'inflicting pain on someone', and that this is the most morally relevant description of the action. This does not mean that for any case in which an action can be described as 'inflicting pain on someone' we should take this to be the most relevant act-description. In the case of a doctor treating a patient, the morally relevant act-description is more likely to be something along the lines of 'helping someone', 'fulfilling her professional duty' or 'saving a life', even though the action can also be correctly described as 'inflicting pain on someone'.[181]

Moreover, even if an act-description is relevant in two cases, it might be relevant in very different ways. Consider again the analogy with the aesthetic description of a building. I might describe one building as a flat rectangle in order to convince you of its high aesthetic value, and I might describe another building as a flat rectangle to express my negative aesthetic judgement of it. In both cases the description of the building as a flat rectangle is relevant, but the way in which it is relevant – its purpose in my overall story as it were – is very different. Whether it is an aesthetic 'plus' or 'minus' will depend on what else I add to my description of the building. Similarly, the description of an act as 'promoting pleasure' can be morally relevant in very different ways. In one case I might describe a sick person who gains pleasure from being visited in hospital and in another case a torturer gaining pleasure from inflicting pain on her innocent victim. In the first case the act-description 'gaining pleasure' functions as a moral plus in my overall story of the situation. In the second case it functions as a moral minus: the pleasure that the torturer takes in her activity makes her action even worse.

That the relevance of act-descriptions is contextually grounded in this sense seems so obviously true that it is hard to see how anyone could deny it. It would be absurd to claim that generalists have been unaware of the fact that moral judgements need to be context-sensitive. Even a utilitarian like Bentham acknowledges the need for context-sensitivity. He remarks:

In some circumstances even to kill a man may be a beneficial act: in others, to set food before him may be a pernicious matter.[182]

So why do particularists think that the context-sensitivity of moral relevance constitutes a problem for generalists? The answer lies in the nature of moral principles. Moral principles contain act-descriptions of certain *types* of actions. They pick out certain act-descriptions as morally relevant and take a stance with regard to actions of this type. That is, moral principles prescribe, forbid, recommend or condemn certain act-types.[183] This presupposes that certain act-descriptions are of *general* moral relevance. The principle 'Do not break your promises', for example, takes a negative stance with regard to actions that fall under the act-description 'breaking a promise' and it thereby presupposes that this act-description is of general moral relevance.

Particularists point out that the fact that a particular action falls under a given principle because it can be described so as to correspond to the act-type specified in the principle does not mean that this act-description is relevant with regard to that particular action. Consider the principle 'Do not inflict pain on human beings'. That a particular action can be described as 'inflicting pain on someone' does not mean that this is the act-description under which we should view the action. A doctor who treats a patient can be described as inflicting pain and, thus described, her action falls under the principle. But since this act-description is not relevant, or at least less relevant than other act-descriptions, the principle seems to mislead us in this case.

Defenders of principled ethics not only presuppose that certain act-descriptions are of general moral relevance, they also take a general moral stance with regard to actions of this type. That is, they assume that certain act-types are *generally* morally required, forbidden, recommended, condemnable, valuable, etc. However, even if a description can be said to be relevant in two cases, it might be relevant in very different ways. Describing a building as a flat rectangle can serve to support a positive aesthetic judgement in one case, and a negative one in another. We saw that for Dancy the same is true with regard to moral act-descriptions such as 'promoting pleasure'. If we adopt a principle according to which promoting pleasure is morally valuable, we seem compelled to say that pleasure is a moral plus even in the case of the sadistic torturer mentioned earlier. But it seems that in some cases I can add the act-description 'promoting pleasure' to my 'overall story' in order to support my negative moral verdict of a particular action. For example, if I say 'She tortured the suspect, and she enjoyed it!' I do not describe the torturer as enjoying her activity in order to indicate that there was at least something morally valuable about her action. Rather, the pleasure that she takes in the torturing seems to make her action even worse.

I understand Dancy as arguing that by marking out certain act-types as generally morally relevant, moral principles lead us to misdescribe particular actions: we consider an act-description to be relevant in a particular case when it is not or when it is relevant in a very different sense, or we take an act-description to be much more relevant than it actually is:

> Particularism claims that generalism is the cause of many bad moral decisions, made in the ill-judged and unnecessary attempt to fit what we are to say here to what we have said on another occasion.[184]

According to Dancy, moral principles distort moral judgement. They lead us to pick out certain act-descriptions as relevant, required, forbidden, condemnable or valuable when they are not. The assumption that certain action-descriptions are of general moral relevance seems to conflict with the insight that moral relevance is context-sensitive: whether, and in what ways, an act-description is relevant depends on the particular context in which the action occurs and the whole 'story' I want to tell about the situation. This is the central idea behind Dancy's holism: an act-description that is morally relevant with regard to one action might be irrelevant (although applicable), or relevant in a very different way, with regard to another action.

There are four types of replies that generalists can make at this point. First, they can argue that particularists draw the wrong conclusions from the above examples and that some act-descriptions *are* indeed always morally relevant. Whenever an action can be correctly described so as to correspond to the act-type(s) specified in the moral principle(s) of one's moral theory, this act-description will be morally relevant. According to utilitarians, for instance, the act-description 'inflicting pain' is always morally relevant. But this does not mean that a doctor who in the course of treating her patient has to inflict pain on him is thereby doing something wrong. The doctor is right in treating her patient, although she is thereby causing pain, because the patient would be in even greater pain without the treatment. Her action is in accordance with the principle 'Create the greatest balance of pleasure over pain'. Moreover, utilitarians can agree with many of Dancy's other examples. For instance, they can agree that there are cases in which it is right to lie and wrong to return what has been borrowed.[185] For utilitarians these act-descriptions are, strictly speaking, not of general moral relevance. If they are morally relevant they are so in virtue of their impact on the overall balance of pleasure and pain. Thus, if they are relevant we can always redescribe the action as one of causing pleasure or pain. This explains Bentham's remark quoted earlier. Bentham points out that there can be cases in which to kill a man is a beneficial act and other cases in which to set food before him a pernicious matter. According to Bentham, whether – and in what way – killing and offering someone food are morally relevant is context-sensitive. It depends on the consequences of a particular act of killing or offering food for the overall balance of pleasure and pain. But this is not the kind of context-sensitivity particularists have in mind when they question moral principles. According to particularists, context-sensitivity does not stop short of act-descriptions which generalists take to be *intrinsically* morally relevant. For utilitarians, maximizing pleasure is such an intrinsically morally relevant act-description. Particularists believe that an act-description that is intrinsically morally relevant – i.e. *the* morally relevant act-description – in one case, may be irrelevant in another case, or fulfil a very different function in our overall story. The example of the sadistic torturer I mentioned earlier will be especially problematic for utilitarians. They will have difficulties to say that the enjoyment the torturer takes in the suffering of her victim makes her action worse. At least on a simple utilitarian account the overall balance of pleasure and pain is higher in the case of the sadistic torturer than in the case of an indifferent or reluctant torturer.

The second way in which generalists can try to accommodate the particularists' examples is by adopting something along the lines of Ross' theory of *prima facie* principles. Like utilitarians, Ross-style pluralists would reply to the particularists by insisting that some act-descriptions are always morally relevant. However, in contrast to monists, Rossian pluralists believe that there is an irreducible plurality of basic moral principles. These principles pick out different act-descriptions as morally relevant. With regard to the case of the doctor, for example, the Rossian pluralist would point out that more than one principle applies. One principle tells the doctor not to inflict pain, another to help others, and a third principle may stress the importance of fulfilling one's professional duties. These principles mark out different act-descriptions as morally relevant, but since they are *prima facie* principles they do not conflict. The doctor will need to decide which of the relevant act-descriptions is the most relevant one in her particular situation and then act on the corresponding principle. Particularists like Dancy who believe that any act-description can be morally relevant, if the circumstances are right, will view this pluralism as a step in the right direction. But they argue that it does not go far enough. According to particularists, it does not go far enough because Rossian pluralists are unable to account for examples in which one of the act-descriptions picked out by the principles is not relevant at all. They allow for a certain form of context-sensitivity. Rossian pluralists emphasize that the *degree* of relevance can change from context to context. However, they insist that the act-types specified by the principles are always relevant to some degree. If there is a *prima facie* principle that condemns breaking promises, 'breaking a promise' need not be the most relevant act-description, but it will always be morally relevant that an action can be described as breaking a promise and it will always be relevant in a negative way. But how can we know this in advance? How can we be so sure that breaking a promise is always a moral minus? Particularists believe that we cannot know it.

A third way in which generalists can try to accommodate the particularists' examples is by making the act-descriptions contained in the principles more specific.[186] If presented with the example of the doctor, the generalist could argue that instead of 'Do not inflict pain on human beings' the relevant principle is 'Do not inflict *unnecessary* pain on human beings'. The doctor does not violate this latter, qualified principle. The same strategy can be applied in the case of the sadistic torturer. If our principle is 'Non-sadistic pleasure is morally valuable' or 'Promote pleasure if and only if the pleasure is non-sadistic' we will have no difficulty in saying that the torturer's delight in his victim's suffering is a moral minus. The action simply does not fall under the principle. This is the manoeuvre McKeever and Ridge employ in order to show that holism does not provide any positive support for Dancy's particularism. I outlined McKeever and Ridge's argument in the context of my discussion of Dancy's conception of reasons, but it will be illuminating to have a brief look at it again.

McKeever and Ridge claim that even strong forms of principled ethics such as utilitarianism can account for holism. Their argument is based on the insight that holism is a claim about context-sensitivity, but neutral with respect to the question of whether this context-sensitivity is codifiable in terms of moral principles. McKeever and Ridge quote the following principle as an example of a principle that is compatible with holism: 'The fact that an action would promote pleasure is a reason to perform the action if and only if the pleasure is non-sadistic'. This principle includes an exception clause which specifies the conditions under which pleasure fails to be a moral plus. The principle is compatible with holism because whether or not the fact that an action would promote pleasure is a moral plus depends on the context; in particular, it depends on whether the pleasure is sadistic. McKeever and Ridge's argument is formally correct. However, Dancy rightly points out that a principle of the above kind would only be possible 'if we were lucky enough to be dealing with a set of morally relevant features whose defeasibility conditions [...] are finitely specifiable'.[187] The truth of the principle hinges on whether sadism is actually the only case in which pleasure is a moral minus rather than a plus. Dancy claims that even if the strategy of 'fine-tuning' our principles were successful in some cases, in most cases the process of making the act-type contained in the principle more and more specific would soon get out of hand. The act-description contained in the principle would become unmanageably long. In many cases it will not suffice to add one or two exception clauses to a moral principle in order to account for the context-sensitivity of the relevance and moral polarity of certain act-types. Think, for example, of the principle 'Do not lie' and the number of exception clauses we would need to add to this principle in order to account for the various circumstances in which we take lying to be morally permissible. Once one takes the context-sensitivity of the moral relevance and polarity of act-descriptions seriously, it is hard to deny that this context-sensitivity at least sometimes transcends codifiability. It seems overly optimistic to assume that we could codify all the conditions under which an act-type is morally relevant – and in which way it is relevant – in finite and manageable terms.

This assumption of uncodifiability is crucial to particularism and it is, therefore, important to be clear about what is meant by it. The thesis of uncodifiability comes in different strengths. In its strongest version it claims that it would not even be theoretically possible to specify all the exceptions of moral principles. It is hard to see how particularists could prove this strong point. Given that our cognitive capacities are limited, it is difficult for us to decide whether or not it would be possible to spell out all the exceptions of moral principles if our cognitive capacities were not limited. Furthermore, if codification is understood in terms of purely descriptive coding, the strong thesis of uncodifiability – and hence particularism – seems to collapse into non-naturalism. Some of Dancy's remarks substantiate this suspicion. For example, he points out that 'moral considerations are naturally shapeless'.[188] Little claims that 'the model backing particularism clearly belongs in the non-naturalist camp'.[189] Jackson, Pettit and Smith define particularism as the view that there 'is no codifiable pattern to be found in the passage from the descriptive to the ethical, and vice versa'.[190] However, it seems odd to suppose that particularism, which is a doctrine about the roles and nature of moral principles, is only available to those who adopt a non-naturalistic metaphysics.[191] Moreover, since there are non-naturalist generalists – think for example of Ross or G. E. Moore – there has to be more to particularism than the claim that moral considerations are naturally shapeless.

Particularists are, therefore, well advised to opt for a weaker version of the thesis of uncodifiability. Understood in a weaker sense, the thesis of uncodifiability is based on the insight that even if it were theoretically possible to specify all the exceptions to our moral principles, these principles would be highly complex. In order to cover all different circumstances, such principles would have to include various exception clauses which would render their antecedents unmanageably long. Given our limited mental capacities, it is highly doubtful whether we would be able to formulate and understand such a set of moral principles, let alone use it. With regard to the generalist's strategy of 'fine-tuning' moral principles, Dancy remarks:

> It is hard not to wonder what the point of such a process is and whether the complexities of its eventual product are ones that we could hope to grasp and operate. For the particularist, if principles have got to be like this, we would be better off without any such things at all.[192]

Holism itself does not preclude the possibility of accounting for context-sensitivity by making our principles more and more specific. However, holism renders the weak thesis of uncodifiability extremely plausible. Holism is the thesis that the moral relevance of an act-description depends on the context in which the action occurs; the thesis of uncodifiability states that this context-sensitivity cannot be specified in finite and manageable terms.

All three generalist responses to the particularists' examples discussed so far assume that some act-descriptions are always morally relevant and always relevant in either a positive or a negative way. But generalists do not need to insist on this point. Generalists are committed to the claim that certain act-descriptions are of *general* moral relevance, not that they are *always* morally relevant. The fourth way in which generalists can account for the examples particularists bring forward is by pointing out that an act-description which is of general moral significance can fail to exert this significance in particular cases. Moreover, an act-type that is generally a moral plus can under certain conditions be a moral minus, and vice versa. On this model, moral principles select certain act-descriptions as *generally* morally relevant and tell us that certain act-types are *generally* prescribed, forbidden, recommended, condemned, etc. Generalists who adopt this model of moral principles can agree with particularists on the thesis of uncodifiability. They acknowledge that moral principles are ineliminably exception-laden. Instead of spelling out the conditions under which a certain act-type is, or is not, morally relevant, they quantify over them. They might conceive of moral principles as being hedged by a *ceteris paribus* qualifier, for example. So we could say that lying is a moral minus, *other things being equal*.[193] I will say more about this generalist solution to context-sensitivity in Chapter Three. At this point it is important to note that, as it stands, particularists are unlikely to be impressed by this model of moral principles. What do we gain by adopting principles of the above kind? All that such principles seem to tell us is that certain types of actions are morally relevant unless they are not. What is the use of a principle that tells us that lying is wrong, except in those cases where it is not? Hedged principles will be empty unless we can give an account of what exactly we mean by qualifications such as 'generally', 'ceteris paribus', 'defeasibly', 'in standard conditions', or 'subject to provisos'. Generalists have to explain what it means for an act-type to be *generally* right, wrong, obligatory, forbidden, unjust, etc.

In this section I argued that particularists urge generalists to explain how the generality of moral principles is compatible with the need for context-sensitivity. In the next section I will present the second part of the particularist challenge.

Why not judgement all the way?

Moral principles contain act-descriptions of certain *types* of actions. This means that moral principles neither tell us whether a particular action is a token of this type, nor what exact course of action to take in a given situation. An action can be correctly described in numerous different ways and we need to view it under a certain description before we apply or follow a moral principle. If we fail to see that an act-token is of the type specified in a moral principle, we will not be able to apply or follow the principle. Moreover, if we misdescribe a particular action as being of the type specified in the principle, reliance on the principle will lead to wrong moral verdicts and actions. The same holds true if we are mistaken about which act-token best implements the act-type prescribed by the principle.

Generalists will normally be happy to grant particularists these points. They acknowledge that moral principles are not sufficient to guide moral thought and action: moral principles need to be supplemented by a capacity of moral judgement. It requires sensitivity, imagination, interpretation and experience to decide whether a principle applies, and to act upon it. We need judgement to bridge the gap between moral principles which contain act-descriptions of certain types of actions on the one hand, and the particular act-tokens to be done or assessed on the other. However, particularists ask why we cannot rely on this capacity of moral judgement alone. Why do moral principles need to be supplemented, but are not supplanted by judgement? Generalists acknowledge that we need to view an action under a certain description in order to make any use of moral principles. Particularists challenge generalists by pointing out that very often viewing an action under the right descriptions seems to be enough. They argue that just as I offer you a description of a building in order to convince you of its aesthetic value, I might convince you to share my moral verdict about a particular action by describing it in a certain way.[194] Moreover, it often seems that once we view a situation under a certain description, it is clear what course of action we ought to take. It seems that we 'just see' what is the right thing to do. According to many particularists, what is required for a sound moral judgement is not knowledge of general moral principles, but 'a way of seeing, a way of being sensitive to the moral facts'.[195] Particularists challenge generalists to show why moral principles are supposed to be necessary for moral thought and action.

This challenge is especially pressing for generalists who try to solve the problem of context-sensitivity by understanding moral principles as *prima facie* or *ceteris paribus* principles. According to Rossian pluralists, for example, moral principles tell us that we have a *prima facie* duty to perform a particular action, but the principles do not determine our overall duty or *duty proper*. There are no further, second-order principles which tell us how to weigh our different *prima facie* duties. Determining the overall status of a particular action and deciding what to do is a matter of judgement. But if we need to rely on our judgement anyway, why not judgement all the way?

The particularist challenge is thus twofold. First, generalists are challenged to explain how the generality of moral principles is compatible with the context-sensitivity of moral relevance. Once freed from the terminology of reasons, the important claim that remains from Dancy's holism is that moral relevance is contextually grounded. If one finds holism plausible one should not expect the context-sensitivity of moral considerations to be specifiable in finite and manageable terms. As we have seen, this combination of holism and uncodifiability raises real problems for generalists. The second part of the particularist challenge is to show why moral principles are supplemented but not supplanted by moral judgement. Why do we need moral principles?

Before I conclude this section I would like to revisit Dancy's remarks about the link between generalism and atomism. This will help to clarify further the particularists' target.

Atomism revisited: Universalizability and thought experiments

In the previous section I argued that understood in terms of the relevance of act-descriptions Dancy's holism poses a real challenge for defenders of principled ethics. I now want to show that the link which Dancy draws between generalism and atomism also becomes clearer once we drop his terminology of reasons.

In 'The current partucularist/generalist debate' (pp. 10–31). I argued that the debate between atomists and holists in the theory of reasons is orthogonal to the debate between generalists and particularists: generalists can be holists and particularists can be atomists. Dancy's diagnosis of what has driven so many philosophers to embrace generalism in ethics is implausible. It seems absurd to claim that historical defenders of principled ethics like Kant, Mill or Ross have been committed to generalism because of a prior commitment to atomism. In this context McKeever and Ridge rightly point out:

> [M]oral philosophers' two thousand-plus-year love affair with moral principles has little or nothing to do with a prior infatuation with atomism about reasons.[196]

However, I will show that *suitably rephrased and qualified* the idea behind atomism proves to be more central to the generalist tradition than it first seems.

Dancy defines atomism as the view that a feature that is a reason in one case must remain a reason, and retain the same polarity, in any other. I suggest rephrasing this idea in the terminology of morally relevant act-descriptions introduced in the previous section: atomism is the assumption that if an act-description is morally relevant in one case it has to be relevant with regard to any particular action that can be so described, and it must always be relevant in either a positive or a negative sense. This assumption underlies some historical forms of generalism, but only in a qualified form. In the previous section I pointed out that for a hedonistic utilitarian, for example, pleasure is always morally relevant, and always morally relevant in a positive sense. However, utilitarians are happy to grant that an act-description that is morally relevant in one case might be irrelevant (though applicable) in another case, or might be relevant in a very different way. I quoted Bentham's remark about the context-sensitivity of the moral import of killing and offering someone food in order to illustrate this point. For utilitarians, considerations such as, for instance, that an action involves killing or offering someone food derive their moral relevance from the impact these actions have on promoting pleasure and avoiding pain. Utilitarians are atomists only about these latter, *intrinsically* relevant act-descriptions.

The same holds true with regard to Rossian pluralists. A Rossian pluralist can argue that refraining from lying, for example, is not a *prima facie* duty, but a derivative duty. Derivative duties are not on the list of basic *prima facie* duties because the act-types they specify are not themselves morally significant. However, they still count as duties because actions of these types generally possess one or more of the morally fundamental characteristics that figure on the Rossian pluralist's basic list. For example, one might argue that lying normally involves promise-breaking and causing harm. Given that we have a *prima facie* duty not to break promises and cause harm, a particular action of lying will be *prima facie* wrong in virtue of being a case of promise-breaking or causing harm.[197] The Rossian pluralist is an atomist with regard to the *prima facie* duties specified on his list of basic duties, but he can be a holist about derivative duties. For example, if there is a basic *prima facie* duty not to cause harm, causing harm will always be morally significant and it will always be a moral minus. By contrast, if refraining from lying is only a derivative duty, Rossian pluralists will have no problems in acknowledging that there are cases – for example when one is playing the game Cheat – where the fact that an action can be described as lying is morally irrelevant.[198] So while it will be hard to find a generalist who is an atomist with regard to everything that might be morally relevant in some particular situation, many generalists are atomists when it comes to the act-descriptions they specify in their *basic* moral principles. The assumption of atomism thus plays some role in the generalist tradition. However, there are certain types of arguments in moral philosophy that can be shown to rely more heavily on the form of atomism Dancy is attacking.

One example to be mentioned in this context is Hare's thesis of universalizability. Hare argues that if we make any moral judgement about a particular situation, we must be prepared to make it about any relevantly similar situation. He believes that moral judgements share this feature of universalizability with descriptive judgements:

> If I call a thing red, I am committed to calling anything else like it red. And if I call a thing a good X, I am committed to calling any X like it good.[199]

Hare claims that if a person says 'I ought to act in a certain way, but nobody else ought to act in that way in relevantly similar circumstances', then she is abusing the word 'ought'; she is implicitly contradicting herself. Her offence against the thesis of universalizability is, according to Hare, logical, not moral. The logical offence lies in the conjunction of two moral judgements, not in either one of them by itself. The thesis of universalizability, therefore, does not render self-contradictory any single moral judgement. What it does is to force people to choose between judgements which cannot both be asserted without self-contradiction.[200]

On the face of it, Hare's thesis of universalizability might seem trivially true. Of course, one should not judge differently objects or state of affairs which are *exactly* like each other. But thus understood the thesis of universalizability collapses into supervenience. If we accept supervenience, we are committed to making the same moral judgement about situations which are exactly like each other in their non-moral properties.[201] Since, as Hare himself notes, nothing is ever exactly like anything else, little seems to be gained by the thesis thus understood.[202] Accordingly, Hare extends his thesis of universalizability to objects and state of affairs that are like each other 'in the relevant respects'.[203] The crucial question is then how we know what the relevant respects *are*. When are two situations, actions, objects or state of affairs relevantly similar? Because universalizability is a feature of descriptive as well as prescriptive judgements, Hare can answer this question by means of a descriptive example. The thesis of universalizability requires that if a person says that a thing is red, she is committed to the view that anything which is like it in the relevant respects is also red. To say that something is red while denying that some other thing which resembles it in the relevant respects is red would be to misuse the word 'red'.[204] Hare argues that:

> The difficulty of formulating precisely the respect in which the two objects have to be similar is simply the difficulty of determining the precise meaning in which the speaker was using the term.[205]

That is, the speaker needs to be able to say what it was about a given object that made her call it red, good or right. Her explanation, if she can give it, will pick out those features which are relevant and every other object or situation which possesses the same features will be like the first in the relevant respects, and hence should not be judged differently.[206] Hare grants that the speaker may be very unclear about the precise boundaries of the concepts she is employing. After all, we can use the term 'red' without having decided what we would say about borderline cases. But Hare insists:

> There must be *something* about the object in question which, if it were repeated in another object, he would (provided that he went on using the word in the same sense) treat as entitling him to call that object red too.[207]

In Hare's view a particular judgement commits us to a universal rule which states that any object, action or state of affairs X with the property (or set of properties) P is q. The thesis of universalizability requires us to make the same judgement wherever the limited set of properties that let us to make the judgement in one case recurs. Hare's argument is based on the assumption that we can isolate a property or a set of properties from our judgement about a particular situation and declare these properties to be *always* relevant and always relevant in the same way. This is atomism in its crudest form and it quickly becomes clear that Dancy is right to point out that it is a highly problematic assumption. The fact that I call a certain object, state of affairs, situation or action q because it possesses the property or set of properties P does not imply that any object or situation with P is q. The fact that I call an action morally wrong because it is the telling of a falsehood does not commit me to calling all actions which involve the telling of a falsehood morally wrong. What I treat as entitling me to call something red in one case does not necessarily entitle me to call something red in another case. It fails to entitle me to call an object red, for example, if I know that I have taken a drug that makes blue things look red and red things look blue.[208] Hare could reply to this objection by including the fact that one has not taken any mind-altering drugs into the set of properties that entitle me to call something 'red'. However, in standard cases the fact that I have not taken any mind-altering drugs does not seem to be among the things that make me call something red. I normally do not even think about it. In addition, particularists are sceptical about the prospect of broadening the universalizability base so as to include all respects whose presence or absence would have affected our initial judgement. The larger the universalizability base of a particular judgement gets, the more it will resemble the supervenience base of the judgement. So at some point 'relevantly similar' will collapse into 'precisely similar'. Particularists doubt that we can find a stable stopping point short of this trivializing result.[209] This doubt leads particularists to adopt the thesis of uncodifiability I introduced earlier.

One might think that Hare stands quite alone in his rather crude presupposition of atomism and that even he has just been careless in his attempt to spell out the notion of relevant similarity. However, a look at the use of thought experiments in moral philosophy shows that Hare is not the only one whose arguments rely heavily on the assumption of atomism. In ethics thought experiments are often used to test whether a certain act-description, factor or distinction is morally relevant. They are, for instance, widely employed in discussions about whether any moral weight should be given to such distinctions as that between what one does and what one merely allows or the distinction between what one intends as a means and what one merely foresees as a side effect. The literature on the doctrine of double effect and the doing/allowing distinction is rife with discussions of runaway trolleys,[210] organ transplants[211] and drowning children.[212] In these examples the reader is usually presented with a pair of cases that are claimed to differ only in terms of the distinction in question. The assumption is that if we judge the two cases to be morally different, this difference must arise from the distinction in question – since everything else is being held constant – and so the distinction must be morally relevant. If, however, we judge the cases to be similar, this is taken to show that the distinction is not actually morally relevant after all. Shelly Kagan labels arguments of this sort 'contrast arguments' because the arguments turn on the presence or absence of a contrast in our judgements about the cases.[213] Consider for example the following argument made by Michael Tooley in an attempt to refute the distinction between doing and allowing:

(1) Jones sees that Smith will be killed by a bomb unless he warns him. Jones's reaction is: 'How lucky, it will save me the trouble of killing Smith myself'. So Jones allows Smith to be killed by the bomb, even though he could easily have warned him. (2) Jones wants Smith dead and therefore shoots him. Is one to say that there is a significant different between the wrongness of Jones's behaviour in these two cases? Surely not. This shows the mistake of drawing a distinction between positive and negative duties and holding that the latter impose stricter obligations than the former.[214]

Contrast arguments of this sort are used by critics as well as advocates of the doing/allowing distinction. Richard Trammell, for instance, argues that Tooley's example is misleading because Jones's extreme hatred for Smith has a 'masking' effect. Trammell proposes to modify the case as follows:

Jones's attitude toward Smith is neutral in both cases. It costs Jones $1000 to save Smith from the bomb. It costs Jones $1000 to avoid shooting Smith. [...] [N]ow it ceases to appear that Jones has the same obligation to save Smith as not to kill Smith.[215]

Such contrast arguments are common in moral philosophy. However, they are based on a very problematic assumption. Kagan shows that the contrast strategy assumes that if a factor has genuine moral relevance, then for any pair of cases, where the given factor varies while others are held constant, the case in that pair will differ in moral status. The difference does not need to be so extreme as to make, say, one action permissible and the other action impermissible. The crucial point is that there will be some difference in moral status between the cases. A look at the literature on the doctrine of double effect and the doing/allowing distinction shows that while the opposing parties disagree about the proper construction and assessment of the various contrast cases brought forward, they tacitly agree that in principle any one pair of cases should be sufficient to settle the question of whether the given factor or distinction is of intrinsic moral relevance. They tacitly assume that, as Kagan puts it, if something 'makes a difference *somewhere* it must make a difference *everywhere*'.[216] Conversely, if something fails to be morally relevant in one case, it can *never* be of intrinsic moral relevance. An example of an author who is unusually clear about his acceptance of this thesis is Jonathan Bennett. With regard to the doing/allowing distinction Bennett remarks:

I believe that distinction is morally neutral. I mean by this that it *never* makes a moral difference, the only alternative being that it always makes one. [...] I don't see how the answer could be that sometimes it has significance and sometimes it doesn't. [217]

Kagan calls this the ubiquity thesis, but the idea should be familiar by now. It is the same idea that Dancy subsumes under the label of atomism. Kagan rightly points out that without the assumption of this thesis from the mere fact that some particular pair of contrast cases differs in moral status, advocates of the doing/allowing distinction or the doctrine of double effect could not conclude that these distinctions must make a difference in other cases where they are present. Without the assumption of atomism the distinctions might well fail to make a moral difference in some cases, even though they are of genuine moral significance in the particular pair of contrast cases at issue. In the same way, without atomism, from the mere fact that some particular pair of contrast cases does not differ in moral status, critics of the given distinction could not go on to conclude that it must lack intrinsic moral significance. The distinction might well make a difference in other cases, even though it did not make one in the cases at hand. Recognizing that the contrast strategy assumes atomism also helps to explain why both critics and advocates of the doing/allowing distinction and the doctrine of double effect spend so much time trying to disarm the contrast cases offered by the other side. For if atomism were correct, a single well-constructed and properly assessed pair of cases from either side would be decisive.[218]

Contrast arguments are not the only form of thought experiments that presuppose atomism. Another strategy often used in moral philosophy is to try to determine what we want to say about a particularly complex or controversial case by isolating the supposedly morally relevant features of this case and to see what we think about them in a simpler case. Once we have made up our mind about this simpler case we transfer this information back to the more complex case. Judith Jarvis Thomson's 'famous violinist' offers a prominent example of this strategy. Thomson argues for the permissibility of abortion by asking us to imagine a case where we are kidnapped and hooked up to a famous violinist who is in a coma and who will need to stay hooked up to us for nine months in order to survive. It would be very generous to stay attached and in bed for nine months, but we do not seem to be morally obliged to do it. The fact that the violinist has a 'right to life' does not seem to matter here. There is a difference between a 'right to life' and 'a right to what is needed to sustain life'. Thomson suggests that we can transfer this moral conclusion back to the controversial case of abortion: even if the foetus has a right to life, there are cases where it is morally permissible to abort.[219] If this argument purports to be conclusive and the claim is that (given that the cases are properly constructed and assessed) what we say in the first case forces us to say the same about the second case, it presupposes atomism. That is, we assume that we can isolate what we take to be morally relevant in one particular case and conclude that it is always morally relevant.

It is important to stress that I do not claim that Thomson's argument, and the use of thought experiments in ethics in general, *necessarily* presuppose atomism. The appeal to other, imaginary or actual, cases can be helpful even if it does not dictate what to say about a particular case at hand. Thought experiments are often illuminating because they can help to reveal biases and other distortions that cloud our moral judgement in the original case. Thomson's 'famous violinist' thought experiment, for example, could help to reveal a latent sexism which might subconsciously influence at least some people to oppose abortion. Since the person kidnapped and hooked up to the violinist in Thomson's scenario need not be a women, the thought experiment helps to bracket the morally irrelevant fact that only women can get pregnant and give birth. Particularists like Dancy are opposed to atomism, but they do not want to ban the use of imaginary cases and thought experiments from moral philosophy. In this context Dancy points out that '[o]f course it often happens that our judgement here is enlightened by a comparison between the new case and others in our experience (or outside it)'.[220] The crucial point is 'that this is enlightenment, not coercion'.[221] Given holism, the move from what we say about one case to what we say about another can never be automatic, but we may appeal to other cases in order to reveal the moral importance that something *can* have.[222] The problem is that moral philosophers often do not content themselves with this modest claim and instead treat thought experiments as conclusive arguments. This can be clearly seen in the case of contrast arguments, but a closer look at the literature reveals many more examples. There is a widespread reliance on the possibility of making progress by extracting what we take to be morally relevant in one particular situation and transplanting it into a new hypothetical situation, and vice versa. The assumption is that if something is morally relevant in one case it must remain relevant, and relevant in a similar way, in any other. This atomism is rarely openly admitted, and, if asked, most moral philosophers would probably deny it. However, many arguments nevertheless implicitly rely on atomism and – suitably rephrased – Dancy's theory helps to expose this assumption.

Conclusion

Particularism is a highly heterogeneous movement. Particularists oppose principled ethics for different reasons and to different

degrees. However, they share an unfortunate tendency to misconstrue or fail to specify their target. I showed how Dancy's narrow
definition of a principled ethics and his notion of moral reasons
seriously undermine his particularist critique. So far Dancy, and
particularists in general, have failed to provide a conclusive
argument against the generalist tradition. Recently, Dancy himself
has conceded that '[p]articularism in general is more a sort of a
suspicion than a thesis'.[223] Particularism is best understood as a
challenge. The challenge is to show how *particular* moral judgements can – and why they should – be based on *general* moral
principles. Moral agents are faced with decisions about what to do
in particular situations, and they need to be able to judge particular
actions, institutions and characters. The challenge which follows
from this for generalists is twofold. First, generalists have to
explain how the generality of moral principles is compatible with
the need for context-sensitivity. The second part of the particularist challenge is to show why moral principles are necessary for
moral thought and action. Moral principles are not sufficient to
guide moral thought and action: they have to be supplemented
by a capacity for moral judgement. Particularists ask why moral
principles need to be supplemented, but are not supplanted, by
judgement. Generalists cannot ignore these questions.

The main aim of this book is to answer the particularist
challenge as defined above. However, before setting out to do so I
will discuss three recent attempts to defend moral principles against
particularists.

Notes

1 Jonathan Dancy, *Ethics Without Principles* (Oxford: Oxford
   University Press, 2004), p. 1.

2 Aristotle, *Nicomachean Ethics*, 2nd edn (Indianapolis: Hackett
   Publishing Company, 1999), translated and introduced by Terence
   Irwin, 1094b.

3 Ibid.

4 See for example John McDowell, 'Comments on "some rational
   aspects of incontinence"', *Southern Journal of Philosophy* 27
   (1988), pp. 89–102, p. 93.

5 See Aristotle, *Nicomachean Ethics*, 1109b, 1126a.

6 Ibid., p. 1143a.

7 Ibid.

8 See Martha C. Nussbaum, *Love's Knowledge: Essays on philosophy and literature* (Oxford: Oxford University Press, 1990), p. 68; *The Fragility of Goodness. Luck and Ethics in Greek Tragedy and Philosophy*, rev. edn (Cambridge: Cambridge University Press, 2001), p. 299.

9 Terence R. Irwin, 'Ethics as an inexact science: Aristotle's ambitions for moral theory', in Brad Hooker and Margaret Olivia Little (eds), *Moral Particularism* (Oxford: Oxford University Press, 2000), pp. 100–29, pp. 110–11.

10 Aristotle, *Nicomachean Ethics*, 1098a; Irwin, 'Ethics as an inexact science', p. 114.

11 Aristotle, *Nicomachean Ethics*, 1126b–7a, 1128a; Irwin, 'Ethics as an inexact science', p. 111.

12 Irwin, 'Ethics as an inexact science', p. 122.

13 See Aristotle, *Nicomachean Ethics*, 1179b–81b.

14 Hugo Adam Bedau, *Making Moral Choices. Three Exercises in Moral Casuistry* (Oxford: Oxford University Press, 1997), p. 101.

15 Albert R. Jonsen and Stephen Toulmin, *The Abuse of Casuistry. A history of moral reasoning* (Berkeley: University of California Press, 1989), p. 89.

16 Ibid., p. 102, pp. 47–74, pp. 281.

17 Ibid., *The Abuse of Casuistry*, p. 258.

18 Ibid., p. 131.

19 Quoted in Jonsen and Toulmin, *The Abuse of Casuistry*, p. 135.

20 Marcus Tullius Cicero, *On Obligations. Translated with an introduction and notes by P. G. Walsh* (Oxford: Oxford University Press, 2011), p. 117.

21 Ibid., p. 116.

22 Ibid., pp. 116–17.

23 See Ibid., p. 251.

24 See ibid., pp. 155; pp. 251–2.

25 See ibid., pp. 154–5.

26 See ibid., pp. 252–3.

27 Ibid., p. 257.

28 R. M. Hare, *Freedom and Reason* (Oxford: Oxford University Press, 1963), p. 18.

29 Michael Sandel, *Liberalism and the Limits of Justice* (Cambridge: Cambridge University Press 1998), p. 11.

30 See Alasdair MacIntyre, *After Virtue* (Notre Dame: University of Notre Dame Press, 1981); Michael Walzer, *Spheres of Justice: A Defense of Pluralism and Equality* (New York: Basic Books, 1983); Sandel, *Liberalism and the Limits of Justice*.

31 MacIntyre, *After Virtue*, p. 21.

32 Ibid., p. 119.

33 See Tom L. Beauchamp and James F. Childress, *Principles of Biomedical Ethics*, 5th edn (Oxford: Oxford University Press, 2001).

34 Jonsen and Toulmin, *The Abuse of Casuistry*, p. 4.

35 Ibid., p. 4.

36 See ibid., pp. 306–7.

37 Albert R. Jonsen, 'Casuistry: An alternative or complement to principles?', *Kennedy Institute of Ethics Journal* 5 (1995), pp. 237–51, p. 248. Also see Carson Strong, 'Specified Principlism: What is it, and does it really resolve cases better than casuistry?', *Journal of Medicine and Philosophy* 25 (2000), pp. 323–41, p. 337.

38 Ibid., p. 9.

39 Tom L. Beauchamp and David DeGrazia, 'Principles and principlism', in George Khushf (ed.), *Handbook of Bioethics* (Dordrecht: Springer, 2004), pp. 55–74, pp. 60–1.

40 Ibid., p. 68.

41 See John D. Arras, 'Getting down to cases: The revival of casuistry in bioethics', *Journal of Medicine and Philosophy* 16 (1991), pp. 29–51, p. 31. For discussion see Jonsen and Toulmin, *The Abuse of Casuistry*, pp. 306–31; Jonsen, 'Casuistry: An alternative or complement to principles?', p. 248.

42 See Carol Gilligan, *In a Different Voice. Psychological Theory and Women's Development* (Cambridge, MA: Harvard University Press, 1982); Nel Noddings, *Caring. A Feminine Approach to Ethics and Moral Education* (Berkeley: University of California Press, 1984).

43 Noddings, *Caring*, p. 83.

44 Ibid.

45 Ibid., p. 13.

46 Ibid.

47 Ibid., p. 47.

48 See Bernard Williams, *Ethics and the Limits of Philosophy* (London: Routledge, 1985), pp. 174–96; 'Persons, character and morality', in Bernard Williams, *Moral Luck. Philosophical Papers 1973–1980* (Cambridge: Cambridge University Press, 1981), pp. 1–19.

49 See for example G. E. M. Anscombe, 'Modern moral philosophy', *Philosophy* 33 (1958), pp. 1–19; Lawrence Blum, *Moral Perception and Particularity* (Cambridge: Cambridge University Press, 1994); John McDowell, 'Virtue and reason', in John McDowell, *Mind, Value, and Reality* (Cambridge, MA: Harvard University Press, 1998), pp. 50–73; Nussbaum, *The Fragility of Goodness*.

50 Nussbaum, *Love's Knowledge*, p. 156.

51 Ibid.

52 Ibid.

53 Jonathan Dancy, 'An unprincipled morality', in Russ Shafer-Landau (ed.), *Ethical Theory. An Anthology* (Oxford: Oxford University Press, 2007), pp. 771–4, p. 774.

54 See David McNaughton, *Moral Vision. An Introduction to Ethics* (Oxford: Wiley-Blackwell, 1988); McNaughton and Rawling, 'Unprincipled ethics', in Brad Hooker and Margaret Olivia Little (eds), *Moral Particularism* (Oxford: Oxford University Press, 2000); Jonathan Dancy, 'Intuitionism in meta-epistemology', *Philosophical Studies* 42 (1982), pp. 395–408.

55 See Jonathan Dancy, *Moral Reasons* (Oxford: Blackwell, 1993), p. 76; Margaret Olivia Little, 'Moral generalities revisited', in Hooker and Little (eds), *Moral Particularism*, pp. 276–304.

56 See Jonathan Dancy, 'Holism in the theory of reasons', *Cogito* 6 (1992), pp. 136–8; *Moral Reasons*, pp. 60–2; 'What do reasons do?', in Terry Horgan and Marc Timmons (eds), *Metaethics After Moore* (Oxford: Oxford University Press, 2006), pp. 39–59; *Ethics Without Principles*, pp. 193–8; 'When reasons don't rhyme', *The Philosopher's Magazine* 37 (2007), pp. 19–24.

57 See McDowell, 'Virtue and reason', pp. 58–65; Jay L. Garfield, 'Particularity and principle: The structure of moral knowledge', in Hooker and Little (eds), *Moral Particularism*, pp. 178–204; Dancy, *Moral Reasons*, pp. 83–4.

58 See Dancy, *Ethics Without Principles*, pp. 71–93.

59 Some remarks of John McDowell can be read as endorsing this form of particularism. For instance, he remarks 'that particular moral cases may stubbornly resist capture in any general net' (John McDowell, 'Values and secondary qualities', in John McDowell, *Mind, Value and Reality* [Cambridge, MA: Harvard University Press, 1998], pp. 131–50, 149). Later in this chapter, I will show that how radical this claim is depends crucially on the underlying understanding of moral principles. For a more detailed taxonomy of different forms of particularism see McKeever and Ridge, *Principled Ethics*, pp. 14–21.

60 See McNaughton and Rawling, 'Unprincipled ethics'.

61 Margaret Little, for instance, argues that 'we have reason to doubt that there are any moral principles, *even* very complicated ones', (Little, 'Moral generalities revisited', p. 277). However, Little is a particularist only with regard to moral principles understood as exceptionless generalizations. She argues for a conception of moral principles as defeasible generalizations. I will say something about Little's notion of moral principles in the second chapter of the book.

62 McNaughton, *Moral Vision*, p. 190.

63 Dancy, *Ethics Without Principles*, p. 7.

64 Ibid., p. 140.

65 Ibid., p. 2.

66 Sean McKeever and Michael Ridge, *Principled Ethics. Generalism as a Regulative Ideal* (Oxford: Clarendon Press, 2006), pp. 5–6.

67 Dancy, *Ethics Without Principles*, pp. 87–8.

68 Ibid., p. 87.

69 McKeever and Ridge, 'Preempting principles: Recent debates in moral particularism', *Philosophy Compass* 3/6 (2008), pp. 1177–92, p. 1180.

70 See McKeever and Ridge, *Principled Ethics*, pp. 7–8; Pekka Väyrynen, 'Moral generalism: Enjoy in moderation', *Ethics* 116 (2006), pp. 707–41, p. 717 footnote; Frank Jackson, Philip Pettit and Michael Smith, 'Ethical particularism and patterns', in Hooker and Little (eds), *Moral Particularism*, pp. 79–99, p. 84; Little, 'Moral generalities revisited', pp. 280–1. Even authors who question supervenience emphasize the irrelevance of supervenience to the particularist/generalist debate. See for example Joseph Raz, 'The truth in particularism', in Hooker and Little (eds), *Moral Particularism*, pp 48–78.

71 McKeever and Ridge, 'Preempting principles', p. 1179.

72 Jonathan Dancy, 'Review: Sean McKeever and Michael Ridge, Principled Ethics: Generalism as a Regulative Ideal. Oxford: Clarendon Press, 2006', *Mind* 116 (2007), pp. 462–7, p. 466.

73 See for example Mark Norris Lance and Margaret Olivia Little, 'From particularism to defeasibility in ethics', in Mark Norris Lance, Matjaz Potrc and Vojko Strahovnik (eds), *Challenging Moral Particularism. Routledge Studies in Ethics and Moral Theory* (New York: Routledge, 2008), pp. 53–74.

74 McKeever and Ridge, *Principled Ethics*, p. 8.

75 See Dancy, *Ethics Without Principles*, p. 116.

76 McKeever and Ridge, *Principled Ethics*, p. 6.

77 Pekka Väyrynen, 'Usable moral principles', in *Challenging Moral Particularism*, pp. 75–106, p. 76.

78 Mark Lance and Margaret Olivia Little, 'Particularism and antitheory', in David Copp (ed.), *The Oxford Handbook of Ethical Theory* (Oxford: Oxford University Press, 2006), pp. 567–94, p. 570.

79 See McKeever and Ridge, *Principled Ethics*, p. 8.

80 Ibid.

81 McKeever and Ridge, 'Preempting principles', p. 1181.

82 McNaughton, *Moral Vision*, pp. 202–3.

83 I borrow this term from McKeever and Ridge, *Principled Ethics*, pp. 9–10.

84 Dancy, *Ethics Without Principles*, p. 117.

85 McNaughton, *Moral Vision*, p. 199.

86 Ibid.

87 McDowell, 'Virtue and reason', p. 58. The classification of McDowell as a particularist is controversial. While McDowell himself resists the particularist label, Dancy repeatedly cites him as one of the major inspirations for his particularist theory (see e.g. Dancy, 'Ethical particularism and morally relevant properties', *Mind* 92 (1983), pp. 530–47). McKeever and Ridge at least tentatively classify McDowell as an anti-transcendental particularist (see Michael Ridge, 'The many moral particularisms', *Canadian Journal of Philosophy* 35 [2005], pp. 83–106; McKeever and Ridge, *Principled Ethics*; see also Pekka Väyrynen, 'Moral particularism', in Christian B. Miller [ed.], *Continuum Companion to Ethics* [London: Continuum, 2011], pp. 247–60; Benedict Smith,

Particularism and the Space of Moral Reasons [New York: Palgrave Macmillan, 2011]).

88 Dancy, *Ethics Without Principles*, p. 192.

89 Immanuel Kant, *Groundwork of the Metaphysics of Morals*, in Mary J. Gregor (ed.), *Immanuel Kant. Practical philosophy* (Cambridge: Cambridge University Press, 1996), p. 45; Kant, *Kants Werke*, edited by Preußische Akademie der Wissenschaften (Berlin: Walter de Gruyter, 1903/11), vol. 4, p. 389, abr. Ak 4:389.

90 Dancy, *Ethics Without Principles*, pp. 116–17.

91 Ibid., p. 117.

92 Ibid., pp. 111–12.

93 McKeever and Ridge, *Principled Ethics*, p. 139.

94 Ibid., pp. 196–223. For another generalist who accepts Dancy's four conditions see Väyrynen, 'Moral generalism: Enjoy in moderation'; 'Usable moral principles'.

95 W. D. Ross, *The Right and the Good* (Oxford: Oxford University Press, 2002, first published 1930), edited by Philip Stratton-Lake, p. 46.

96 Ibid.

97 Ibid., p. 19.

98 Jackson, Pettit and Smith, 'Ethical particularism and patterns'. For Dancy's discussion of this approach see Dancy, 'Can the particularist learn the difference between right and wrong?', in K. Brinkmann (ed.), *The Proceedings of the Twentieth World Congress of Philosophy. Vol. 1 Ethics* (Bowling Green: Philosophy Documentation Center, 1999), pp. 59–72; *Ethics Without Principles*, pp. 109–11. I borrow the label 'constitutive generalism' from McKeever and Ridge, *Principled Ethics*, p. 12.

99 Jackson, Pettit and Smith, 'Ethical particularism and patterns', p. 87.

100 Ibid., p. 91.

101 Ibid.

102 A generalist who makes this point very clear is Väyrynen. See Väyrynen, 'Moral generalism: Enjoy in moderation', p. 708.

103 Dancy, *Ethics Without Principles*, p. 7.

104 Ibid., p. 2.

105 Väyrynen, 'Particularism and default reasons', *Ethical Theory and Moral Practice* 7 (2004), pp. 53–79, p. 67.

106 Väyrynen, 'Moral generalism: Enjoy in moderation', p. 728.

107 McKeever and Ridge, *Principled Ethics*, pp. 120–1.

108 Joseph Raz, *Engaging Reason: On the Theory of Value and Action* (Oxford: Oxford University Press, 1999), p. 67.

109 Dancy, 'When reasons don't rhyme', p. 20.

110 Allan Gibbard, *Wise Choices, Apt Feelings. A Theory of Normative Judgment* (Oxford: Oxford University Press, 1990), pp. 160–4.

111 Roger Crisp, 'Particularizing particularism', in Hooker and Little (eds), *Moral Particularism*, pp. 23–47; 'Ethics without reasons?', *Journal of Moral Philosophy* 4 (2007), pp. 40–9.

112 John Broome, 'Reasons', in Jay Wallace, Philip Pettit, Samuel Scheffler and Michael Smith (eds), *Reasons and Values. Themes from the Philosophy of Joseph Raz* (Oxford: Oxford University Press, 2004), pp. 28–55.

113 *Ibid.*

114 Dancy, *Ethics Without Principles*, pp. 15–37.

115 Garrett Cullity, 'Particularism and presumptive reasons', *Proceeding of the Aristotelian Society, Supplementary Volumes* 76 (2002), pp. 169–90.

116 See for example Väyrynen, 'Particularism and default reasons'; McKeever and Ridge, *Principled Ethics*, pp. 46–75, John F. Horty, 'Reasons as defaults', *Philosophers' Imprint* 7 (2007), pp. 1–28; Simon Kirchin, 'Particularism and default valency', *Journal of Moral Philosophy* 4 (2007), pp. 16–32.

117 Shelly Kagan, *The Limits of Morality* (Oxford: Oxford University Press, 1989); Frances Kamm, *Morality, Mortality*, vol. 2 (Oxford: Oxford University Press, 1996), p. 231.

118 See Jonathan Dancy, 'Enticing reasons', in *Reasons and Values. Themes from the Philosophy of Joseph Raz*, pp. 91–118; Raz, *Engaging Reason*, pp. 101–2.

119 T. M. Scanlon, *What We Owe to Each Other* (Cambridge, Mass.: Harvard University Press 2000, first published 1998), p. 19.

120 Väyrynen, 'Moral generalism: Enjoy in moderation', p. 717.

121 For an author who criticizes the preoccupation with the notion of reasons in the philosophy of normativity see Broome, 'Reasons'.

122 Dancy, *Ethics Without Principles*, p. 7.

123 Ibid., p. 81.

124 Ibid., p. 15.

125 Ibid.

126 Dancy, 'An unprincipled morality', p. 772.

127 Dancy, 'Review: Sean McKeever and Michael Ridge', p. 462.

128 Dancy, *Ethics Without Principles*, p. 76.

129 Ibid., p. 7.

130 See Dancy, 'Review: Sean McKeever and Michael Ridge', p. 466.

131 Dancy, *Ethics Without Principles*, p. 7.

132 See Dancy, *Moral Reasons*, pp. 60–2. According to Dancy, holism holds true for reasons containing only descriptive concepts well as reasons based on thick moral concepts. So the fact that something would be cruel, for example, might function just as holistically as the fact that a book has been borrowed (see Dancy, *Ethics Without Principles*, pp. 84–5; 'Moral particularism', in *The Stanford Encyclopedia of Philosophy* [Fall 2013 Edition], edited by Edward N. Zalta, http://plato.stanford.edu/archives/fall2013/entries/moral-particularism/ [accessed 5 January 2014]; see also Simon Kirchin, 'Particularism, generalism and the counting argument', *European Journal of Philosophy* 11 [2003], pp. 54–71). More moderate particularists who allow for the possibility of intra-moral principles restrict the purview of reasons-holism to reasons describable entirely in non-moral terms (see Little, 'Moral generalities revisited'; David McNaughton and Piers Rawling, 'Unprincipled ethics', in Brad Hooker and Margaret Olivia Little (eds), *Moral Particularism* [Oxford: Oxford University Press, 2000], pp. 256–75).

133 See Dancy, *Moral Reasons*, pp. 60–1.

134 Ibid., p. 61.

135 Dancy, *Ethics Without Principles*, p. 81.

136 Ibid., p. 77.

137 Ibid.

138 McKeever and Ridge, *Principled Ethics*, pp. 31–2. Other generalists have made arguments to a similar effect. See Joseph Raz, 'The trouble with particularism', *Mind* 115 (2006), pp. 99–120; Jackson, Pettit and Smith, 'Ethical particularism and patterns', pp. 96–9.

139 I will say more about codifiability in the second part of this chapter.

140 See Crisp, 'Ethics without reasons?', p. 46.

141 See Dancy, *Ethics Without Principles*, pp. 41–2.

142 Crisp, for instance, claims that 'what Dancy alleges to be a mere enabler is best understood as part of a favourer' (Crisp, 'Ethics without reasons?', p. 47).

143 Raz, 'The truth in particularism', pp. 61–70.

144 Ibid., pp. 68–70.

145 Dancy, *Ethics Without Principles*, p. 7.

146 Dancy, 'An unprincipled morality', p. 772.

147 Kant, *Groundwork of the Metaphysics of Morals*, 4: 421.

148 Barbara Herman, *The Practice of Moral Judgment* (Cambridge, MA: Harvard University Press, 1996), p. 75.

149 Ibid., p. 77.

150 See Dancy, *Moral Reasons*, pp. 112–13.

151 Ibid., p. 63.

152 See Kant, *Groundwork of the Metaphysics of Morals*, 4: 402–4: 403.

153 One way in which particularists could try to challenge Kantian ethics would be to claim that there are no maxims that can be willed as a universal law. The debate between Kantians and particularists would then turn on which maxims are universalizable and what scope universalizable maxims leave for judgement in deciding on right action. Thus understood, however, the particularists' challenge adds nothing to what Kantians have been discussing for centuries.

154 Selim Berker, 'Particular reasons', *Ethics* 118 (2007), pp. 109–39.

155 See Dancy, *Ethics Without Principles*, pp. 15–25.

156 See Berker, 'Particular reasons', pp. 114–15.

157 Ibid., pp. 120–1.

158 Dancy, *Ethics Without Principles*, p. 190.

159 Berker, 'Particular reasons', p. 130.

160 Ibid., p. 112.

161 Berker, 'Particular reasons', p. 125.

162 Berker makes a similar point. See Berker, 'Particular reasons', p. 138.

163 For Dancy's notion of default reasons see Dancy, *Ethics Without Principles*, pp. 112–13; 'Defending the right', *Journal of Moral Philosophy* 4 (2007), pp. 85–98, pp. 88–92.

164 Dancy, *Ethics Without Principles*, p. 41.

165 See for example McNaughton, *Moral Vision*, p. 205; Dancy, *Ethics Without Principles*, pp. 146–7; McKeever and Ridge, *Principled Ethics*, pp. 122–3.

166 See for example Dancy, *Ethics Without Principles*, p. 32; Väyrynen, 'Moral generalism: Enjoy in moderation'; McKeever and Ridge, *Principled Ethics*, p. 62.

167 See for example Dancy, 'On moral properties', *Mind* 90 (1981), pp. 367–85.

168 Dancy, *Ethics Without Principles*, pp. 140–1.

169 J. L. Austin, 'A plea for excuses', in J. L. Austin, *Philosophical Papers* (Oxford: Oxford University Press, 1961), pp. 121–52, p. 148.

170 Donald Davidson, 'The logical form of action sentences', in Donald Davidson, *Essays on Actions and Events*, 2nd edn (Oxford: Oxford University Press, 2001), pp. 105–22; 'The individuation of events', in Donald Davidson, *Essays on Actions and Events*, pp. 163–80.

171 Ross, *The Right and the Good*, p. 42.

172 G. E. M. Anscombe, *Intention* (Cambridge, MA: Harvard University Press 2000, first published 1957), pp. 37–49.

173 See Dancy, 'Ethical particularism and morally relevant properties'; 'Intuitionism in meta-epistemology'; 'On moral properties'.

174 Dancy, 'Intuitionism in meta-epistemology', p. 404.

175 Dancy, 'Ethical particularism and morally relevant properties', p. 534.

176 See ibid., p. 546. Also see Dancy, *Moral Reasons*, pp. 112–16.

177 Dancy, *Moral Reasons*, pp. 112–13.

178 Ibid., p. 113.

179 Ibid., pp. 112–13.

180 Ibid., p. 115.

181 Dancy discusses the example of a dentist who causes a patient pain when giving him an injection. See Dancy, 'Holism in the theory of reasons', pp. 136–7.

182 Jeremy Bentham, *An Introduction to the Principles of Morals and Legislation* (Oxford: Oxford University Press, 1996, first published 1789), J. H. Burns and H. L. A. Hart (eds), p. 79.

183 Second-order moral principles like the categorical imperative, Scanlon's contractualist principle or a rule-consequentialist principle contain very abstract act-descriptions and take a stance towards them, but they do not concern specific act-types such as breaking promises, lying or helping someone in need. Rather, they offer criteria for assessing our first-order principles. However, since second-order principles presuppose the existence of first-order principles they are indirectly subject to the same problems.

184 Dancy, *Moral Reasons*, p. 64.

185 Ibid., pp. 60–1.

186 For an elaborate example of this approach see Henry S. Richardson, 'Specifying norms as a way to resolve concrete ethical problems', *Philosophy and Public Affairs* 19 (1990), pp. 279–310.

187 Dancy, *Ethics Without Principles*, p. 81.

188 Ibid., p. 141.

189 Little, 'Moral generalities revisited', p. 279.

190 Jackson, Pettit and Smith, 'Ethical particularism and patterns', p. 80.

191 Dancy himself makes this point. See Dancy, 'Can the particularist learn the difference between right and wrong?', p. 66.

192 Dancy, *Ethics Without Principles*, p. 12.

193 See for example Paul M. Pietroski, 'Prima facie obligations, ceteris paribus laws in moral theory', *Ethics* 103 (1993), pp. 489–515; Robert L. Frazier, 'Moral relevance and ceteris paribus principles', *Ratio* 8 (1995), pp. 113–27; Garrett Cullity and Richard Holton, 'Particularism and moral theory', *Proceedings of the Aristotelian Society, Supplementary Volumes* 76 (2002), pp. 169–209.

194 See Dancy, *Moral Reasons*, p. 113.

195 McNaughton, *Moral Vision*, p. 205.

196 McKeever and Ridge, *Principled Ethics*, p. 39.

197 See McNaughton, 'An unconnected heap of duties?', pp. 437–8.

198 See ibid., p. 437.

199 Hare, *Freedom and Reason*, p. 15.

200 Ibid., p. 32. Also see R. M. Hare, *Moral Thinking: Its Levels, Method, and Point* (Oxford: Oxford University Press, 1981), p. 12.

201 In *Moral Thinking* Hare indeed seems to use the term 'universalizability' in this sense of supervenience. He remarks that the 'thesis of universalizability requires that if we make any moral judgement about this situation, we must be prepared to make it about any of the other precisely similar situations' (p. 42, emphasis added). I am here discussing Hare's earlier definition of universalizability. For a discussion of the later notion see Dancy, *Moral Reasons*, pp. 258–60.

202 Hare, *Freedom and Reason*, p. 12.

203 Ibid.

204 Ibid., p. 11.

205 Ibid., p. 13.

206 Ibid., pp. 13–14.

207 Ibid., p. 13.

208 See Dancy, *Ethics Without Principles*, p. 74.

209 See Dancy, *Moral Reasons*, p. 81.

210 See Philippa Foot, 'The problem of abortion and the doctrine of the double effect', in Philippa Foot, *Virtues and Vices and Other Essays in Moral Philosophy* (Oxford: Oxford University Press, 1978), pp. 19–32, p. 23. For a more recent and highly sophisticated discussion of Trolley cases and other well-known thought experiments in ethics see Francis M. Kamm, *Intricate Ethics. Rights, Responsibilities, and Permissible Harms* (Oxford: Oxford University Press, 2007).

211 See Judith Jarvis Thomson, 'The Trolley problem', in Judith Jarvis Thomson, *Rights, Restitution, and Risk. Essays in Moral Theory* (Cambridge, MA: Harvard University Press, 1986), pp. 94–114.

212 See James Rachels, 'Active and passive euthanasia', *The New England Journal of Medicine* 292 (1975), pp. 78–90, p. 79.

213 Shelly Kagan, 'The additive fallacy', *Ethics* 99 (1988), pp. 5–31, p. 6.

214 Michael Tooley, 'Abortion and infanticide', *Philosophy and Public Affairs* 2 (1972), pp. 37–65, pp. 59–60.

215 Richard Trammell, 'Saving life and taking life', *Journal of Philosophy* 72 (1975), pp. 131–7, p. 132.

216 Kagan, 'The additive fallacy', p. 13.

217 Jonathan Bennett, 'Morality and consequences', in Sterling McMurrin, *The Tanner Lectures on Human Values* vol. 2 (Cambridge: Cambridge University Press 1981), pp. 45–116, p. 73.

218 Kagan, 'The additive fallacy', p. 12.

219 Judith Jarvis Thomson, 'A defence of abortion', *Philosophy and Public Affairs* 1 (1971), pp. 47–66.

220 Dancy, *Moral Reasons*, p. 65.

221 Ibid.

222 See Dancy, 'The role of imaginary cases in ethics', *Pacific Philosophical Quarterly* 66 (1985), pp. 141–53; *Moral Reasons*, pp. 64–66.; *Ethics Without Principles*, pp. 155–8.

223 Andreas Lind and Johann Brännmark, 'Particularism in question: an interview with Jonathan Dancy', *Theoria* 74 (2008), p. 3.

CHAPTER TWO

Three Recent Attempts to Defend Moral Principles

This chapter discusses three recent attempts to defend the importance of moral principles: McKeever and Ridge's 'generalism as a regulative ideal', Väyrynen's theory of hedged moral principles, and Lance and Little's theory of defeasible generalizations. Since all three theories can be understood as direct responses to Dancy's particularism, I will refer to the above authors as Dancy's generalist critics. They take seriously the fact that Dancy's particularism attacks the very basis of principled ethics. Dancy's particularist critics want to defend the importance of moral principles at this fundamental level. I share this metaethical approach with Dancy's generalist critics, but I believe that the theories of moral principles they propose face serious problems.

The aim of this part of the book is twofold. First, it provides a survey of the most prominent recent attempts to fend off the particularists' attack. Secondly, and more importantly, the discussion of the problems of Dancy's generalist critics will help to clarify what it is that we want from a theory of moral principles. It thus helps to prepare the ground for the third chapter of the book which develops an alternative account of the nature and roles of moral principles.

The first section offers an internal critique of Dancy's generalist critics. I will show that all three theories face serious problems even when judged by their own standards. This approach requires me to take a number of things for granted. Most notably, I will follow Dancy's generalist critics in using realist language. Although not all authors in the current generalist/particularist debate are moral realists – Michael Ridge for instance is an avowed expressivist – they all use realist language. They speak of moral properties, moral truths and moral facts, of features that make actions right and wrong, etc. The current generalist/particularist debate takes place against the background assumption that moral knowledge is possible and that indeed we have quite a bit of it. Moreover, Dancy's generalist critics make extensive use of the terminology of reasons which I criticized in the first chapter of this book. However, for the sake of the argument I will need to bracket this problem as far as possible in the following discussion.

After the internal critique in the first section of this chapter, the second section will highlight a general problem of Dancy's generalist critics. I will show that Dancy's generalist critics – as well as Dancy himself – ignore the practical, action-guiding nature of moral principles.

Dancy's generalist critics

McKeever and Ridge's generalism as a regulative ideal

I start my discussion of Dancy's generalist critics with McKeever and Ridge's 'generalism as a regulative ideal'. McKeever and Ridge offer the first, and so far only, book-length metaethical defence of moral principles. Their aim is to show 'that the presuppositions of traditional moral philosophy are justified'.[1]

In making their positive case for generalism, McKeever and Ridge start from ground that is common between current generalists and particularists: the possibility of moral knowledge in particular cases. According to McKeever and Ridge, knowledge that a given action is right or wrong is based on the recognition of the relevant moral reasons which speak in favour of or against performing the action. They understand these reasons as descriptive facts and argue that the relation between these facts and the rightness or wrongness of a given action can be captured in the form of moral principles.[2] Many particularists believe that the number of possible moral reasons is incomprehensibly large and, therefore, cannot be captured in the form of moral principles. For instance, Dancy remarks that 'anything whatever might make a practical difference, or provide a reason, if the circumstances were suitable'.[3] McKeever and Ridge object that in order for there to be moral knowledge, the number of possible moral reasons must be 'finite and humanly comprehensible'.[4] They argue that this is especially clear in the case of moral knowledge by description. McKeever and Ridge point out that if, for example, we do not directly witness a crime but only hear about it from someone else, then our moral judgement that it was wrong must be based on the finite and comprehensible set of facts included in our interlocutor's description. Moreover, even in cases where we literally see someone performing an immoral action, our perceptual faculties are limited and the features of a situation in virtue of which we judge a given action to be wrong must thus themselves be limited. From this McKeever and Ridge conclude that if particularists want to account for the possibility of moral knowledge in particular cases, they have to acknowledge that the number of possible moral reasons is finite and humanly comprehensible.[5]

McKeever and Ridge explicate that on an atomistic conception of moral reasons, this conclusion would already be enough to establish that we could extract moral principles from our particular moral judgements. In Chapter One, I introduced atomism as the view that a feature which is a reason in one case must remain a reason, and retain the same polarity, in any other. Given that the facts in virtue of which an action can be morally right or wrong are finite and humanly comprehensible, we can know that a particular action is, say, morally wrong because it involves deception and no other moral reasons are present. We could then deduce a principle from this particular moral judgement according to which any action involving deception is morally wrong so long as no other moral reasons are present.[6] However, once one accepts the holistic conception of moral reasons which contemporary particularists defend, matters become more complicated. For given holism, a feature that is a reason in one case may be no reason at all, or an opposite reason, in another. So the fact that a particular action is wrong because it involves deception, and no other reasons are present, does not entitle us to conclude that all cases where deception is the only reason-giving feature are morally wrong. Holists insist that there are other morally significant features apart from moral reasons which can enable or disable the latter to be the reasons they are. It is thus not possible to articulate a principle to the effect that whenever an action is a case of deception and there are no other reasons present then it is morally wrong.[7]

In order to account for this difficulty, McKeever and Ridge stipulate that a claim to moral knowledge in a particular case commits us to the thesis that we have not overlooked any morally significant features which would overturn our moral judgement.[8] So McKeever and Ridge grant particularists that the moral judgement we take to follow from one set of facts could be overturned by further facts. But they insist that our judgement amounts only to knowledge if we have not overlooked any further facts which would overturn it. The next step in the argument is to show that this rational commitment, allegedly implicit in any claim to moral knowledge, can be built into a moral principle and that our moral knowledge in a given case can thus be captured in a principled way. McKeever and Ridge claim that we can 'simply quantify'[9] over all the possible morally significant features which, if present, would overturn our moral judgement. Consider, for example, a case in which someone has killed a rational agent and no other feature of the situation seems morally relevant. We conclude that the action was wrong in virtue of the fact that it was the killing of a rational agent. Our statement that we know that the action was wrong commits us to the claim that the situation is indeed an instance of the killing of a rational agent, that we have not overlooked any morally significant facts which prevent this fact from functioning as a reason, and that there are no countervailing reasons which outweigh it. McKeever and Ridge claim that we can extract the following default principle from this particular moral judgement:

(K) For all actions (x): If (a) x is an instance of killing a rational agent and (b) no other feature of the situation explains why the fact that x is the killing of a rational agent is not a moral reason not to perform the action and (c) any reasons to x do not (when taken collectively) outweigh the fact that x is the killing of a rational agent, then x is wrong in virtue of being an instance of killing a rational agent.[10]

McKeever and Ridge refer to principles of the above kind as default or hedged moral principles because nothing is said about which features might act as possible defeaters or countervailing reasons. We move from hedged to unhedged moral principles when we begin to list all the different possible defeaters and countervailing reasons in the antecedent of the principle and claim that none of them is present.

McKeever and Ridge argue that we can and need to move from hedged to non-hedged moral principles, i.e. 'principles whose defeating and enabling conditions have been fully and finitely articulated'.[11] They give two reasons for this need to move beyond default principles. First, there is the worry that 'there might be infinitely or unmanageably many moral principles'.[12] According to McKeever and Ridge, this would render moral knowledge unattainable, because there is no satisfactory model for how normal human beings could be sensitive to an infinite number of distinct types of morally relevant considerations.[13] However, by rejecting default principles as insufficient on the grounds that they are unmanageably large in number, McKeever and Ridge are contradicting one of their own premises, namely that the number of moral reasons is finite and humanly comprehensible. If the number of moral reasons is finite, the number of default principles that instantiate these reasons cannot be infinite. McKeever and Ridge cannot reject default principles on the grounds that they are infinite or unmanageably large in number, on pain of contradiction.

The second reason McKeever and Ridge mention for moving from hedged to unhedged principles is that 'default principles are insufficient to guide action without an independent ability to judge whether relevant defeaters are present'.[14] That is, we need to be able to judge whether, in a particular case, a consideration that is generally reason-giving is outweighed, annulled or reversed. McKeever and Ridge seem to demand too much of moral principles at this point. No principles or rules – other than probably algorithms – are fully action-guiding. Principles and rules can at most require or recommend some act-*type*. It requires judgement to decide which act-token best conforms to that requirement or recommendation in a particular situation.[15] Like all principles, default principles need to be supplemented by judgement. McKeever and Ridge fail to show that default principles are in some serious sense deficient. However, I will bracket this point in order to follow their overall line of argument. According to McKeever and Ridge:

[T]he best account of practical wisdom entails that practical wisdom involves the internalization of a finite and manageable set of non-hedged moral principles which together codify all of morality.[16]

They present their argument as an inference to the best explanation. What is to be explained is how practical wisdom is possible. McKeever and Ridge argue that the best explanation of 'how a person of practical wisdom can reliably know what there is most reason to do will invoke the idea that she already knows all of the kinds of considerations which can function as reasons, defeaters, enablers, intensifiers, and diminishers'.[17] This, in turn, requires that the list of considerations which can assume moral significance is finite and manageably short.[18] What follows from this is that it is possible to move from hedged default principles to unhedged moral principles by enumerating all defeating and enabling conditions. In the case of default principles, we quantify over all the features which, if present, would overturn our moral judgement. Once it is established that the number of these morally significant features is limited, McKeever and Ridge can announce the possibility of unhedged moral principles.

But McKeever and Ridge want to claim more than this. They purport to have shown that the possibility of moral thought and judgement depends on the provision of a suitable supply of unhedged moral principles. The claim is that unhedged moral principles are *necessary* for moral thought and judgement, not only that morality *can* be captured in a set of principles:

[M]oral thought and judgement presuppose the possibility of our having available to us a set of unhedged moral principles (which go from descriptive antecedents to moral consequents) which codifies all of morality.[19]

McKeever and Ridge fail to provide an argument for this alleged epistemic necessity of unhedged moral principles.

However, the real problem with McKeever and Ridge's defence of generalism lies in their understanding of moral principles itself. To begin with, McKeever and Ridge take moral principles to go from 'purely descriptive antecedents'[20] to moral consequents. They believe that the whole of morality is codifiable in terms of moral principles, where codifiability is understood as follows:

A set of moral principles S codifies all of morality in our sense of 'codifies' just in case (a) the moral principles in question have purely descriptive antecedents and moral consequents [...] and (b) for any moral truth, there is a moral principle or a set of principles in S such that the principle(s) in question together with the relevant descriptive facts entail the moral truth in question.[21]

This presupposes the truth of some form of reductive naturalism. Non-naturalist generalists – famous examples include W. D. Ross and G. E. Moore – will not be able to adopt McKeever and Ridge's defence of generalism. Non-naturalists deny that the moral realm is codifiable in purely descriptive terms. Given McKeever and Ridge's pretensions to defend the principled basis of traditional ethics, it is unfortunate that their conception of moral principles excludes non-naturalist generalists.

What is more, McKeever and Ridge do not only claim that the whole of morality is codifiable in a finite set of principles, but that these principles are also *manageably* short. However, even if we assume with McKeever and Ridge that the number of morally significant features is limited, we have to acknowledge that these features can interact and combine in various different ways. Let me illustrate this point with a rather artificial example. Assume that the number of morally significant considerations is highly limited, and that there are only five descriptive facts which can ever be morally significant. That is, assume there are only five features which can ever provide a moral reason or disable, enable, intensify or diminish another feature's reason-giving force. It will not be enough to enumerate these five morally significant features in the antecedents of our moral principles. We also have to account for the various ways in which these five features can interact and combine to yield the particular moral outcomes they do. McKeever and Ridge's notion of unhedged moral principles not only presupposes the enumerability of all morally significant features, but also the codifiability of their combinatorial patterns. Five morally significant features can combine in 31 different ways, and McKeever and Ridge would have to say that we can and need to account for all these 31 combinations in the formulation of our moral principles. While such principles already seem to be difficult to manage, things are likely to be even more complicated. The above combinatorial function assumes that the order in which the features occur does not matter, i.e. *a-b* and *b-a* do not count as two separate possibilities but as one. However, it seems plausible to assume that the order in which the morally significant features occur does matter at least sometimes. It matters, for example, whether someone has been threatened before or after he made a promise. If order matters, five morally significant features can combine in 251 ways. Moreover, some of the five features might happen to occur only, or never, in combination with one or more of the other five features. For example, feature *a* might be right-making if and only if *b* and *c* are absent, *d* and *e* are present and *e* is occurring before *d*. This would reduce the number of possible combinations, but at the same time render the combinatorial function even more complicated. So even if the number of morally significant features were highly limited, the antecedents of unhedged principles would be unmanageably long and complex.

McKeever and Ridge's account of unhedged moral principles is too demanding. So far no satisfactory set of unhedged principles has been presented and it is telling that McKeever and Ridge themselves do not offer even an example of an unhedged moral principle. It is important to note that they do not claim that the right set of moral unhedged moral principles which codifies all of morality could easily be found and articulated. McKeever and Ridge emphasize that that generalism is a regulative ideal and 'that moral theorising remains a work in progress, just as scientific theorising remains a work in progress'.[22] They acknowledge 'that the practice of moral theorising is [not] guaranteed ever to terminate in a moral theory we know is absolutely complete'.[23] However, my point is that even if there were a set of unhedged principles which codifies all of morality, yet to be discovered, it would be highly complex. In order to cover all different circumstances such principles would have to include various exception clauses that would render their antecedents unmanageably long. This is not to deny that there could be some general, unhedged moral principles. 'Do not inflict suffering on others for your own enjoyment', for example, is a promising candidate for an unhedged moral principle. However, some isolated exceptionless principles here and there are not enough to support McKeever and Ridge's assertion of the possibility of a set of unhedged principles which together codify all of morality. What is more, I have argued that

McKeever and Ridge fail to show that we need such a set of principles. In the absence of such an argument, we do not have any reason to adopt their form of generalism as a regulative ideal and search for the right set of unhedged moral principles.

Väyrynen's theory of hedged moral principles

In a series of papers Väyrynen has recently defended a form of moral generalism that rests on a notion of 'hedged' moral principles.[24] In contrast to McKeever and Ridge, Väyrynen does not aim to defend the principled basis of traditional moral theories. Rather, he believes that there is a need for a new, moderate form of generalism. According to Väyrynen, there is a need for a new form of generalism that can accommodate and explain reasons-holism, the thesis that lies at the heart of Dancy's particularism. Väyrynen's aim is 'to hijack holism into a generalist framework'[25] by developing 'a novel account of moral principles as a kind of "hedged" principles'.[26]

However, the motivation for Väyrynen's project needs qualification. In Chapter One, I showed that the debate between atomists and holists in the theory of reasons is orthogonal to the particularist/generalist debate. Generalists can be holists and particularists can be atomists. In order to account for holism, generalists do not need to employ any novel account of moral principles of the sort Väyrynen advances. Even strong, traditional forms of principled ethics such as utilitarianism can account for holism. I argued that it is the combination of holism and the assumption of uncodifiability that poses a threat to traditional forms of generalism. Holism is the thesis that moral reasons are context-sensitive; uncodifiability is the view that this context-sensitivity at least sometimes transcends codifiability. With regard to McKeever and Ridge's generalism as a regulative ideal, I suggested that it is unrealistic to assume that the whole of morality could be codified in a set of finite and manageable principles. In many cases it will not suffice to add one or two exception clauses to a moral principle in order to account for the context-sensitivity of the moral reasons which the principle is supposed to specify. Once one takes the context-sensitivity of moral reasons seriously, it is hard to deny that this context-sensitivity sometimes transcends codifiability. Väyrynen seems to agree on this point since he remarks that 'holism treats normative reasons as *irreducibly* context dependent'.[27] He acknowledges that holism raises the possibility 'that we cannot state the conditions for the presence of reasons in finite and useful terms'.[28] Generalists like Väyrynen, who claim to take the particularist challenge seriously and who see a need for a new, 'moderate' form of generalism, cannot ignore the problem of uncodifiability. Otherwise their quest for a new theory of moral principles will be unmotivated. Väyrynen's account of hedged moral principles thus has to account not only for reasons-holism, i.e. the context-sensitivity of moral reasons, but also for the fact that this context-sensitivity is at least sometimes uncodifiable. In what follows I will examine whether Väyrynen's model of hedged moral principles fulfils this requirement.

According to Väyrynen, moral principles 'specify the form and nature of conditions that would license one to treat some considerations as moral reasons'.[29] He believes that moral principles have an explanatory function and points out that 'a substantive principle that killing persons is wrong would identify killing a person as a feature that would be explanatory of wrongness'.[30]

The crucial question for Väyrynen is how moral principles of the above kind can account for the potentially uncodifiable context-sensitivity of moral considerations. The first step is to accept that moral principles have exceptions. We then need an account of how moral principles can tolerate exceptions. Väyrynen argues that moral principles can account for exceptions only if they have a more complex structure than they seem to have on the surface. If a moral principle such as 'All promises ought to be kept' were just a simple universal generalization, any exception to the principle would refute it.[31] One possible way to account for exceptions is to add an 'unless' clause to the principle and try to spell out the unsuitable conditions associated with it. This is McKeever and Ridge's strategy which I discussed in the first part of this chapter. Väyrynen rightly points out that 'we might not generally be able to state the unsuitable conditions associated with a given principle in a finite and manageable form'.[32]

Väyrynen's proposal is to build a reference to what he dubs the 'normative bases' of moral reasons into the moral principles. He starts his argument with the following thesis:

> For any consideration C that is a moral reason to ø, the normative fact that C is a moral reason to ø requires a basis that explains why C is a moral reason to ø.[33]

Väyrynen claims that this so-called 'basis thesis' should be uncontroversial even to particularists. I will say more about this thesis later. For the moment, I shall assume with Väyrynen that 'when some fact is a moral reason of a certain type, there should be something because of which it is such a reason'.[34] There needs to be something that explains, for instance, why promising to do something is a moral reason to do it when it is. For Väyrynen this is tantamount to the claim that every moral reason requires a normative basis that is the source of the kind of normative significance that the reason has and thus explains why it is a reason. He points out that what exactly one regards as the basis of a moral reason will depend on one's substantive moral theory. According to utilitarians, promising gives a reason insofar as, and because, fulfilling the promise sustains a social institution which has co-operative and other benefits to people. Other moral theories offer different explanations of why promising gives moral reasons. Contractualists, for example, might argue that keeping a promise gives due weight to the expectations that a promise creates concerning one's future behaviour.[35]

Väyrynen states that the bases of moral reasons have a relational structure. Moral theories of the above kind describe a relation R between a property F and a moral property M such that x's being F is a reason for x's being M when, and because, x instantiates R.[36] While the content of R is subject to substantive normative disputes, the following principle is supposed to be neutral between different first-order moral theories:

> (P) Necessarily, any act that one has promised to do is *pro tanto* right in virtue of one's having promised to do it, provided the act instantiates the designated relation for promising and *pro tanto* rightness.[37]

Principle (P) is hedged by reference to the relation that defines the normative basis of promising. Väyrynen claims that 'there always seems to be available a moral principle [...] that affirms the existence of the designated relation for F and M and selects it as the basis of the reason that something's being F gives for its being M'.[38] He thus reaches the following general model of hedged moral principles:

(HP) Necessarily, any x that is F is M in virtue of x's being F, provided x instantiates the designated relation for F and M.[39]

According to Väyrynen, the great advantage of his model lies in its ability to explain when and why something is a reason of a certain kind, and when and why it is not. We can appeal to one and the same normative basis to explain, for instance, why promising gives a reason to fulfil the promise and why the fact that being extracted by manipulation is an unsuitable condition for promising to give a reason to fulfil the promise.[40] So hedged moral principles do not only allow for exceptions, but also tell us when and why something counts as an exception. Väyrynen takes it to be an important achievement of his theory that it reconciles reasons-holism and generalism. He stresses that his model of hedged moral principles is compatible with holism since 'a feature that a hedged principle identifies as giving moral reasons of a certain type may fail in some context to give a reason of that type, and this happens when, and because, the relevant designated relation fails to be instantiated'.[41] However, as I pointed out earlier, holism itself does not generate any need for a new conception of moral principles. It is the acknowledgement that the context-sensitivity of moral considerations is at least sometimes uncodifiable which would earn Väyrynen the title of a *moderate* generalist.

Unfortunately, his proposed model of hedged moral principles only postpones the problem of context-sensitivity. It leaves the task of dealing with exceptions to substantive, first-order moral theory. The question of how to deal with exceptions will re-emerge at the level of normative bases when we try to formulate the relation between a property F and a moral property M. Väyrynen insists that his theory can grant that we might be unable to state the potential unsuitable conditions in a manageable list.[42] Hedged moral principles imply that a feature of a situation is unsuitable for x's being F to be a reason for x's being M when, and because, x fails to instantiate the designated relation for F and M. Väyrynen emphasizes that this does not presuppose that the potential unsuitable conditions themselves form a manageably short list.[43] However, this is only the case because Väyrynen's model presupposes an even stronger sense of codifiability. It assumes that for every moral reason we can identify a relation R that tells us that necessarily whenever F then M. Our first-order moral theory is supposed to determine when and why certain moral reasons obtain. In addition, Väyrynen holds that the basis of a moral reason cannot be normatively disjoint. That is, he denies that killing a person, for instance, can sometimes be morally wrong because it frustrates the victim's prudential interests, sometimes because it destroys the kind of intrinsic good that the individual person is, and sometimes because it violates her dignity.[44] Väyrynen postulates that 'there is a unique property which fills the designated normative basis role'.[45] If we accept this 'uniqueness condition',[46] the designated relation R not only tells us that a feature F always gives us a reason of a certain kind, but also that there is no other feature which can give us that reason. So once we have specified R, our moral principle would tell us, for instance, that necessarily any act of killing is wrong *if and only if* it frustrates the victim's prudential interests. Accordingly, there is no need to enumerate all the circumstances in which killing fails to be wrong-making. If we knew that killing is wrong *if and only if* it frustrates the victim's prudential interests, there would obviously be no further need to specify the conditions which could enable or disable killing to be the reason it is. Väyrynen's account of hedged moral principles presupposes that the context-sensitivity of moral reasons is fully codifiable. Despite Väyrynen's claims to the contrary, such an account of moral generalism can hardly be said to be moderate.

This result should not be too surprising, considering that Väyrynen's hedged moral principles have an inbuilt reference to the normative bases of moral reasons, and hence to traditional first-order moral theory. It is traditional first-order moral theories, such as utilitarianism, which are supposed to tell us when and why something is a moral reason. Väyrynen faces a dilemma. Either there is a need for a *new, moderate* form of generalism because there is something wrong with traditional, principle-based first-order moral theories, or there is not. If there is a need for a new form of generalism, we cannot offer a conception of moral principles that incorporates, and leaves untouched, traditional principle-based ethics. If we believe that there is nothing wrong with traditional principle-based ethics, then there is no need for a new, moderate form of generalism.[47]

But the problems with Väyrynen's argument start even earlier, namely with his apparently uncontroversial 'basis thesis'. This thesis, according to which every moral reason requires a normative basis that explains it, is supposed to be acceptable even to particularists. Väyrynen is right insofar as '[g]eneralists and particularists agree that nothing is barely right, but rather is right in virtue of having some other, "right-making" properties'.[48] Dancy, for instance, acknowledges that 'nothing is just wrong; a wrong action is wrong because of other features that it has'.[49] If this is what the basis thesis is about, it is simply saying that moral properties are resultant. Väyrynen's normative basis would then be the same as the resultance base of moral properties. Resultance is a relation between a property of an object and the features that 'give' it that property.[50] Generalists and particularists agree that moral properties are resultant. But in contrast to Väyrynen, particularists deny that there is such thing as a *general* resultance base for a moral property. In this context Dancy remarks:

> I want to agree that every particular moral truth will need and have an explanation, but deny that the explanation has any need to be run in terms of general moral truths. The explanation will be given in terms of the properties from which the thin properties of rightness and wrongness result. This has no need to be generalized.[51]

Thus, according to Dancy, resultance is not a generalizable relation. Dancy points out that 'there are many different ways in which an action can get to be wrong'.[52] He emphasizes that we cannot assume that what explains why an action is wrong in one case will explain why a similar type of action is wrong in another case. To be clear, particularists do not deny that if an action is wrong, every other action that is exactly the same in all non-moral respects must also be wrong. That is, particularists acknowledge that moral properties supervene on non-moral properties in the sense that if an action has a moral property, then any other action exactly similar to the first in non-moral respects will have that property too.[53] While the supervenience base of an action consists in *all* the non-moral properties of the action, the resultance base contains only those properties that 'give' the action its moral status. What particularists deny is that if an action is wrong, every other action that shares the features that make the first one wrong must also be wrong. They point out that two actions may be similar to each other in a limited way, that is, in the respects that make the first action wrong, but differ in other respects so that the second is not wrong. For example, two actions can share the feature of being the breaking of a promise, but differ in moral status because one of the promises was given under duress. The properties that make one action wrong are prevented from doing so in the other case because of variations that lie beyond the common resultance base.[54] Why should we think that particularists are wrong and that moral resultance is generalizable? By describing the normative bases of moral properties in terms of traditional, i.e. principle-based, moral theories, Väyrynen is begging the question against particularists.

However, Väyrynen's basis thesis is problematic even if we presuppose the truth of generalism. At some point Väyrynen remarks that moral principles identify 'conditions that explain why some such moral property as rightness is instantiated'.[55] This suggests that what we are looking for is the general resultance base of certain moral properties. That is, we are looking for the property (or the set of properties) that, say, makes right actions right. We thus assume that all right actions share a common non-moral property, or a set of non-moral properties, which always instantiates the same moral property. Utilitarianism, for instance, tells us that all right actions share the common property of being conducive to the general happiness. The utilitarian principle explains when and why the moral property 'rightness' is instantiated. If this is what Väyrynen wants to deduce from his basis thesis, it not only conflicts with particularism, but also with ethical pluralism. Both particularists and ethical pluralists, like W. D. Ross, believe that there are many ways in which an action can become right or wrong. For instance, Ross remarks that:

> There is no reason to anticipate that every act that is our duty is so for one and the same reason. Why should two sets of circumstances, or one set of circumstances, *not* possess different characteristics, any one of which makes a certain act our prima facie duty?[56]

Thus, pluralists deny that there is such a thing as the common resultance base of right actions *per se*. But unlike particularists they believe that we can generalize the resultance base of certain types or groups of actions. So ethical pluralists hold that we can specify the property (or the set of properties) that makes, for example, acts of killing wrong. What explains the wrongness of acts of killing might be different from, say, the explanation of the wrongness of acts of lying. For instance, we might formulate a principle according to which killing is wrong if, and because, it violates the victim's dignity, and another principle that states that lying is wrong if, and because, it undermines a social institution that has co-operative and other benefits to people.

But the demand for an explanatory basis can be read in yet another way. So far we have been looking for features that explain why an action is right or wrong, i.e. right- and wrong-making features. According to Väyrynen, 'hedged principles [...] explain which features are right- and which are wrong-making'.[57] But at some points he seems to demand not only an explanation of why an action is right or wrong, but also an explanation of why certain features 'make' an action right or wrong. Väyrynen believes that 'when we judge some specific consideration C to be (that is, to have the property of being) a reason for an act's being right or wrong, we should be able to explain why C is the kind of reason it is'.[58] Part of what makes it so difficult to understand the basis thesis is Väyrynen's use of the term 'moral reason'. Väyrynen talks about 'right- and wrong-making reasons'[59] and seems to conceive of moral reasons as features or facts that 'make' actions right or wrong. He refers to the normative basis of moral reasons as 'some evaluative or deontic condition (property, relation, etc.) the presence of which explains why C is a reason (when it is) for an action to be right or wrong'.[60] We are thus no longer concerned with explanations of the wrongness or rightness of actions, but with 'explanations of right-making features'.[61] What is at issue now is the source and explanation of the normative significance of the features that make actions right or wrong. Thus understood, the 'basis thesis' is even further away from being the uncontroversial thesis Väyrynen claims it to be. It goes beyond the notion of resultance as well as what traditional principle-based theories offer. This in turn means that Väyrynen cannot fix the normative bases of moral reasons by reference to traditional first-order moral theory. Let me explain.

While the notion of resultance is concerned with the explanation of why an action is right or wrong, Väyrynen seems to ask for an explanation of why the features that explain why an action is right or wrong – i.e. the right- or wrong-making features – are right- or wrong-making. Traditional principle-based theories generally do not satisfy this explanatory demand, nor do they aim to do so. The utilitarian principle, for example, tells us that an action is right because it is conducive to the general happiness, but it does not tell us why the fact that an action is conducive to the general happiness is of normative significance. In this context Bentham remarked that 'to give such proof is as impossible as it is needless'.[62] Väyrynen apparently disagrees since he demands an explanation of 'why the circumstances that count as reasons [...] are morally relevant in the ways they are'.[63] He notes that:

> Even if one accepts 'Causing pain is wrong' out of a direct concern for not causing pain to others [...] one would presumably be a defective moral agent if one accepted the principle even if one thought that there was no basis for regarding the property of causing pain as a wrong-making feature.[64]

This might be true for some right- and wrong-making features, but I believe that it is far from clear that all moral reasons require such a normative basis. If we were to tell someone that an action is wrong because it causes needless suffering, and if the person were then to ask us why causing needless suffering is a wrong-making feature (or a reason not to do the action), we would presumably think of her as morally defective. Väyrynen might try to answer this objection by pointing out that what explains why some consideration is a reason of a certain kind, need not be distinct from the consideration itself. He emphasizes that the basis thesis does not entail that any explanation as to why something is a reason will be related to a further reason.[65] He wants to allow for the possibility that promoting overall happiness is a moral reason to ø because 'for there to be a moral reason to ø just is for ø-ing to promote overall happiness'.[66] It is debatable whether this qualifies as an explanation. However, this is not my point. My objection is not that Väyrynen's basis thesis is vulnerable to an infinite regress of explanations. To quote Bentham again, the point is not that 'a chain of proofs must have their commencement somewhere',[67] but rather that with regard to some reasons proof or explanation seems *needless*. My example above shows that it is at least questionable whether we need to explain, for instance, why causing needless suffering is wrong-making. The basis thesis is supposed to be intuitively plausible.[68] However, understood as a demand for explanation of right- and wrong-making features, Väyrynen's basis thesis is far from uncontroversial. Read as a claim about resultance, the thesis is largely uncontroversial, but of little use for Väyrynen's overall argument since we cannot simply assume that resultance is a generalizable relation without begging the question against particularism.

Väyrynen's model of hedged moral principles does not live up to the expectations it raises. It fails to show why morality needs to be principled and presupposes a strong sense of codifiability that sits badly with Väyrynen's aspirations to offer a moderate form of generalism.

Lance and Little's theory of defeasible generalizations

In contrast to McKeever, Ridge and Väyrynen, Lance and Little take themselves to have departed so far from traditional principled ethics that they used to identify themselves as particularists. However, they quickly realized that since their main objective is to defend the importance of moral principles, this label is rather misleading.[69] Lance and Little emphasize that they are not 'anti-generalists',[70] but that they reject a certain version of generalism according to which moral principles have to be exceptionless in order to be explanatory. They believe that moral principles are ineliminably exception-laden. Moral principles are 'shot through with exceptions we cannot eliminate'.[71] Lance and Little's aim is to show that these defeasible generalizations can nevertheless be 'robustly explanatory and insightful'.[72]

Lance and Little's argument starts with the observation that the sciences and our everyday life are rife with explanatory defeasible generalizations: defeasibly, matches light when struck; normally red cups look red; ceteris paribus, fish eggs develop into fish.[73] Qualifications such as 'defeasibly', 'normally' or 'ceteris paribus' are widely used. But what do we mean when we advance generalizations thus qualified? According to Lance and Little, defeasible generalizations are exception-laden generalizations that hold *in privileged conditions*:

> Sometimes when we issue a generalization to the effect that something has a certain feature, what we really want to say is not that such a connection always, or even usually holds, but that the conditions in which it *does* hold are particularly revealing of that item's nature, or of the broader part of reality in which the item is known.[74]

Thus, for any x, conditions C are privileged relative to x just in case C either (a) is particularly revealing of x's nature or (b) is particularly revealing of the broader part of reality in which x is known. Little and Lance argue that defeasible generalizations 'tell us both what happens in conditions that are thus privileged *and* what compensatory moves are required by the ways in which one's situation may stand in distance from the privileged ones'.[75] They point out that there are a number of distinct types of privilege, each with its own structure of compensatory relations to the non-privileged. They specify three different types of privileging moves.

First, the privileging can take the form of a relation between a paradigm and a 'riff'. Lance and Little give the following example. Defeasibly, football is played with 11 players on a side. This is only defeasibly so, for there are many variants such as 20-on-20 little league games or 5-on-5 pick up games. The rules of FIFA football define a paradigm that admits of all kinds of riffs.[76] Acceptable variations of football are motivated by their relation to this paradigm. Non-standard football games carry a trace of the paradigmatic FIFA football: if we move to 5-on-5 football we ought to make other commensurate adjustments in the field, the goal, etc. so as to be true to the spirit of the game. For instance, with fewer players on the field it is much easier to get into position to have an open shot at a goal. The goals are, therefore, typically reduced in size to maintain similarity in the difficulty of scoring.[77] According to Lance and Little, this paradigm/riff move can also be found in the moral realm. Consider the following example: defeasibly, pain is bad-making. Lance and Little claim that in cases where pain contains a phenomenological element of pleasure (e.g. for someone with certain sadomasochistic preferences) we recognize this as a 'conceptual extension'[78] of the paradigm case where pain is bad-making. However, it is difficult to see how to unpack the metaphor of 'carrying a trace' in this case. To what extent do cases of sadomasochistic pain carry a trace of the paradigm of bad-making pain? Maybe a second example helps to make things clearer. Let us assume with Lance and Little that pain is not only not bad-making, but actually good-making when it is constitutive of athletic accomplishment. Lance and Little claim that this instance of good-making pain carries a trace of the paradigm case of bad-making pain insofar as 'it is only because pain is paradigmatically something to be avoided that the notion of physical challenge has the meaning, and the status of constitutive good, that it does'.[79] The idea seems to be that the understanding of how pain can be constitutive of athletic accomplishment requires an understanding of how pain is normally bad-making and something to be avoided. However, the explanation of why pain constitutes athletic accomplishment seems to be not so much that it is normally to be avoided, but rather that it makes the accomplishment difficult, that it makes it a challenge and tests one's will.[80] It seems that someone could understand this without having a prior understanding of how pain is normally something to be avoided. Again it is not clear how to unpack the metaphor of a trace.

Lance and Little's second type of privileging move is constituted by a form of justificatory dependence. Having the perception of a red cup provides me with a defeasible justification for believing that there is a red cup. Thus, defeasibly, appearances that P justify beliefs that P.[81] There are of course circumstances where our appearances are misleading and where having the appearances pushes in the direction of not believing its content. For example, if one has knowingly taken a drug that leads one to perceive blue things as red, one has good reason to believe that the cup is not red. However, Lance and Little claim that there is nevertheless an intimate connection between appearances and justification. For when appearances are unreliable, one's knowledge of this fact itself must rely on justification provided by contexts in which one *can* rely on appearances.[82] Appearances carry the property of being defeasibly trustworthy 'as a trace even into situations in which their justificatory import changes from trustworthy to non-trustworthy'.[83] Consider the analogous moral example. Lying is defeasibly wrong-making. In cases where lying is right-making or morally neutral, justifying that moral status makes essential reference to contexts in which lying has its paradigmatic negative valence. Lance and Little ask us to imagine lying while playing the game Diplomacy. In this case lying is morally neutral because people agree to play a game in which the point is to lie at the crucial moment in a convincing and strategic manner. It is morally neutral because of prior agreements that have been made in a context where the normal moral valence of lying holds. Lance and Little argue that the paradigm of wrong-making lying leaves a trace insofar as a proper understanding of one's situation when playing Diplomacy includes an awareness of the fact that one is in a non-privileged situation.[84] They see this as an illustration of how defeasible generalizations play an essential role in moral understanding. Lance and Little claim that defeasible generalizations have 'a power a list of instances does not, for it situates instances within a framework that maintains some as exceptions to others' rule'.[85]

However, what the above example actually shows is that mastery of the concept 'lie' requires knowledge of a set of paradigm cases or prototypes and the ability to understand non-paradigm cases in relation to these prototypes. Let me explain. Lance and Little are right to emphasize that conceptual knowledge is more than knowledge of a list of instances of a concept. However, they assume that knowledge and mastery of moral concepts just *is* knowledge of defeasible generalizations. They remark that defeasible generalizations 'function explanatory in virtue of the fact that to understand them is to understand the sort of difference various deviations from a posited set of standard conditions makes'.[86] But what is actually doing the explanatory work in Lance and Little's model are the concepts themselves with their often complex structure of a core of paradigm cases and non-paradigm cases clustering around and relating to this core. At some point Lance and Little themselves speak of an 'explanatory paradigm'[87] rather than of explanatory generalizations. The picture of conceptual competence Lance and Little present is compatible with the particularist idea that we learn and master moral concepts without explicitly formulating any moral principles or generalizations. For instance, Dancy argues that we can learn moral concepts by developing a set of prototypes, clearest cases, or best examples, in such a way that we conceive of the less clear cases in terms of their distance from the prototype or prototypes.[88] In order to defend the importance of moral principles

Lance and Little would have to show what explanation, insight or other use moral principles provide above and beyond knowledge of paradigm cases and the skill to relate non-paradigm cases to the paradigmatic core of moral concepts.

The third and final type of privileging Lance and Little mention is idealization-approximation. The example they discuss is the ideal gas law $pv = nrt$. A wide range of actual gases approximates the behaviour of ideal gases. As one gets a natural system increasingly similar to the description of an ideal gas, the ideal gas law predictions become increasingly accurate. Lance and Little point out that one could thus say that there is a gas law of the form *defeasibly* $(pv = nrt)$ that governs both the actual and the ideal world.[89] Similarly, the generalization 'Lying is wrong-making' can be read as holding true under idealized conditions. Since things are often far from ideal the generalization is defeasible. But it is essential to our understanding of the concept of a person, for instance, that in conditions of full information, genuine autonomy and basic trust, persons are owed the truth. In idealized conditions lying is wrong-making.[90] So according to Lance and Little, the paradigmatic instances of a moral concept all have the same moral valence. Lance and Little believe that all paradigmatic lies, for example, are morally wrong. But this does not seem to be right. Is it not possible to think of a paradigmatic lie that is morally neutral or even right-making? Lance and Little seem to conflate the question of whether we are dealing with a case of a paradigm lie with the question of whether the principle 'Lying is wrong-making' is defeated in that case. There is a difference between lying while playing the game Diplomacy or lying to save someone's life and cases that are at the periphery of the concept of lying such as mistakes, jokes, exaggerations or oversimplifications. With regard to the former cases, we need to decide whether we make an exception to our principle 'Lying is wrong-making'; with regard to the latter we need to decide whether we are dealing with cases of lying at all. Mistakes, jokes, exaggerations and oversimplifications are – if we assume that they fall under the concept 'lie' at all – non-paradigmatic cases of lying. Non-paradigmatic lies can be just as wrong as – or worse than – paradigm lies. So it is one question whether something is a paradigmatic or non-paradigmatic instance of the concept 'lying' and quite another question whether a given action is right- or wrong-making. The paradigm/non-paradigm distinction is orthogonal to the indefeasible/defeasible distinction. People might agree that the principle 'Do not torture' is indefeasible, but disagree about what counts as torture.

In contrast to McKeever, Ridge and Väyrynen, Lance and Little acknowledge that moral principles are ineliminably defeasible. The problem is that they fail to provide a convincing account of defeasibility. Without such an account, a principle telling us that lying is defeasibly wrong-making does not seem to say more than 'Lying is wrong, except in those cases where it is not'.

So far I have shown that Dancy's generalist critics face a number of serious internal problems. In the next chapter I will argue that all three accounts share a common shortcoming, namely their disregard for the practical use of moral principles.

Moral principles and practical reasoning

The distinction between practical and theoretical principles

Moral principles are commonly believed to be something, as R. M. Hare puts it, 'that we can act on, or in conformity with, or, on the other hand, in breach of'.[91] We comply with, subscribe to, follow and breach moral principles. Moral principles are inherently practical. However, Dancy and his generalist critics present a very different picture of the nature and role of moral principles. They conceive of moral principles as descriptive, truth-apt and explanatory propositions. According to Dancy, the function of moral principles is to fix the truth-conditions of moral judgements by determining the moral status of actions.[92] Moreover, he stipulates that moral principles, if there were any, would have to be explanatory insofar as 'of each action that has a moral status, the principle must somehow tell us *why* it has that status'.[93] McKeever and Ridge claim 'that there are moral principles which are true [and] explanatory'.[94] They believe that moral principles 'provide the truth-conditions for the application of a moral concept'.[95] According to Väyrynen, a moral principle is a 'proposition that identifies conditions or properties in virtue of which something has a given moral property such as rightness, and which are thus explanatory of why it is right'.[96] For Lance and Little moral principles are 'explanatory, interrelated moral generalizations that are capable of serving key epistemic functions'.[97] In the previous chapter we saw that Lance and Little's notion of moral principles is based on the analogy with defeasible generalizations in the sciences. Like scientific principles, the moral principles discussed by Dancy and his generalist critics are descriptive and explanatory, rather than prescriptive and action-guiding. They are theoretical rather than practical. Lance and Little explicitly refer to moral principles as '*theoretical* moral generalizations'.[98] This conception of moral principles proves to be seriously misleading. In order to see why, we need to have a closer look at the distinction between theoretical and practical principles and the different roles that these two types of principles can play in moral reasoning.

What exactly is it that distinguishes practical from theoretical principles? Onora O'Neill understands practical principles as 'principles that could at least sometimes be used in working out how to live our lives, or some parts or aspects of our lives'.[99] She points out that, in contrast to theoretical principles like the empirical principles of the special sciences, practical principles 'are for agents'.[100] That is to say, practical principles are action-guiding. They prescribe or forbid, recommend or warn and are used to guide, control or change our behaviour. Theoretical principles, by contrast, are used to describe and explain the world. However, while the capacity to guide action seems to be undoubtedly an essential feature of practical principles, it is not clear that theoretical principles lack this capacity altogether. Theoretical principles shape our beliefs about the world and can thereby have an effect on our behaviour. Thus, in this respect theoretical principles can be said to be action-guiding as well. In order to distinguish practical from theoretical principles, it is not enough, therefore, to point to the action-guiding capacity of practical principles.

One might try to specify further the distinction by following O'Neill's remark that practical principles of all sorts contain act-descriptions.[101] However, the same holds true for some theoretical principles. Many psychological, economic or socio-logical principles – which are usually classified as theoretical principles – contain act-descriptions. They make general statements about how people act in certain situations or circumstances.

Another feature that comes into one's mind when trying to distinguish practical from theoretical principles is the normative semantic content of the former. Practical principles seem to possess a normative semantic content which theoretical principles lack. This normative content is either expressed by deontic terms such as 'ought', 'may', 'must' and 'should', or conveyed through the use of imperatives. This way of distinguishing practical from theoretical principles is helpful insofar as theoretical principles indeed lack normative semantic content. But the criterion of normative semantic content fails as a necessary condition for being a practical principle. Imagine, for example, the regulations of a primary school stating the following rule: 'Parents will collect their children from the hall entrance at 4pm'. Although we normally read this as a command, the normativity of this rule cannot be read off the semantic content of the sentence alone; the sentence could as well be read as a prediction or as an empirical generalization.

Action-guiding capacity and normative semantic content are important features of practical principles, but the above examples show that these criteria fail as sufficient and necessary conditions, respectively. In what follows, I will understand the distinction between theoretical and practical principles in terms of truth-aptness. Theoretical principles are propositions and as such they are capable of being true or false.[102] Practical principles, by contrast, are not propositions and strictly speaking it does not make sense to describe a practical principle such as 'Love your neighbour as yourself' or 'Eat at least five portions of fruit or vegetables a day' as true or false. I say 'strictly speaking' because we sometimes say that a practical principle such as 'Eat at least five portions of fruit or vegetables a day' is correct or true. However, what we mean by this is that the principle is justified. What is true or false is not the practical principle itself, but rather the proposition *that* eating five portions of fruit and vegetables is a good thing to do. Thus, while a practical principle such as 'Do not lie' cannot be true or false, the moral judgement *that* lying is wrong is capable of being true or false. Prohibitions, obligations, permissions, recommendations or warnings can be justified and we can utter true or false propositions about them. But it does not make sense to say that the practical principles themselves are true or false. Practical principles are something we comply with, subscribe to, follow or break, but which cannot be true or false. Theoretical principles, by contrast, are something we believe to be right or wrong; but we do not comply with, subscribe to, follow or break theoretical principles. We can believe the Darwinian principle of natural selection, the law of gravity, the economic principle of supply and demand or the ideal gas law to be true or false, but we cannot follow or break them.[103]

On the face of it, there seem to be examples in our everyday talk about principles and rules which challenge this distinction. The rules of chess, for example, are practical principles. Problems arise because in discussing chess, one can express the rule governing moves of the bishop as the rule *that* the bishop moves only diagonally, and this seems to suggest that we are dealing with a proposition. However, this problem is easily solved by distinguishing the rule so described from the proposition that the bishop moves only diagonally. The proposition is strictly speaking false, because the bishop is often moved in a nondiagonal manner by learners and people not concentrating, but the rule is neither true nor false. Of course, it is true that it is a rule of chess that the bishop moves only diagonally, but what is true in this case is a proposition about the rule, not the rule itself. Furthermore, it does not make sense to describe someone as complying or failing to comply with the proposition that the bishop moves only diagonally. What does make sense is to describe someone as complying or failing to comply with the rule or practical principles that the bishop only moves diagonally.[104]

The distinction between theoretical and practical principles can be illustrated in terms of the notion of 'direction of fit'.[105] Theoretical principles are word-to-world directed. That is, they purport to make true statements about the world and are used to describe and explain it. Practical principles are world-to-word directed. Instead of reflecting the world, the primary function of practical principles is to change it. They are used to change, guide or control the behaviour of agents with decision-making capacities. However, in order to guide agents effectively in the world they live in, practical principles must not be based on a total misrepresentation of this world. Following the practical principle 'Eat at least five portions of fruit or vegetables a day' makes sense because it is true that eating a certain amount of fruit and vegetables is conducive to our health. It would be silly to continue adherence to the principle if it should turn out that eating fruit and vegetables was actually harmful. Practical principles can thus also be said to reflect the world, but their function is to change, guide and control the behaviour of agents within this world. Moreover, theoretical principles might be said to be to a certain extent action-guiding insofar as they shape our beliefs about the world and thereby have an effect on our behaviour. However, their primary function is to describe and explain the world. In contrast to theoretical principles, practical principles are action-guiding because we can follow them.

A theoretical principle such as 'Lying is wrong' might help us to appreciate and assess the moral status of a given action, character or institution. Theoretical moral reasoning is often retrospective and based on a third-person perspective. Reasoning of this kind is involved when we try to understand, explain or justify our own or other people's past actions. Theoretical reasoning is not confined to actual actions or situations. We can also reason about the moral status of imaginary cases. What is important is that theoretical reasoning is about something – an actual situation, an imaginary case, an institution or a person – that is already there to be judged or at least sufficiently specified. By contrast, practical reasoning is prospective; it is directed at action that has yet to be performed.[106] The challenge of practical reasoning is not that of determining the moral status of a particular situation, institution or agent, but that of moving from this moral appraisal to moral action. The judgement that a certain action is wrong, or that an institution is unjust, does not tell us how to respond to this wrongness or injustice. Practical reasoning is reasoning about what to do once we believe that the action, institution or agent with which we deal is of a certain kind. Imagine, for example, that you notice someone being bullied by another person.[107] Making this observation and judging that something morally bad is happening will not be enough. You will also need to decide whether or not to intervene, and if you decide to intervene you need to judge which approach will be most likely to improve rather than to worsen the victim's lot. As moral agents we need not only appraise and assess actions, we also have to be able to *act* morally. Moral reasoning is not only theoretical reasoning about how to describe, assess or explain a given action, character or institution, it is also practical reasoning about what to do.

Particularists and their generalist interlocutors ignore this form of moral reasoning. Dancy, for example, describes the task of moral reasoning as 'an attempt to capture the moral nature of the situation one is confronted with'[108] and the capacity of moral judgement as a 'skill of discernment'.[109] This is theoretical reasoning about the moral status of a given action and not practical reasoning about what to do. After we have 'discerned' the morally relevant features of the situation we are 'confronted with', we still need to decide how to act. The exclusive focus on the assessment of actions, and the disregard for the question of what to do, is not only problematic because it leads to an incomplete picture of moral reasoning. It also reflects what O'Neill has aptly described as a 'view of ethics as a spectator sport'.[110] Both sides of the current particularist/generalist debate portray the moral agent as a disinterested bystander who assesses the moral status of a given situation or past action, rather than as someone who asks herself what she should, morally speaking, do given that situation or past action.

What explains the preoccupation with the theoretical function of moral principles in the current particularist/generalist debate? One reason is surely that all the authors discussed here take Dancy's particularism as their main target. Dancy presents his theory as a view in moral epistemology and metaphysics. Moral practice plays only a marginal role in his argument against principled ethics.[111] In trying to answer Dancy's particularist challenge, current generalists tend not to question this focus of the debate. A further explanation for the theoretical conception of moral principles prevalent in the current particularist/generalist debate lies in the assumption of moral realism. Dancy and his generalist critics presuppose a form of moral realism or at least use realist terminology. Many moral realists seem to conceive of moral principles as a class of theoretical principles. Russ Shafer-Landau, for instance, identifies two major roles of moral principles. The first role is investigative or epistemic: the awareness of moral principles helps us to appreciate the ethical status of the options we confront. The second role of moral principles is to fix the truth status of moral conclusions.[112] According to Shafer-Landau, moral principles state 'a relation claimed to obtain between a moral property and other, grounding properties that are correlated with its instantiation'.[113] Thus understood, moral principles are theoretical principles that have to fit the world, rather than practical principles which are designed to change the world by guiding the behaviour of the agents within it. Moral realists often try to support their objectivist position by drawing analogies between morality and the sciences. In particular, moral principles are represented as resembling scientific laws or other empirical generalizations.[114] This naturally leads to a focus on the theoretical role of moral principles.

Dancy's generalist critics and action-guidance

At least some participants in the particularist/generalist debate will protest that they *do* take account of the practical, action-guiding function of moral principles, even though this function is not at the centre of their theories. McKeever and Ridge, for example, claim that 'moral principles can and should play an important role in guiding action'.[115] They aim to show that moral principles are explanatory *as well as* action-guiding. Recall that McKeever and Ridge defend exceptionless moral principles which link purely descriptive antecedents to moral consequents. I argued that, if they are possible at all, such principles would be unmanageably complex. McKeever and Ridge deny this. However, they concede that moral standards will have to have a certain level of complexity, and they are aware of 'the seemingly vast distance between the kinds of thoughts or rules that might claim to figure explicitly in moral reasoning and anything that could count as an ultimate standard'.[116] McKeever and Ridge point out that '[m]oral agents seem regularly to be guided by shockingly crude rules';[117] rules that could never function as moral standards understood in their sense. They try to solve this problem by distinguishing moral principles understood as standards from moral guides. According to McKeever and Ridge, moral standards 'are good in theory but might be useless in practice'.[118] In contrast to moral standards, guides do not need to provide entirely accurate application conditions for moral concepts. They do not need to cover all cases and might even have some false implications. Since McKeever and Ridge want to claim that 'moral principles can and should play an important role in guiding action',[119] they have to show how we can get from their form of moral standards to action-guiding principles. How can their form of moral standards provide us with valuable tools for guiding action? McKeever and Ridge offer two alternative generalist accounts of moral guidance. They do not argue for one model in favour of the other because they believe that the question of which model is most plausible will depend on the content of one's moral standards, and they wish to be neutral with regard to such first-order moral questions.[120]

McKeever and Ridge's first model of principled guidance – the model of 'local specification' – starts with the assumption that moral standards are highly abstract principles which do not apply straightforwardly and invariably to our actual circumstances. Action-guiding principles, on this model, are ways of applying these abstract principles to our local circumstances. Formulating action-guiding principles, on this model, are ways of applying these abstract principles to our local circumstances. The adoption of a specific guiding principle is justified if and only if it provides a morally defensible interpretation of the standard.[121] One problem with this model of principled guidance is that it fits badly with McKeever and Ridge's notion of moral standards. According to McKeever and Ridge, moral standards articulate the truth-conditions for the application of moral concepts by referring to those descriptive features of the world which explain why the concepts apply when they do. It is hard to see how moral standards of this form could be said to be too abstract. Moral standards understood in McKeever and Ridge's sense would lead us from the descriptive features of a particular case to the verdict of its moral status. They would apply straightforwardly and invariably to our actual circumstances. On McKeever and Ridge's conception of moral standards there is thus no need for principles which help us to interpret or specify these standards. More important, the principles would not be practical. They would be interpretations of theoretical moral standards for the moral assessment of particular actions, characters or institutions, and not guides about what to do once such an assessment is made.

McKeever and Ridge's second model of principle guidance – the model of 'deliberative simplification' – builds on the idea of moral guides being useful oversimplifications. McKeever and Ridge point out that this model is widely associated with consequentialism.[122] Indeed it is hard to see how the model could ever work outside a consequentialist framework. According to this model, the principles we typically employ in deliberation are not standards of right conduct. However, an agent who employs them in deliberation will regularly and systematically act rightly.[123] A popular example of this model has been defended by Hare, who distinguishes between *intuitive* or *prima facie* moral principles and *critical* principles. According to Hare, the former are employed at the level of intuitive moral thinking. They are relatively simple and general moral guides that have proven to be useful in moral practice. *Critical* principles, by contrast, can be highly specific and complex. They are used at the level of critical thinking which proceeds in terms of the actual standards of moral conduct.[124] Thus, on the model of deliberative simplification, action-guiding principles are simplified and rather crude versions of ultimate moral standards. They function as second-best strategies. That is, defenders of the model acknowledge that if we were able to remember and apply complex principles in our everyday moral lives, we would be better off being guided directly by the ultimate moral standards. However, we lack the time and the cognitive abilities to do so. Moreover, there is a danger that complex moral standards are too flexible to constrain those moral agents who are prone to self-deception and special pleading. The idea is that, unlike moral standards, crude action-guiding principles do not invite deliberation about possible exceptions and special circumstances. What justifies the use of moral principles that fall short of ultimate standards, is that doing so will systematically lead us to act well – where what counts as acting well is determined by the standards. Defenders of the model of deliberative simplification concede that adherence to crude action-guiding principles will also have costs and sometimes lead us astray, but they insist that the benefits of following these principles will outweigh the costs.[125]

McKeever and Ridge follow this model of deliberative simplification and claim that moral principles have an important role to play in offsetting biases built into ordinary human reasoning. In particular, they discuss the problem of special pleading and so-called framing effects.[126] With regard to the problem of framing effects, McKeever and Ridge avail themselves of some recent findings in empirical psychology. The difficulty with this strategy is that empirical data alone are unlikely to speak in favour of either generalism or particularism. While McKeever and Ridge view moral principles as a way of dealing with the problem of framing effects, a number of experiments suggest that it is exactly the use of moral heuristics – crude action-guiding principles – that leads to this problem in the first place. Experiments show that people use moral heuristics – moral short-cuts, or rules of thumb – that lead to mistaken and sometimes even absurd moral judgements.

This is not to deny that there are contexts in which intuitive moral rules are useful and justified, but it shows that we should be aware of the fact that such heuristics are error-prone.[127] McKeever and Ridge would probably answer this challenge by pointing out that their argument is not supposed to extend to any old action-guiding principle or moral heuristic, but only to those which are '*suitably framed*'.[128] The fact that bad moral principles lead people to make bad moral decisions, they will insist, does nothing to undermine their argument. But this does not solve the problem. The problem is that McKeever and Ridge accept a model of principled guidance according to which action-guiding principles are second-best strategies. What justified the use of these second-best strategies is their utility, i.e. that following these principles will generally lead people to act well. Following second-best strategies will inevitably lead to errors and bad decisions. The assumption is that these costs are outweighed by the overall benefits of following the principles. Part of the success of McKeever and Ridge's defence of the practical importance of moral principles thus depends on whether the benefits of following action-guiding principles – understood as simplified and rather crude versions of moral standards – do actually outweigh the number of bad moral decisions to which this will inevitably lead. This is an empirical question. By making the justification of action-guiding principles depend on their utility, the question of whether a moral principle is justified becomes an empirical matter. My point is that, at least so far, the empirical data is not conclusive. Moreover, if at all, the empirical question can be settled only with regard to a concrete set of action-guiding principles and this would mean that McKeever and Ridge could no longer remain neutral on the content of morality.

Even if it could be empirically shown that following a certain set of moral heuristics systematically leads people to act well, and that the benefits of following these heuristics outweigh the costs, the model of deliberative simplification would remain highly problematic. According to the model of deliberative simplification, the justification of action-guiding principles is purely instrumental, and gets detached from questions of moral rightness and wrongness. Action-guiding principles will be justified and their observance required even if they lead to morally wrong or even disastrous actions in particular cases, as long as the overall utility of following the principles outweighs these costs. This conclusion is deeply unsatisfactory. To a large extent it is this rigorism which has led many particularists to condemn principle-based ethics as morally disastrous. If we were to follow McKeever and Ridge's model of deliberative simplification, particularists like David McNaughton would be right in claiming that moral principles are often 'a hindrance in trying to find out which is the right action'.[129]

Moreover, understood as useful oversimplifications, action-guiding principles cannot, and are not meant to, account for the context-dependence of moral verdicts. Particularists hold that the context-sensitivity of moral considerations, i.e. reasons-holism, blocks principled articulation. McKeever and Ridge devote a large part of their book to the refutation of this thesis. They argue for the possibility of a set of unhedged, exceptionless moral principles that is compatible with the holistic conception of moral considerations which particularists defend. However, to accept the model of deliberative simplification means to concede that while principle-based ethics can account for the fact of context-sensitivity in their theoretical moral standards, they fail to do so in moral practice. Instead of trying to incorporate some element of context-sensitivity in their notion of action-guiding principles, defenders of the model of deliberative simplification capitulate and conclude that action-guiding principles are necessarily suboptimal. This is an unsatisfactory answer to the particularist challenge. If one acknowledges that context-sensitivity poses a challenge for principled ethics, as McKeever and Ridge purport to do, one should not ignore this challenge when it comes to moral action.

Most importantly, however, McKeever and Ridge's model of deliberative simplification fails to generate practical principles. Merely simplifying a theoretical principle does not make it a practical principle. A simplified version of the ideal gas law or the law of gravity is not a practical principle, but rather a defective theoretical principle.[130] McKeever and Ridge's complex descriptive, truth-apt and explanatory moral principles do not become practical by simplifying their content. The principles which McKeever and Ridge bring forward as action-guiding principles are in fact theoretical principles.

Let us briefly look at Väyrynen's attempt to account for the practical role of moral principles. Like McKeever and Ridge, Väyrynen distinguishes between moral principles understood as standards and principles that function as moral guides. He claims that the 'explanatory and the guiding function of moral principles are logically distinct'.[131] That is, a principle might accurately explain why a certain moral property is instantiated without being of much use when it comes to moral practice, and 'a simplified guide may provide us with more reliable direction than an accurate but complex standard of right action'.[132] Like McKeever and Ridge, Väyrynen refers to Hare's distinction between intuitive and critical moral principles in order to illustrate this point. However, it is not clear whether Väyrynen actually wants to defend this model. He stresses that we should not 'treat [moral guides] as free-standing moral principles because they lead to systematic mistakes when generalized outside that range of problems to situations in which their justifications no longer operate'.[133] This remark does not fit well with the model of action-guiding principles as useful oversimplifications. Maybe Väyrynen is best understood as highlighting the distinction between two *functions* of moral principles, rather than postulating two distinct *types* of principles. This would mean that Väyrynen's hedged moral principles purport to be explanatory as well as action-guiding. So given that this is what Väyrynen intends to argue, how are his hedged moral principles supposed to guide action?

According to Väyrynen, moral principles provide adequate guidance if they 'contribute non-trivially to a reliable overall strategy for doing the right thing for the right reasons that is available to the practical thinking of conscientious, morally committed agents'.[134] He argues that hedged moral principles are action-guiding because their acceptance makes a difference to the dispositions of agents by shaping their moral sensibility.[135] He presents an account of moral judgement as 'sensitivity to the details of the case at hand'.[136] But Väyrynen has nothing to say about how we decide what to do once we have determined the details of the case. As O'Neill rightly points out, '[a]ccounts of judgement as sensitivity to circumstances or cases are accounts of *theoretical* judgement'.[137]

Moreover, it is worth noting how moderate Väyrynen's claims about moral guidance are in comparison to his claims about the explanatory function of hedged moral principles. With regard to the latter, he purports to show that the 'possibility of sound moral judgement depends on the existence of a comprehensive set of moral principles'.[138] When it comes to the action-guiding function of principles, Väyrynen is far less ambitious. He claims only that his 'generalist model of moral guidance is at least no worse off than extant particularist models'.[139] The practical nature of moral principles evidently plays a subordinate role in Väyrynen's theory. According to Väyrynen, moral principles are neither necessary nor sufficient for moral action. He believes that principles are not necessary for moral action because 'particularists can coherently allow that there are true moral principles but insist that proper responsiveness to the moral reasons that those principles identify only requires responsiveness to moral reasons that need not be grounded by acceptance of any principles as guides'.[140] Principles are not sufficient for acting well since applying and following them requires moral judgement.[141] Most defenders of principled ethics acknowledge that principles cannot fully guide action and, therefore, stress the importance of moral judgement. What they have to show is why we cannot rely on this capacity of judgement alone and make moral judgements on a case-by-case basis without any reference to moral principles. Väyrynen insists that 'generalists can deny that sensitivity and judgement supplant principles in guiding action […] [because] grasp of hedged principles can help to improve and refine these skills'.[142] But this is too weak a response. Generalists should be able to give an account of how moral action can, and why it should, be based on principles. In order to answer this challenge, more needs to be said about the interplay between moral principles and judgement. I will offer such an account in Chapter Three.

In contrast to McKeever, Ridge and Väyrynen, Lance and Little do not address the problem of action-guidance at all. Their theory of defeasible generalizations focuses exclusively on the theoretical, explanatory function of moral principles. It is striking that this disregard for the practical use of moral principles extends to Lance and Little's understanding of the tradition of principled ethics. They state that the 'classical conception of moral principles'[143] is characterized by three features:

1. Classical Principles are universal, exceptionless, law-like moral generalizations that mark the moral import of considerations. […]

2. The conditionals implicit in classical principles serve genuine inferential roles in determining, criticizing, or justifying particular moral claims. They are supposed

to name a genuinely possible move from noting that
something is *F* to concluding that it is *G*.

3. Classical Principles are members of theoretical systems.
   [...] [S]omething is not a classical principle unless it
   fits into a structure of other principles that purport to
   systematic illumination.[144]

I strongly doubt that this 'classical' conception of moral principles
has ever been a widely held view among defenders of principled
ethics, but I will not argue for this point here. What I would like
to stress is that Lance and Little do not mention the practical,
action-guiding function of moral principles. Their conception
of moral principles as theoretical principles is at odds with
the common, traditional understanding of moral principles as
practical principles. When we think of 'classical' moral principles
we typically think of principles such as 'You shall not murder'
or 'Do not lie', which are practical principles. They are used to
prescribe and guide moral actions, rather than to describe and
explain the world. To be clear, I do not want to deny that moral
principles cannot also play important theoretical roles. We can, and
do, use moral principles in many different ways, some of which
are theoretical and some of which are practical. What I want to
claim is that a theory of moral principles which ignores their
practical function is seriously defective. Dancy and his generalist
critics do not recognize that moral reasoning is not only reasoning
about how to assess the moral status of a given action or state of
affairs, but also reasoning about what to do in the light of this
assessment. As a result they are left with an impoverished picture
of moral reasoning. This is a serious charge. Is there anything that
current particularists and their generalist interlocutors could say in
response? They could reply by denying that there is any genuine
difference between theoretical and practical reasoning. In the next
section I will explore whether current particularists and their generalist interlocutors could construe moral reasoning about what to
do as a form of theoretical reasoning and thereby escape the charge
of providing an incomplete picture of moral reasoning.

Reasoning about what to do as theoretical reasoning?

Particularists and their generalist interlocutors could argue that what we do when we reason about how to act in a certain situation is to choose between a set of possible courses of actions or options. We assess and then decide among these options in the same way in which we assess the moral status of a given action, character or institution.[145] Call this the 'option-choice' model. On the option-choice model of moral reasoning there seems to be no need for a separate account of practical reasoning. Options are construed as act-types whose moral status can be determined in the same manner as we determine the moral status of past actions. Moral reasoning is one form of reasoning about what is the case. In this context Gilbert Harman claims that:

> Reasoning as to whether a certain act is wrong is reasoning as to whether to classify the act as wrong. Similarly, reasoning as to whether to do a certain act is reasoning as to whether to classify the act as something to do.[146]

Harman argues that reasoning about what one ought to do 'is really a particular kind of theoretical reasoning [...] since reasoning that is concerned with what to believe about what one ought to do [...] is still reasoning concerned with what one ought to believe'.[147]

The first thing to say in response to this argument is that practical reasoning is not merely reasoning about whether or not to do a certain action. When we classify a particular act as wrong the act is already there to be judged. By contrast, it does not make sense to say that we classify an act as 'something to do' because the act purportedly to be so classified has not yet been performed. What we *can* classify as 'something to do' is a more or less specific range of act-types or options. However, it requires practical reasoning to specify these options and to realize one of them. When we think about what to do, normally we do not have a range of options readily available to us to choose from. The option-choice model sketched above ignores this fact and depicts reasoning about what to do as a matter of picking and choosing from an already specified range of options. It thus presupposes that there is a finite list of options from which an agent can choose in a particular situation. This is a radical oversimplification which renders the option-choice model overly epistemologically demanding as well as ethically dubious. Let me start with the epistemological problems.

In most situations we are not able to compile a finite list of all the options open to us, because there will simply be too many such options and our time and mental capacities are limited. Consider the rather mundane example of a person doing her weekly shopping in a supermarket. Her options of what to buy are virtually endless and she would not have much time for anything else in her life if she set out to assess all of these options. Trying to make practical decisions in accordance with the option-choice model is at best extremely time- and energy-intensive, and at worst impossible for finite beings like us.

Depicting practical reasoning as a matter of picking and choosing from an already specified range of options is not only epistemologically but also ethically dubious. The option-choice model is morally misleading because it suggests that we need not worry about which options are options worth considering. When we think about what to do, many of the options open to us will be irrelevant. The crucial question is how we decide which options are the important or relevant ones. Overlooking an important option can have disastrous consequences for our final decision about what to do. In addition, the question of which options are relevant can itself be a moral question. For example, it is a moral question whether, when thinking about what to do with one's salary, it is wrong not to consider the option of giving half of it to charity. Furthermore, there are cases where considering certain kinds of actions as options signifies a lack of moral character. Bernard Williams illustrates this idea nicely:

> One does not feel easy with the man who in the course of a discussion of how to deal with political or business rivals says, 'Of course, we could have them killed, but we should lay that aside right from the beginning'. It should never have come into his hands to be laid aside.[148]

Since the option-choice model is implicitly presupposed by a number of metaethical and first-order moral theories, I will discuss it in more detail in Chapter Three. However, it should already be clear that the option-choice model comes with considerable epistemological and ethical costs attached to it. Generalists have therefore a good reason to look for an alternative model of practical reasoning. So could Dancy's generalist critics avail themselves of another account of reasoning about what to do?

One author whom Dancy and his generalist critics might hope to draw on in order to show that there is no genuine difference between theoretical and practical reasoning is David Velleman. Velleman argues that we can understand reasons for acting by analogy with reasons for belief.[149] For Velleman, 'practical reasoning is a kind of theoretical reasoning, and [...] practical conclusions, or intentions, are the corresponding theoretical conclusions, or beliefs'.[150] The aim of theoretical reasoning is knowledge or at least justified belief. Velleman claims that when we reason about what to do we also aim at knowledge, namely at self-knowledge. As agents we want our actions and ourselves to make sense to us. When an agent is trying to make sense of what someone else is about to do, she compiles evidence until she has enough to indicate the truth of a determinate conclusion, and then she draws the conclusion whose truth is indicated. Velleman points out that when the agent is forming a similar belief about herself, she compiles only enough evidence to indicate a set of alternative conclusions, each of which she would be moved to make true if she drew it. The agent then draws whichever conclusion she likes, in the confidence that she will thereby be moved to make it true. She thus arrives at a belief that is true of her action partly by relying on herself to perform an action that is true to her belief.[151] In the case of reasoning about what to do, we obtain knowledge about our actions and ourselves by 'making it up' in advance.[152]

Particularists and their generalist critics might be attracted to this model of reasoning about what to do because Velleman promises that it is theoretical 'only in a thoroughly inoffensive sense'.[153] Earlier I claimed that accounts of moral reasoning as exclusively theoretical reasoning wrongly picture ethics as a spectator sport. They conceive of the moral agent as a disinterested bystander who describes and assesses the moral status of a given action, rather than as someone who steps in and acts. Velleman addresses this criticism. He points out that his model of reasoning about what to do is theoretical in the sense that it aims at knowledge and yields, if not knowledge, then at least justified belief. But it is not intended to be theoretical in the sense of being contemplative, reactive, or passive. To the contrary, Velleman views the agent as an 'inventor, creator, and author' in the sense that the agent attains her understanding of what she is doing by making up a story in the confidence that she will then be moved to live it out.[154] Particularists and their generalist critics might thus hope that by adopting a model of moral reasoning along Velleman's lines, they could fend off the criticism I levelled against them in the previous section.

However, if we look at what Velleman has to say about moral reasoning, this quickly turns out to be a false hope. For Velleman, '[b]eing moral is the ultimate form of making sense'.[155] An agent who cares about her future self-knowledge will not be content with continually identifying her motives at the last minute, as they become relevant to her next decision. Rather, she will want to prepare for future decisions by learning in advance what motives she always has and what motives she is likely to have in various foreseeable circumstances.[156] Velleman argues that our desire to make sense of our future actions leads us to form and pursue long-term plans.[157] By adopting long-term plans we ensure that our desires follow more regular patterns and this, in turn, enables us to forecast our behaviour. According to Velleman, an agent can gain even more intelligibility by adopting impartial policies toward various kinds of behaviour.[158] For example, an agent 'can have a policy of standing up for truthfulness [...] or never tolerating lies'.[159] What Velleman calls policies can equally be called principles. In contrast to plans, they are commitments which are perpetually in force. Policies 'are plans to the effect that we shall act in a particular way on every occasion of a particular kind'.[160] On Velleman's account our desire for self-understanding leads us to cultivate a set of moral principles. As policies moral principles 'enhance the generality and simplicity of one's self-conception'.[161] Understood as long-term plans or policies, moral principles are inherently practical. The purpose of plans and policies is not to make true statements about the world, but to regulate, mould and change it. Since plans and policies play a central role in Velleman's account of reasoning about what to do, and since Velleman classifies moral principles as policies, the theory is not compatible with the conception of moral principles prevalent in the current particularist/generalist debate. Particularists and their generalist interlocutors thus cannot avail themselves of Velleman's account in order to make sense about how we reason about what we should, morally speaking, do.

I do not want to take a stance on the overall plausibility of Velleman's ingenious account of practical reasoning. I will present my own model of practical moral reasoning in Chapter Three. According to this model, practical reasoning is reasoning about how to jointly implement a plurality of moral and non-moral practical principles understood as long-term commitments. While Velleman also attaches considerable importance to long-term commitments, his account starts with the notion of a desire for self-understanding. It is plausible to assume that adopting long-term commitments is conducive to our self-understanding. But it is much more controversial to claim, as Velleman does, that we adopt these long-term commitments *because* we aim at better self-understanding. The charge of over-intellectualization looms large here. In contrast to Velleman, I will start with the much less controversial assumption that in order to qualify as an action, an activity has to be purposeful, and an agent's commitments fix this purpose. Action starts with commitment and an agent's long-term commitments structure her reasoning about how to act. However, what is important for my present argument is that, contrary to first impressions, Dancy and his generalist critics cannot draw on Velleman's account in order to show that there is no genuine difference between theoretical and practical reasoning.

In order to neutralize the charge of drawing an incomplete picture of moral reasoning by focusing exclusively on theoretical principles, current particularists and their generalist interlocutors would have to provide a plausible account of reasoning about what to do as a form of theoretical reasoning. If my above arguments are sound, the prospects of developing such an account look bleak. I do not claim to have shown that it is impossible to construct a model of moral reasoning as exclusively theoretical reasoning. What I claim is that the burden of proof is on those who want to deny the distinction between theoretical and practical reasoning. In the absence of convincing considerations to the contrary, it is plausible to assume that there is an important difference between theoretical moral reasoning and practical moral reasoning. If this is true, current particularists and their generalist critics fail to account for a central aspect of moral reasoning and the role of moral principles in this form of reasoning.

Conclusion

The discussion of Dancy's generalist critics revealed serious problems and deficiencies. What can other generalists learn from this? To begin with, generalists should give up on the idea of finding a set of exceptionless principles which codifies all of morality. My discussion of McKeever and Ridge's theory of unhedged moral principles showed that this project is doomed to failure. The shortcomings of Väyrynen's argument reinforced this point. I argued that generalists who purport to take the context-sensitivity of moral considerations seriously should not deny that this context-sensitivity is at least sometimes uncodifiable. In contrast to McKeever, Ridge and Väyrynen, Lance and Little accept that moral principles are ineliminably exception-laden or defeasible. However, they fail to provide a convincing account of what it is for a moral principle to be exception-laden. Lance and Little's account does not distinguish sufficiently between the defeasibility and the indeterminacy of moral principles. One of the main objectives of the next chapter of this book is to develop a plausible account of what it means for a principle to be defeasible and to distinguish the defeasibility of moral principles from their indeterminacy. Finally, generalists have to show how moral action can, and why it should, be based on moral principles. In the final section of this chapter, I argued that by ignoring the importance moral principles play in reasoning about what to do, Dancy and his generalist critics offer an impoverished picture of moral reasoning. The practical use of moral principles deserves to be at the centre of a defence of moral generalism, rather than at its periphery. In the next and final chapter of this book I will put these insights into practice, and present an alternative conception of the nature and roles of moral principles.

Notes

1   Sean McKeever and Michael Ridge, *Principled Ethics*, *Generalism as a Regulative Ideal* (Oxford: Clarendon Press, 2006), p. 3.

2   Ibid., p. 115.

3   Jonathan Dancy, *Ethics Without Principles* (Oxford: Oxford University Press, 2004), p. 111.

4   McKeever and Ridge, *Principled Ethics*, p. 115.

5   Ibid., pp. 115–16. This conclusion is questionable. Mark Schroeder points out that while McKeever and Ridge claim that moral reasons must be relatively few in number, they allow that just about any old fact can be a reason for belief, i.e. an epistemic reason. If we can manage an infinite number of epistemic reasons, why cannot we also manage an infinite number of moral reasons? See Mark Schroeder, 'A matter of principle', *Nous* 43 (2009), pp. 568–80, pp. 577–8.

6   McKeever and Ridge, *Principled Ethics*, p. 116.

7   Ibid., pp. 116–17.

8   Ibid., p. 117.

9   Ibid., p. 118.

10 Ibid.

11 Ibid., p. 177.

12 Ibid., p. 137. McKeever and Ridge are best understood as using the term 'infinite' very loosely here. There is of course a difference between 'infinite' and 'unmanageably large in number'. Unless qualified otherwise, whether a set of principles is unmanageably large in number will depend on the agent who uses these principles and the purpose that these principles are supposed to serve.

13 McKeever and Ridge, *Principled Ethics*, pp. 144–5.

14 Ibid., p. 138.

15 Onora O'Neill makes this point very clear. See Onora O'Neill, 'Practical principles and practical judgement', *Hastings Center Report* 31 (2001), pp. 15–23, p. 18.

16 McKeever and Ridge, *Principled Ethics*, p. 139. At this point McKeever and Ridge switch, without notice, from moral knowledge to the notion of practical wisdom. Their idealized conception of the person of practical wisdom is highly problematic, but for the sake of the argument I will ignore these problems.

17 McKeever and Ridge, *Principled Ethics*, p. 142.

18 Ibid.

19 Ibid., p. 170.

20 Ibid., pp. 139–40.

21 Ibid., p. 17.

22 Ibid., p. 179.

23 Ibid., p. 24.

24 See Pekka Väyrynen, 'Moral generalism: Enjoy in moderation', *Ethics*, 116 (2006), pp. 707–41; 'Ethical theories and moral guidance', *Utilitas* 18 (2006), pp. 291–309; 'Usable moral principles' in Mark Norris Lance, Matijaz Potrc, and Vojko Strahovnik (eds), Challenging Moral Particularism. Routledge Studies in Ethics and Moral Theory (New York: Routledge, 2008), pp. 75–106; 'A theory of hedged moral principles', in Russ Shafer Landau (ed.), *Oxford Studies in Metaethics* vol. 4 (Oxford: Oxford University Press, 2009), pp. 91–132.

25 Väyrynen, 'Moral generalism: Enjoy in moderation', p. 710.

26 Ibid.

27 Ibid., p. 711, emphasis added.

28 Ibid., p. 736.

29 Väyrynen, 'Usable moral principles', p. 82.

30 Väyrynen, 'Moral generalism: Enjoy in moderation', p. 716.

31 Ibid., p. 725. Note that this argument presupposes a theoretical conception of moral principles which I will challenge later in this chapter. It presupposes that moral principles are descriptive and that they are refuted if they fail to reflect some sort of moral reality. Practical principles are not refuted by counterexamples in this sense because they have a world-to-word direction of fit.

32 Ibid.

33 Ibid., p. 719.

34 Väyrynen, 'Moral generalism: Enjoy in moderation', p. 719.

35 Ibid., pp. 722–3.

36 Ibid., p. 726.

37 Ibid.

38 Ibid.

39 Ibid.

40 Väyrynen, 'Moral generalism: Enjoy in moderation', p. 724.

41 Ibid., pp. 727–8.

42 Ibid.

43 Ibid., p. 737.

44 Väyrynen, 'Moral generalism: Enjoy in moderation', p. 734. This assumption is highly controversial. Ross, for instance, who is often referred to as a paradigm generalist, explicitly allows for disjoint normative bases. He points out that derived duties 'are compounded together in highly complex ways' (W. D. Ross, *The Right and the Good*, Philip Stratton-Lake [ed.] [Oxford: Oxford University Press, 2002, first published 1930], p. 27). The duty not to lie, for example, stems from the basic duties of non-maleficence and fidelity. See Ross, *The Right and the Good*, pp. 54–6; David McNaughton, 'An unconnected heap of duties?', *The Philosophical Quarterly* 46 (1996), pp. 436–47.

45 Väyrynen, 'A theory of hedged moral principles', p. 111.

46 Ibid.

47 The focus here is on the need for a *new, moderate* form of generalism. The generalist project of justifying the importance of moral principles is a valuable one even if one is a convinced utilitarian or Kantian. One does not need to reject traditional principled ethics in order to find exciting and fruitful the recent attempts by particularists and generalists to discuss the nature and role of moral principles independently of any particular first-order moral theory.

48 Väyrynen, 'Moral generalism: Enjoy in moderation', p. 716.

49 Dancy, *Ethics Without Principles*, p. 85.

50 Ibid.

51 Jonathan Dancy, *Moral Reasons* (Oxford: Blackwell, 1993), p. 106.

52 Dancy, *Ethics Without Principles*, p. 86.

53 Ibid.

54 Dancy, *Ethics Without Principles*, p. 87.

55 Väyrynen, 'Usable moral principles', p. 77.

56 Ross, *The Right and the Good*, p. 24.

57 Väyrynen, 'Usable moral principles', p. 89.

58 Ibid., p. 85.

59 Väyrynen, 'Moral generalism: Enjoy in moderation', p. 717.

60 Väyrynen, 'Usable moral principles', p. 86.

61 Ibid.

62 Jeremy Bentham, *An Introduction to the Principles of Morals and Legislation*, J. H. Burns and H. L. A. Hart (eds) (Oxford: Oxford University Press, 1996, first published 1789), p. 13.

63 Väyrynen, 'Usable moral principles', p. 87.

64 Ibid., p. 89.

65 Väyrynen, 'Moral generalism: Enjoy in moderation', p. 722.

66 Ibid., p. 721, footnote.

67 Bentham, *An Introduction to the Principles of Morals and Legislation*, p. 13.

68 Väyrynen, 'Moral generalism: Enjoy in moderation', p. 719.

69 Mark Norris Lance, and Margaret Olivia Little, 'From particularism to defeasibility in ethics', in Mark Norris Lance, Matjaz Potrc and Vojko Strahovnik (eds), *Challenging Moral Particularism. Routledge Studies in Ethics and Moral Theory* (New York: Routledge, 2008), p. 54.

70 Ibid., p. 73.

71 Ibid.

72 Ibid.

73 Mark Norris Lance and Margaret Olivia Little, 'Defeasibility and the normative grasp of context', *Erkenntnis* 61 (2004), pp. 435–55, p. 438.

74 Lance and Little, 'From particularism to defeasibility in ethics', p. 62.

75 Mark Norris Lance and Margaret Olivia Little, 'Where the laws are', in Russ Shafer-Landau (ed.), *Oxford Studies in Metaethics* (Oxford: Oxford University Press, 2007), pp. 149–71, p. 152.

76 Lance and Little, 'From particularism to defeasibility in ethics', p. 63.

77 Ibid.

78 Ibid., p. 66.

79 Ibid.

80 See McKeever and Ridge, *Principled Ethics*, p. 71.

81 Lance and Little, 'From particularism to defeasibility in ethics', p. 65.

82 Ibid., p. 66.

83 Ibid.

84 Lance and Little, 'From particularism to defeasibility in ethics', p. 69.

85 Ibid., p. 73.

86 Ibid., p. 66.

87 Ibid., p. 70.

88 Dancy, 'Can the particularist learn the difference between right and wrong?', in K. Brinkmann (ed.), *The Proceedings of the Twentieth World Congress of Philosophy. Vol. 1 Ethics* (Bowling Green: Philosophy Documentation Center, 1999), p. 70.

89 Lance and Little, 'From particularism to defeasibility in ethics', p. 66.

90 Ibid., p. 70.

91 R. M. Hare, 'Principles', in R. M. Hare, *Essays in Ethical Theory* (Oxford: Oxford University Press, 1989), p. 49.

92 See ibid.

93 Dancy, *Ethics Without Principles*, p. 116.

94 McKeever and Ridge, *Principled Ethics*, p. 109.

95 Ibid., p. 7.

96 Väyrynen, 'Usable moral principles', p. 76.

97 Mark Norris Lance and Margaret Olivia Little, 'Particularism and antitheory', in D. Copp (ed.), *The Oxford Handbook of Ethical Theory* (Oxford: Oxford University Press, 2006), pp. 567–94, p. 570.

98 Lance and Little, 'From particularism to defeasibility in ethics', p. 53.

99 Onora O'Neill, 'Practical principles and practical judgement', *Hastings Center Report* 31 (2001), pp. 15–23, p. 16.

100 Ibid.

101 Ibid.

102 The following paragraph is based on an argument made by David Copp in the context of a discussion of confirmation theories in ethics. Although Copp is not concerned with the distinction between theoretical and practical principles, his remarks are highly illuminating with regard to this problem. See David Copp, 'Explanation and justification in ethics', *Ethics* 100 (1990), pp. 237–58, pp. 254–6.

103 Principles of epistemic rationality and some principles of logic such as *modus ponens* are more problematic. They are not descriptive in the same way that the empirical principles of the special sciences are. Agents can follow or violate these principles. According to my

definition of theoretical and practical principles, *modus ponens* and other logical and epistemic principles fall in the category of practical principles. I do not see this as a problem. The category of practical principles is very broad and diverse. Some practical principles might be more normative than others.

104 See Copp, 'Explanation and justification in ethics', p. 256.

105 See G. E. M Anscombe, *Intention* (Cambridge, MA: Harvard University Press, 2000, first published 1957), pp. 56–7.

106 See Onora O'Neill, 'Instituting principles: Between duty and action', in Mark Timmons (ed.), *Kant's Metaphysics of Morals: Interpretative Essays* (Oxford: Oxford University Press, 2002), pp. 331–47, p. 333.

107 I borrow this example from O'Neill, 'Instituting principles: Between duty and action', p. 333.

108 Ibid., Dancy, *Ethics Without Principles*, p. 103.

109 Ibid., p. 143.

110 O'Neill, 'Instituting principles: Between duty and action', p. 336.

111 For Dancy's discussion of moral practice see Dancy, *Ethics Without Principles*, pp. 133–4.

112 Russ Shafer-Landau, 'Moral Rules', *Ethics* 107 (1997), pp. 584–611, p. 586.

113 Ibid., p. 584.

114 See for example Richard N. Boyd, 'How to be a moral realist', in Geoffrey Sayre-McCord (ed.), *Essays on Moral Realism* (New York: Cornell University Press, 1988), pp. 181–228; Paul M. Pietroski, 'Prima facie obligations, ceteris paribus laws in moral theory', *Ethics* 103 (1993), pp. 489–515.

115 McKeever and Ridge, *Principled Ethics*, p. 109, Ethics 103 (1993), pp. 489–515.

116 Ibid., p. 197.

117 Ibid.

118 Ibid., p. 8.

119 Ibid., p. 109.

120 Ibid., p. 198.

121 Ibid., p. 201.

122 Ibid., p. 198.

123 Ibid.

124 See R. M. Hare, *Moral Thinking: Its Levels, Method, and Point* (Oxford: Oxford University Press, 1981).

125 McKeever and Ridge, *Principled Ethics*, pp. 199–200.

126 *Ibid.,* pp. 202–15.

127 See Cass R. Sunstein, 'Moral heuristics', *Behavioral and Brain Sciences* 28 (2005), pp. 531–73.

128 McKeever and Ridge, *Principled Ethics*, p. 215, emphasis added.

129 David McNaughton, *Moral Vision, An Introduction to Ethics* (Oxford: Wiley-Blackwell, 1988), p. 190.

130 This is not to deny that in some cases simplified versions of theoretical principles can be useful heuristics or *ceteris paribus* principles. However, these principles are still theoretical principles; they have a clear word-to-world direction of fit.

131 Väyrynen, 'Usable moral principles', p. 77.

132 Väyrynen, 'Ethical theories and moral guidance', p. 294.

133 Väyrynen, 'Usable moral principles', pp. 91–2.

134 Ibid., p. 77.

135 Ibid., p. 94.

136 Ibid., p. 93.

137 O'Neill, 'Instituting principles: Between duty and action', p. 333.

138 Väyrynen, 'Moral generalism: Enjoy in moderation', p. 722.

139 Väyrynen, 'Usable moral principles', p. 95.

140 Ibid., p. 93.

141 Ibid.

142 Ibid., p. 93.

143 Lance and Little, 'Particularism and antitheory', p. 570.

144 *Ibid.*

145 Dancy is likely to object that on his model we do not assess options but reasons. However, he will have to acknowledge that we need to assess the various possible courses of action open to us in a given situation (i.e. our options) in order to see which of them we have most reason to perform. This is especially so given Dancy's belief that anything whatever might provide a reason if the circumstances are suitable.

146 Gilbert Harman, 'Moral particularism and transduction', *Philosophical Issues* 14 (2005), pp. 44–55, p. 52.

147 Gilbert Harman, *Change in View. Principles of reasoning* (Cambridge, MA: Harvard University Press, 1986), p. 77. It is important to note that even though Harman refuses to classify

reasoning about what to do as practical reasoning, he nevertheless wants to draw a distinction between theoretical and practical reasoning. He uses the term 'practical reasoning' to refer to the reasoned revision of intentions and plans. Harman argues that practical reasoning revises intentions while theoretical reasoning revises beliefs. According to Harman, intentions are distinctive attitudes that cannot be reduced to either beliefs or desires, and it is the reasoned revision of these distinctive attitudes that he refers to as practical reasoning (see Harman, *Change in View*, pp. 1–2, pp. 77–3, p. 113).

148 Bernard Williams, *Ethics and the Limits of Philosophy* (London: Routledge, 1985), p. 185.

149 J. David Velleman, *The Possibility of Practical Reason* (Oxford: Clarendon Press, 2000), p. 180.

150 J. David Velleman, *Practical Reflection* (Stanford: Center for the Study of Language and Information, 2007), p. 15.

151 Ibid., p. 93.

152 Ibid.

153 Ibid.

154 Ibid.

155 Ibid., p. 318.

156 Ibid., p. 15, p. 271.

157 Ibid., pp. 215–18.

158 Ibid., p. 308.

159 Ibid.

160 Ibid.

161 Ibid.

CHAPTER THREE

The Nature and Roles of Moral Principles

After the mainly analytical and critical focus in the first two chapters of the book, this third chapter offers a positive account of the nature and roles of moral principles. It is divided into four sections. The first two sections develop an account of the nature of moral principles, while the final two show why moral principles so understood are constitutive of the activity and capacity of moral judgement. In order to answer the particularist challenge as defined in the first chapter of the book, generalists have to accomplish two things: first, they have to explain how the generality of moral principles is compatible with the need for context-sensitivity, and second, they need to show why moral principles are a necessary part of our moral thought and action. What roles do they play in moral thought and action?

With regard to the problem of context-sensitivity I will highlight, and distinguish between, two important features of moral principles: their indeterminacy and their defeasibility. It is in virtue of the combination of these two features that moral principles can fulfil the need for context-sensitivity. However, the indeterminacy and defeasibility of moral principles also means that following and applying them requires judgement. In the third and fourth sections, I will, therefore, have to show why moral principles need to be supplemented, but are not supplanted, by judgement. What is the relation between moral principles and moral judgement? Why do we need moral principles?

Indeterminacy

Moral principles, as I shall defend them, are characterized by their indeterminacy and their defeasibility. In this and the next section, I will distinguish and explain the different ways in which I take moral principles to be indeterminate and defeasible. Many of the points I will be making hold good for other principles, especially other practical principles, as well. I will refer to non-moral principles for the purpose of illustration, but my primary focus will be on moral principles. At this point one might wonder what makes a principle a moral principle. I will understand moral principles as principles that employ moral concepts in a specific way. Moral principles take a stance with regard to certain types of actions, institutions or character traits. They classify certain types of actions, institutions or character traits as right or wrong, good or bad, virtuous or vicious, and they prescribe, forbid, recommend or condemn certain types of actions, institutions or character traits. Given the notorious difficulties of distinguishing the moral from the non-moral, this way of distinguishing moral from non-moral principles might seem somewhat arbitrary. However, I will assume that we have an intuitive grasp of the distinction between moral and non-moral concepts and focus on those concepts that fall clearly in the moral realm.

While indeterminacy is widely acknowledged to be a scalar property, moral philosophers pay little attention to the fact that there is more than one form of indeterminacy relevant to morality. I will distinguish between four forms of indeterminacy central to morality: vagueness, open-texture, comparison indeterminacy, and indeterminacy in implementation. Contrary to the impression given by many moral philosophers, none of these four forms of indeterminacy is entailed by the others. It is, therefore, impossible to fully understand the phenomenon of moral indeterminacy, and its implication for the nature and roles of moral principles, by focusing on just one of them.

Vagueness

The form of indeterminacy that is often taken as basic in discussions of moral indeterminacy is vagueness. Typical examples of vague concepts include 'red', 'bald', 'heap', 'tadpole' and 'child'. Such concepts are widely believed to share two essential characteristics.[1] First, vague concepts lack sharp boundaries. For example, there seems to be no exact point at which a creature growing from tadpole to frog ceases to be a tadpole.[2] As result of this lack of sharp boundaries, vague concepts have borderline cases. Certain reddish-orange patches, for example, are borderline red. We can see how this form of indeterminacy might affect moral principles. One might think, for example, that a moral principle that proscribes the killing of a person against her or his will is indeterminate because the concept of personhood is indeterminate. It is unclear if, and if so when, a foetus counts as a person. As with the development of a tadpole into a frog, there seems to be no exact point at which a creature growing from a zygote into an adult human being becomes a person. Consequently, it is unclear whether the principle 'Do not kill a person against her or his will' applies to cases of abortion. The second characteristic of vague concepts is their susceptibility to sorites paradoxes. Intuitively, one grain of sand cannot make a difference to whether or not something qualifies as a heap of sand. This seems part of what it is for 'heap' to lack sharp boundaries. So we have the principle H: if x is a heap of sand, then the result y of removing one grain will still be a heap. However, take a heap and remove grains one by one; repeated applications of H imply absurdly that the solitary last grain is a heap.[3] Again we can see how this might affect moral judgements. Intuitively, one second cannot make a difference to whether or not an abortion is morally permissible. So if it is morally wrong to abort a foetus without medical indication in the thirty-eighth week of pregnancy then it is equally wrong to abort the foetus one second before it reaches the thirty-eighth week. By the same reasoning, we seem forced to conclude that it is wrong to abort a one-cell, 46-chromosome human zygote – a moral conclusion which many will want to deny.

There are semantic, ontological and epistemic accounts of vagueness. Semantic accounts locate the vagueness in natural language. Vagueness arises because the words and phrases of our language are often not specific enough to pick out unique states of affairs in the world.[4] Ontological accounts locate vagueness in the objects or properties themselves. According to ontological accounts, vagueness is not merely a phenomenon of our language but a feature of the world itself.[5] Ontological vagueness implies semantic vagueness: if certain objects or properties are vague it is impossible to correctly capture these objects or properties in non-vague language. By contrast, epistemic accounts attribute vagueness to ignorance. For defenders of such epistemic accounts, vagueness is the result of our limited powers of discrimination. Predicates have well-defined boundaries, but we often fail to see clearly where these boundaries lie.[6] I wish to remain neutral on the question of whether there can be vague objects and properties. It seems possible to have vague language in a non-vague world.[7] Since I assume that moral principles must be capable of being formulated in natural language, it does not matter for my purposes whether vagueness is a feature of the world or 'merely' an ineliminable part of our language. I will, therefore, adhere to a semantic account of vagueness.

What are the implications of vagueness for the nature and roles of moral principles? The existence of vague concepts in the moral realm means that there are no determinately true answers to some moral questions containing these concepts.[8] If we consider this to be a problem, it is a problem for generalists and particularists alike. There will be cases where moral principles fail to provide us with a determinately true answer. But they fail because there is no such answer to be found. No particularist will be able to do better in these cases.

It is important to note that admitting the existence of vague concepts in the moral realm does not force us to accept the sceptical conclusion of all-encompassing vagueness. A non-moral example helps to illustrate this point. The fact that certain reddish-orange patches are borderline red does not undermine our belief in the possibility of making determinately correct colour judgements. In most cases we still feel confident to classify colour patches as determinately red or determinately orange, and even with regard to the reddish-orange patch in question we can still make many determinate judgements, for example that it is determinately not-blue. The same is true for judgements about baldness, heaps, children and tadpoles. The fact that these concepts are vague does not mean that there are no cases where their application is determinately right or wrong. Why is this? Why is it plausible to postulate that some questions lack determinate answers but implausible to claim that all do? The answer lies in the nature of vague concepts itself. We saw that vague concepts are characterized by two central features:

they lack sharp boundaries and they are susceptible to sorites paradoxes. It would make no sense to talk of a concept's lack of sharp boundaries if there were no core of clear cases to which the concept determinately applies. Similarly, sorites paradoxes would not be paradoxical if there were no starting- and end-point where the concept determinately applies and determinately does not apply, respectively. The very definition of vague concepts therefore precludes the possibility of all-encompassing indeterminacy.

This notwithstanding, moral principles which contain vague concepts cannot provide us with necessary and sufficient application conditions for these concepts because vague concepts lack sharp boundaries. This is a problem for generalists if they take the provision of necessary and sufficient application conditions for moral concepts to be part of the role of moral principles. However, moral principles, as I will understand them, do not have to fulfil this role. In this respect my account differs from McKeever and Ridge's conception of moral principles discussed in Chapter Two as well as Jackson, Pettit and Smith's pattern argument discussed in Chapter One. According to my account, moral principles can contain vague moral and non-moral concepts, but it is not their function to fix the boundaries of these concepts.

How do we manage to learn and apply vague concepts if there are no principles which articulate correct, necessary and sufficient conditions for their application? Answering this question will help to shed more light on the nature of moral principles and allow me to show how my account differs from a particularist account of competence with vague concepts. Concepts categorize and organize our perception of the world. In the absence of such a structure we would be overwhelmed by its complexity. Categorization involves viewing two or more distinct entities as in some way similar. According to the classical picture, concepts segregate things into classes by providing a system of 'pigeonholes'.[9] Category membership is presented as an all-or-nothing matter: an object is either *in* a category or *outside* it. The traditional model of categorization presupposes that there are necessary and sufficient criteria for category membership. Since there can be no necessary and sufficient conditions for the application of vague concepts, they seem unable to fulfil their categorizing function. However, concepts can classify without setting boundaries. Mark Sainsbury has made this point especially clear. The colour spectrum, as displayed, for instance, in a book, provides a good example for 'boundaryless' classification. Although the colours stand out as clearly different, there are no sharp divisions. Looking carefully we can see that the colours merge into one another; there are no boundaries. This does nothing to impede the classificatory process: the colour spectrum provides a paradigm of classification.[10] According to Sainsbury, we learn vague concepts with the help of paradigm cases. He argues that we acquire vague concepts from the inside, working outwards from central cases, and locating the central cases of contrary concepts, rather than starting from the outside, identifying boundaries and moving inwards.[11] We acquire the concept 'red', for example, with the help of paradigmatic instantiations of that colour and we grasp the concept of 'not red' via a grasp of yellow, green, blue, etc.

Dancy makes use of a similar idea in order to show that particularists have an attractive model of conceptual learning and competence available to them:

> The general idea is that instead of building up a concept by developing lists of necessary and sufficient conditions for 'being of that sort', we do it rather by developing a set of prototypes, clearest cases, or best examples, in such a way that we conceive of less clear cases or less good examples in terms of distance from the prototype or prototypes.[12]

Dancy substantiates this idea by referring to Eleanor Rosch's prototype theory. In the 1970s, Rosch and her colleagues discovered that not every member of a given category is equally important to our understanding of it. For example, robins turn out to be cognitively more central for the category 'bird' than other members of the category, such as chickens, ostriches or penguins. Rosch found out that the differences between the reaction times to verify good and poor examples of category membership were far more extreme for ten-year-old children than for adults, indicating that the children had learned the category membership of the prototypical members earlier than that of non-prototypical members.[13] Rosch emphasizes that cognitive prototypes do not give us a list of necessary and sufficient conditions for category membership. Her prototype theory provides evidence that we can, and do, acquire concepts with the help of paradigms, prototypes, clearest cases and best examples, rather than by focusing on the boundaries of the concepts.

So far this picture does indeed seem to fit well with particularism. Particularists might think that it provides evidence for their claim that we do not need any principles in order to learn and apply moral concepts. I will address the question of why we need moral principles in the next section. At this point I want to stress that the conceptual knowledge which we acquire through paradigms, prototypes, clearest cases or best examples is *general* knowledge. When we think about less clear cases in terms of their distance to the core of prototypical or paradigm cases we abstract away from the irrelevant, individual features of the prototypical cases. What we see and respond to in prototypical cases is something general. A particular object or case by itself will be of no use in learning a concept unless we are able to view it as an instance of a general type: a proto-*type*. This is at odds with the particularists' claim that our basic moral knowledge is particular.[14] To grasp and master a concept is to be able to see something particular as being of a general kind.

Moral principles which employ vague concepts apply uncontroversially only to those cases that fall in the paradigmatic core of these concepts. However, this does not mean that we can restrict moral principles to a definite set of such cases. It is impossible to draw a sharp line between those cases that clearly fall within the prototypical core of a vague concept and those cases that clearly do not. Bertrand Russell makes this point very clear:

> Someone may seek to obtain precision in the use of words by saying that no word is to be applied in the penumbra, but [...] the penumbra itself is not accurately definable, and all the vaguenesses which apply to the primary use of words apply also when we try to fix the limit to their indubitable applicability.[15]

We cannot turn a vague principle into a non-vague principle by providing a list of necessary and sufficient conditions for falling under the principle. Moral principles that contain vague concepts need to be interpreted. I will say more about the interpretation of moral principles in the context of indeterminacy as open-texture in the next section.

Open-texture

Vagueness is distinct from a second form of indeterminacy, which, following H. L. A. Hart, I call open-texture. In *The Concept of Law* Hart argues for a middle position on judicial interpretation between formalism and rule-scepticism.[16] According to Hart, formalism and rule-scepticism 'are the Scylla and Charybdis of juristic theory; they are great exaggerations, salutary where they correct each other, and the truth lies between them'.[17] Formalists believe that legal rules can be so detailed that the question of whether or not they apply to a particular case is always settled in advance, and never involves, at the point of actual application, a fresh choice between open alternatives.[18] Hart argues that such a system of legal rules would be possible '[i]f the world in which we live were characterized only by a finite number of features, and these together with all the modes in which they could combine were known to us'.[19] But since this is not the world we live in, formalism is not a tenable position. The rule-sceptic is often a disappointed formalist. Having realized that his ideal conception of what it is for a rule to exist is not attained by rules in reality, 'he expresses his disappointment by the denial that there are, or can be, any rules'.[20] Hart points out that rule-scepticism presents us with a false dilemma. It is not the case that '[e]ither rules are what they would be in formalist's heaven and they bind as fetters bind; or there are no rules'.[21] This fits well with what I want to say about moral principles. It is neither the case that moral principles function as algorithms, providing us with determinate answers to all cases, nor that they are of no importance at all. Principles are an essential part of morality despite – and even because of – their indeterminacy.

Hart uses the term 'open-texture' to describe the interpretative nature of the law. According to Hart, the law needs to be interpreted because the concepts it employs are open-textured and open-textured concepts are interpretative. Hart argues that in order to decide whether a legal rule applies to a particular case we need to delimitate the range of meanings of the concepts employed by the rule. The application of the rule 'No vehicles in the park', for example, depends on whether a particular object is regarded as a 'vehicle'. In usual cases the concept seems to need no interpretation: the recognition of instances is unproblematic.[22] However, there will be cases where it no longer seems clear whether the concept should apply or not. A rule that forbids you to take a vehicle into a park clearly prohibits you from driving through the park with your motorcar, but what about bicycles, roller skates, or toy cars? What about aeroplanes?[23] Similarly, consider moral principles such as 'Do not lie' or 'Do not torture sentient beings'. In many cases such principles will need no interpretation. But there are cases where it no longer seems clear whether an action qualifies as a lie or as torturing. For example, is conventional politeness a form of lying? Does sleep deprivation qualify as torture?

In contrast to vagueness, open-texture is at least in principle eliminable. In the case of vagueness an attempt to eliminate indeterminacy would lead to arbitrary distinctions, such as the distinction between grains of sand in the definition of 'heap'. In the case of open-texture we do not encounter the problem of sorites paradoxes and the arbitrariness of drawing any definite boundaries which sorites paradoxes expose. So in contrast to vagueness, open-texture does not entail that some questions necessarily lack determinate answers. Any interpretation of an open-textured concept is an attempt to move from indeterminacy to determinacy. We might think that the boundaries a given interpretation draws are unreasonable or arbitrary, but this will be a criticism of that particular interpretation and not a denial of the possibility of drawing any definite boundaries *per se*.

According to Hart, the open-texture of legal rules is an advantage rather than a disadvantage for our legal practice. It allows rules to be reasonably interpreted when they are applied to situations and problems that the legislator did not foresee or could not have foreseen.[24] I contend that the same is true for moral principles. Due to the open-texture of the concepts they employ, moral principles possess a flexibility that is crucial when we are confronted with new and challenging moral questions as in the case of genetic engineering, for example. Recent developments in biotechnology and genetics raise a host of new ethical questions and problems, many of which could not have been foreseen. The possibilities of genetic engineering are widely believed to challenge our traditional understanding of important concepts such as the concept of human nature, harm or fairness. If moral principles were fully determinate, and hence leave no room for interpretation, they would be of no use in such cases. If the boundaries of these concepts were clearly defined, and fixed once and for all, moral principles containing these concepts would be useless in cases that we did not foresee when we formulated or adopted these principles.[25] Following such inflexible principles would result in counterintuitive and even disastrous decisions. Or the principles would be useless since they would suggest nothing. The open-texture of the concepts employed by moral principles allows us to avoid these problems. This provides an argument against those particularists who claim that a principle-based framework of moral thought and action is necessarily rigid and inflexible.

The open-texture of the concepts embodied in moral principles also gives generalists an advantage over particularists who claim that we should approach novel cases with a set of paradigms, prototypes, clearest cases or best examples, rather than a set of principles. Moral principles are flexible and adaptable in a way that a list of paradigms, prototypes, clearest cases and best examples is not. Having in mind a concrete example or a paradigm case can be a hindrance when deliberating about how to judge a novel and difficult situation. When deliberating about harm in the context of genetic engineering, for example, clinging to a paradigm of harm as one person inflicting bodily injury on another person and thereby making that person worse off is likely to distort our deliberation rather than support it. Moral principles abstract away from the individual features of prototypical cases. They do not describe any particular prototypical cases. This gives moral principles a crucial role in the resolution of disagreements. As long as we disagree only about the interpretation of an open-textured concept contained within a moral principle, and not about the principle itself, we have a common basis from which we can try to resolve the disagreement. Trying to find a common interpretation of the principles will force us to become clearer about what it is that makes a particular case a prototypical instance of a concept. We need to ask ourselves, for example, what it is about a particular lie or a particular killing that makes it prototypical for us. In the course of the discussion we might come to reconsider the status of a particular case as prototypical. Moral principles allow for such reconsiderations because they employ open-textured concepts without specifying any particular, purportedly prototypical, instances of these concepts.

How do we interpret open-textured concepts? Hart points out that when a legal rule is passed, both the legislators and the public have in mind particular situations and problems that are to be avoided.[26] In the case of the legal rule prohibiting vehicles in the park, the image is arguably one of excluding normal motorcar, bus and motorcycle traffic from the park. In deciding whether, for the purpose of the rule, 'vehicle' applies to, for instance, golf cars, aeroplanes, toy cars or roller skates, we consider in what respects and how far these cases resemble the paradigm cases.[27] For example, like a motorcar, roller skates make noise (but not nearly as much), and they threaten safety and order (though the threat is on a much lower scale). Roller skates are far smaller than motorcars and they do not pollute the air.[28] There are thus both similarities and dissimilarities, and we need to decide which are relevant and which are not. Open-textured concepts have a relatively stable core centred around clear paradigm cases. Like legal rules, moral principles apply non-controversially only to those cases that lie at the stable core of the open-textured concepts they employ. In order to interpret a moral principle we begin by reflecting on the stable core of prototypical cases to which the principle clearly applies. For instance, we think about clear cases of lying. In deciding whether white lies, jokes, exaggerations or oversimplifications count as lying, we consider in what respects these cases resemble our paradigm cases. Among the central characteristics of prototypical lies seem to be the uttering of a falsehood and the intention to deceive. Deliberating about these features of a prototypical lie will help us to decide whether we want to count as a lie a social lie that deceives no one.[29]

It is plausible to assume that what counts as a prototypical instance of an open-textured concept is to some extent culturally dependent. What people consider as a prototypical instance of a concept depends at least partly on what instances they have come across. Robins may count as a prototypical instance of the concept 'bird' for people who live in areas where robins are common.[30] But robins are unlikely to be treated as a prototypical instance by people who live in areas where this species of birds does not occur. In the moral case, these differences can lead to disagreement about the interpretation of moral concepts. To say that open-textured concepts have a stable core is not to say that this core can be clearly defined or fixed for all times. When faced with disagreement about a case that we, up to that point, considered to be a prototypical instance of a concept, we might reconsider the case's status as a prototype.

One might worry that rather than being a virtue, this flexibility of open-textured concepts renders principles which contain them effectively meaningless. If there can be disagreement and uncertainty about the status of a case as a paradigm instance of an open-textured concept as well as its interpretative implications for other cases, should we not conclude that there is no correct interpretation of such concepts? Does it not mean that anything goes when it comes to the interpretation of moral principles? In dealing with this worry it is important to remember that, like vagueness, open-texture is not a phenomenon that is unique to moral concepts. Open-texture is normally not thought to render other rules and principles, such as legal rules, meaningless. However, one might think that although many non-moral concepts are open-textured and thus interpretative, moral concepts are special. In the case of moral concepts the disagreements about their correct interpretation are particularly deep and widespread, and this – one might argue – is best explained by the assumption that there is no right and wrong when it comes to interpreting moral principles.[31] The problem with this argument is that it fails to account for the phenomenology of moral disagreement. When we disagree with someone we normally assume, and indeed try to make sure, that we understand what the other person is saying. That is, we assume that we are talking about the same thing, rather than speak past each other. In order for this to be the case there needs to be an overlapping consensus on the core meaning of the concepts employed by the opposing parties. And since there needs to be some shared core understanding of a concept in order for communication about the concept to be possible, interpretations of a moral principle that conflict with that core understanding can be ruled out as incorrect. It is therefore not true that 'anything goes' when we interpret moral principles. Given that it is impossible to believe oneself to be in a genuine disagreement with someone one does not understand, believing oneself to be in a disagreement presupposes the rejection of the sceptical assumption that there is no true and false in interpreting moral principles. While both the status of a case as a paradigm instance of an open-textured concept and its interpretative implications for other cases can be a matter of controversy, there has to be some overlapping consensus on the core meaning of the concept in order for there to be meaningful discussions about it. That is, we do not have to agree on a *definite* set of paradigm cases, but there needs to be *some* shared core understanding of open-textured concepts in order for us to acknowledge differences in its interpretation. Otherwise we would not be disagreeing about the interpretation of one, single concept, but be talking about different concepts. This in turn means that disagreement about, and involving, open-textured moral principles presupposes that some interpretations will be determinately false and others determinately correct.

To value open-texture means to acknowledge that interpreting moral concepts is a work in progress, but it does not entail that there is no true interpretation to be found. On the contrary, acknowledging open-texture is an antidote against the danger of dogmatism and false certainty detrimental to any search for truth in ethics and elsewhere.

Comparison indeterminacy

In contrast to vagueness and open-texture, comparison indeterminacy is, as its name says, unique to comparative judgements.[32] Comparison indeterminacy can obtain between abstract values such as equality and liberty or particular bearers of these values, for example certain social institutions which instantiate the value of equality or liberty. It arises in situations where we need to decide which of two options would be more lucrative or enjoyable, for example, or which available course of action would be more virtuous, which form of government more just, or the fulfilment of which duty more important. In some situations there seems to be no single, determinate answer to these questions and moral principles accordingly seem to fail to guide our moral thought and action.

I follow Ruth Chang's distinction between incomparability and incommensurability.[33] According to Chang, incommensurable values or bearers of value cannot be precisely measured using a single scale. For example, one might think that liberty and equality cannot be reduced to a common measure. Two objects or states of affairs are incomparable if nothing affirmative can be said about what value relation holds between them.[34] According to the majority view, the logical space of positive value relations for any two objects or states of affairs is exhausted by the trichotomy of relations 'better than', 'worse than' and 'equally good'.[35] Given this 'trichotomy thesis', two objects are incomparable if one object is neither better nor worse than the other with respect to some value and yet the objects are not equally good. A particular career as a clarinettist and a particular career as a lawyer, for example, are incomparable if the former is neither better nor worse than the latter with respect to, say, goodness of careers, and yet the two careers are not equally good.[36]

One might think that incommensurability entails incomparability. That is, one might think that if there is no common unit of value in terms of which two items can be measured, they are incomparable. However, comparison does not require a single scale of units of value according to which items can be precisely measured. As Chang points out, one alternative can be morally better than another without being better by, say, 2.34 units.[37] Comparable items can be ordinally ranked, i.e. ranked on a list, but may not be cardinally rankable, i.e. precisely ranked by some unit of value. While it seems relatively clear that many objects and states of affairs are incommensurable, it is a matter of controversy whether or not they are ever incomparable. Whether or not one believes in the existence of value incomparability depends crucially on what kinds of value relations one takes there to be. Some philosophers have argued that there are more value relations than the traditional three. Strong contestants in this context are notions such as 'imprecise equality' and 'rough equality'.[38] Once one acknowledges the existence of such a fourth value relation, the possibility of value incomparability becomes more difficult to defend.[39] I do not want to take a stance on whether or not value incomparability exists. Rather, I wish to explore what would follow for principled ethics, *if* some bearers of value were incomparable.

However, let me first look at the implications of incommensurability for principled ethics. Incommensurability can obtain between different values, different bearers of the same value as well as between bearers of different values. The pleasure of listening to an opera and the pleasure of understanding a complex philosophical argument, for example, are probably not precisely measurable according to some common scale. The same holds true for the pleasure of understanding a complex philosophical argument and, say, the justice of a particular court decision. This means that incommensurability can affect both monistic and pluralistic principled ethics. Utilitarians need to weigh the pleasure or utility produced by different courses of action and Rossian pluralists, for example, have to weigh the justice of one particular action against the beneficence of another. Utilitarians, especially, tend to speak of 'calculating', 'measuring' and 'aggregating' the utility of the consequences of different possible actions. Taken literally, these notions presuppose a single scale of units of value according to which the consequences can be precisely measured. Classical utilitarianism thus seems to presuppose commensurability. However, utilitarians might have ways of circumventing the problems that incommensurability poses.[40] The precise measurement of the value of particular actions, characters or institutions using a common unit of value does not seem to be essential to either utilitarianism or a theory of Rossian *prima facie* duties. What is essential is that the different alternatives can be ranked in some way, and, as I pointed out before, these rankings do not need to be cardinal. It is incomparability, and the resulting breakdown in ranking, that poses the real threat.

If different forms of pleasure were incomparable, we would not be able to employ the utilitarian principle 'Maximize pleasure'. That is, if the pleasure of listening to an opera and the pleasure of understanding a complex philosophical argument were incomparable, the principle would fail to be action-guiding. Maximization does not tolerate incomparability. Utilitarians, and consequentialists in general, have tried to avoid the problem of incomparability by switching from maximizing to satisficing. Satisficing demands only that the agent does an action that has sufficient value – that is 'good enough' – and not that she performs the action with the best consequences. Instead of trying to achieve the best outcome, the agent is asked to settle on the first satisfactory alternative she comes across.[41] A person who has to sell her house because she is moving to another city, for example, may aim to obtain what she takes to be a satisfactory price for the house, rather than to maximize her profit and attempt to get the best price she can. She might be so busy with all the other preparations of moving to and settling in the new city that it is rational for her to sell the house to the first buyer that offers her a satisfactory price.[42] The satisficing model solves the problem of making a choice in cases where an enormous, or even potentially infinite, number of alternatives are to be compared. For satisficing utilitarians an action will be right if it promotes a sufficient amount of pleasure. A satisficing choice can be made as soon as an alternative is found that meets this benchmark. The agent does not need to compare this satisficing choice with other possible actions and their consequences. Incomparability is, therefore, no problem. However, satisficing accounts of morality are controversial. There are many cases in which we will blame others and ourselves for not trying to achieve the best outcome. In morality, settling on the first satisfactory alternative and not trying to do the best can cost lives. This is not to say that we should, or can, ignore that our time, energy and capacities are limited and have to be divided between our various projects and commitments. But it seems that within these constraints we want people to strive to be the best moral agents they can be. It is plausible to argue that when we are concerned with avoiding harm, establishing justice or helping those in need, settling on the first satisfactory alternative is often not good enough.[43] Moreover, those who do not believe that settling on the first satisfactory alternative instead of striving to do the best can ever be morally wrong, are likely to want to make room for supererogatory actions. The problem of incomparability will then reappear at the level of decisions between morally praise-worthy actions that are beyond the call of duty.

Incomparability can obtain between different bearers of the same value specified by a single moral principle, as well as between different bearers of different values specified by a plurality of principles. If the justice of one particular action were incomparable with the beneficence of another, a Rossian pluralist would be unable to determine his *duty proper* in those situations. Incomparability can thus affect the usefulness of a single moral principle, like the principle of utility, as well as our ability to deal with a plurality of principles like Ross' set of *prima facie* principles. However, it is important to note that the possibility of incomparability is not a problem only for generalists. Particularists who want to argue that we decide what to do by weighing the reasons we discern in a particular situation will face the same problems. If the reasons were based on incomparable values, we would not be able to determine which reason has more weight. If incomparability is a problem, it is a problem for generalists and particularists alike.

My answer to the potential threat of incomparability is twofold. First, I assume that moral principles cannot be ranked in a strict hierarchical order. A strict ranking of moral principles is incompatible with incomparability. However, a strict hierarchical ordering of moral principles would be impossible even if all values turned out to be comparable. The impossibility of strict hierarchical ordering is a consequence of the defeasibility of moral principles, which I will discuss in the second part of this section. Because of the lack of a strict priority ordering, moral principles, as I defend them, are compatible with (but do not presuppose) the incomparability of values or certain bearers of value. The second answer to the threat of incomparability lies in the model of practical reasoning I will propose in 'Moral Principles and the Activity of Moral Judgement' (pp. 156–88). According to this model, practical reasoning is not primarily a task of weighing different values *against each other*, but of interpreting and enacting these values in a way that allows us to fulfil them *together*. This model of practical reasoning does not presuppose the comparability of values. Of course, enacting one value can sometimes exclude enacting another. In specific cases, happiness can conflict with knowledge, mercy with justice, economic equality with liberty, and so on. There thus may be situations in which we are unable to find an action that does justice to our different values. However, such situations will be the result of the incompatibility of values (i.e. they cannot both be realized together), not their incomparability.[44] It is important to keep these two notions apart. Bearers of value can be incompatible without being incomparable, and they can be incomparable without being incompatible. We have uncovered incomparability not when we cannot decide how to rank two values or bearers of value, but when we can decide that they are unrankable.[45] Incomparability itself does not constitute a special problem for the theory of moral principles I defend.

Indeterminacy in implementation

The final form of indeterminacy relevant for moral principles emerges in the context of practical reasoning. It concerns the underdetermination of action by practical principles. I call this form of indeterminacy 'indeterminacy in implementation'.

In the first chapter I pointed out that moral principles contain act-descriptions of certain *types* of actions. They pick out certain act-descriptions as morally relevant and take a stance with regard to actions of this type. Practical principles, including moral principles, prescribe, forbid, recommend or condemn certain act-*types*. However, when we follow practical principles we have to perform particular *tokens* of these act-types. Since an act-type can be instantiated by various different act-tokens, practical principles necessarily underdetermine action. A person who has made it her principle to help those in need, for example, can do so by going to the supermarket on behalf of her ill neighbour, looking after the child of an overworked acquaintance, volunteering in a local charity, writing a cheque for UNICEF, and so on. Which act-token a principle of beneficence requires depends on who needs what, the means and actors available, and many more details of the particular situation. Moral principles are indeterminate in the sense of underdetermining action.[46]

Indeterminacy in implementation is easily mistaken as a by-product of one of the other three forms of indeterminacy. For example, one might think that moral principles underdetermine action because in cases of comparison indeterminacy they fail to guide our choice between different courses of action. Or one might think that moral principles underdetermine action because they contain open-textured concepts and thus need to be interpreted before we can act on them. However, although comparison indeterminacy and open-texture can undeniably add to the difficulty of enacting moral principles, indeterminacy in implementation is a separate and distinct form of indeterminacy. Even in cases where there is no question of how to interpret the concepts contained in a principle and where there are no other, conflicting, principles, we need to decide how to enact the principle. Take the principle 'Do not lie' as an example. Even in cases where it is obvious that a particular utterance would be a lie and where there are no countervailing considerations that might outweigh the wrongness of this lie, there will normally be more than one way of avoiding the lie and as moral agents we need to settle on one of them. So even if moral concepts were fully determinate, moral principles would still be indeterminate in their implementation.

One might think that indeterminacy in implementation vanishes once we have specified our principles sufficiently. But even a highly specified principle such as 'Give five per cent of your yearly income to UNICEF' underdetermines action: the agent can donate the money once a year, once a month or once a week; she may use online banking or write a cheque; and she can make out the cheque in blue or black ink. In many cases, it will of course not matter which of the various act-tokens we perform. Arguably it does not matter, for example, whether a cheque is made out in blue or black ink. However, in many other cases the question of how best to implement the act-type prescribed or recommended by a given principle is crucial, and often difficult to answer. Some forms of helping others can be patronizing and degrading, some ways of speaking the truth are unnecessarily cruel and some acts of beneficence can be unjust. Furthermore, there might even be better and worse ways of implementing a highly specified principle such as 'Give five per cent of your yearly income to UNICEF'. For example, using online banking to transfer money will save paper and hence be better for the environment.

Selecting particular act-tokens when acting on a moral principle can be a difficult task requiring serious deliberation.[47] If we want to help someone who is bullied, for example, it can be very difficult to decide whether or not to intervene. After all, intervening might make things worse for the victim. If we decide to intervene we will need to decide which of the various act-tokens available to us will be the most appropriate and efficient. In making these decisions we have to pay close attention to the details of the particular situation in which we find ourselves: where does the bullying take place and how does it manifest itself? What can we say about the victim and those involved in the bullying? In what relation do we stand to those involved? All these considerations play a role in determining which particular token of the act-type specified by a given moral principle we should perform. In another situation helping someone who is bullied might call for a very different act-token. Implementing moral principles thus requires context-sensitivity. This may seem a surprising result given that particularists usually argue that moral principles cannot allow for context-sensitivity. According to my account, the indeterminacy of moral principles entails a need for context-sensitivity in the sense that their enactment must be sensitive to context. Why do particularists think that moral principles are incompatible with context-sensitivity? There are two reasons for this. First, many particularists believe that moral principles prescribe rigidly uniform behaviour which is insensitive to the differences between situations and persons. This charge of ethical rigorism is largely based on a misunderstanding of what moral principles are. It disregards the fact that moral principles are necessarily indeterminate. Moral principles prescribe act-types and not act-tokens. Which act-token best implements the act-type specified by the principle will depend on the details of the particular situation in which we find ourselves. However, that is not all there is to it. There are different forms of context-sensitivity. Indeterminate moral principles leave room for context-sensitive enactments because they prescribe, forbid, recommend or condemn certain act-types, not act-tokens. Which act-token a moral agent should perform in a particular situation depends on the context. The need for context-sensitivity that particularists usually insist on goes deeper than that. What can generalists say about cases where a particular act-token seems permissible even though our principle forbids actions of this type? In some contexts lying is morally forbidden, but in others it is not. It is cases like these that particularists usually have in mind when they argue that moral principles conflict with the need for context-sensitivity. Pointing to the indeterminacy of moral principles will not help to answer this problem. It is the defeasibility of moral principles that is at issue here. I shall, therefore, discuss this form of context-sensitivity in the section on defeasibility below.

Indeterminacy in implementation prevents moral principles from being overly rigid. Due to their indeterminacy in implementation, moral principles allow for a context-sensitivity that is essential for successful moral reasoning and action. However, one might worry that rather than being a virtue, this need for context-sensitive enactment renders moral principles incapable of guiding action. How do we make these, often difficult, context-sensitive decisions, and of what use are moral principles if they do not assist us in making them? In order to answer this question generalists have to provide an account of the roles of moral principles in the activity of moral judgement as well as the relation between moral principles and the capacity of moral judgement. I will offer such an account in the next two sections. I will show that the need for context-sensitive enactment does not undermine the capacity of moral principles to guide action.

Although none of the four forms of moral indeterminacy outlined above is reducible to any of the others, they can of course occur simultaneously. Moral principles which contain both vague and open-textured concepts, for example, will be particularly difficult to interpret. Similarly, comparison indeterminacy can complicate the enactment of moral principles. Moreover, it is not always clear what form of indeterminacy we are dealing with. For example, what on the surface looks like a disagreement about the interpretation of an open-textured concept might really be a disagreement about comparative value judgements. To illustrate this point, take the concept 'liberty' as an example. Following Gerald MacCallum, it is widely agreed that there is one concept of liberty, but many different interpretations or conceptions of liberty.[48] According to MacCallum, liberty is always *of* something (agent or agents), *from* something, *to* do, not do, become, or not become something. So-called negative and positive liberty theorists agree on this basic, core understanding of the concept. Without such a shared core understanding the opposing parties in the debate would simply speak past each other. Disagreements arise over the interpretation of the concept. Different writers on liberty disagree about what counts as an agent, what qualifies as a limitation of liberty, and what counts as a purpose that the agent can be described as being either free or unfree to carry out. However, often it is not clear whether the disagreement is really about the *interpretation* of the concept 'liberty' or rather about the *value* of different aspects of liberty. A standard argument against positive conceptions of liberty, for example, is that by counting internal constraints as constraints on freedom, liberty becomes a dangerous political ideal. Isaiah Berlin famously argued that there is a slippery slope from thinking of liberty as realization of one's true, rational self to licensing the most despicable forms of authoritarian government.[49] This could be read not as criticizing positive liberty theorists for misunderstanding the meaning of liberty, but as valuing an aspect of liberty that is dangerous when taken as a political ideal. We could at least in principle be in full agreement on the interpretation of the concept of liberty but disagree about which aspects of liberty we should strive for in a society and how to weigh liberty in comparison to other moral values. Such disagreements will not be the result of open-texture, but might instead be a symptom of comparison indeterminacy. Determining what form of indeterminacy we are dealing with in a particular case can thus itself be a matter of controversy and require serious deliberation.

This notwithstanding, indeterminacy is a benefit rather than a burden for principle-based ethics. Vagueness, open-texture and indeterminacy in implementation promote a flexibility and context-sensitivity that is essential to sound moral reasoning and action. Comparison indeterminacy raises difficulties when combined with incompatibility and these difficulties need to be taken seriously. In order to answer these difficulties generalists have to provide an account of the roles of moral principles in moral reasoning and the relation between moral principles and the capacity of moral judgement. However, before I proceed to offer such an account, let us look at the second characteristic of moral principles: their defeasibility.

Defeasibility

There are cases where it is necessary to lie in order to save a life or to cause harm in order to prevent greater harm. Killing a person against his or her will is normally seen as morally impermissible, but it might be permissible in cases of self-defence. Lying is normally a moral minus, it makes one's action worse, but it seems to be morally neutral when one is playing the game Diplomacy, where lying is part of the game. Promoting pleasure is normally a good thing, but not when it is the sadist's delight in her victim's agony. Moral principles are defeasible. In what follows, I want to clarify what exactly it is for a moral principle to be defeasible.

To begin with, it is important to distinguish the indeterminacy of moral principles from their potential defeasibility. A moral principle can be blocked, defeated or annulled even in cases that lie at the stable core of the concept the principle contains. Something might be a prototypical lie, for instance, but the obligation to save a person's life might trump our obligation not to lie if the life could not be saved without lying. While generalists have to accept that all moral principles are necessarily indeterminate, they can deny their defeasibility. For instance, one might argue that the principle 'Do not torture' is indefeasible: there are no circumstances under which we should suspend or violate this principle. The principle is absolute or sacrosanct. But the principle is nevertheless indeterminate. This indeterminacy has recently become a real political issue, with some lawyers and politicians arguing that 'waterboarding' does not fall under the concept of torture.[50] These lawyers and politicians purport not to deny the indefeasibility of the principle 'Do not torture', rather they claim to offer only a specific interpretation of the principle. So in contrast to indeterminacy, defeasibility is not a necessary feature of moral principles.

In some cases it will be a matter of dispute whether we are dealing with a case of indeterminacy or defeasibility. One might discuss, for example, whether a promise given under duress fails to fall under the principle 'Keep your promise' because it is not a promise at all or because its normative force has been defeated by the fact that it was given under duress. Another problematic case is the much-quoted example of lying when playing Diplomacy. One might view it as an example where the principle 'Do not lie' is defeated, or as a non-paradigmatic case of lying to which the principle does not apply at all. Lying during a game of Diplomacy might be thought to be a non-paradigmatic case of lying because all the players have freely and knowingly agreed to the practice of mutual deception, and the lying takes place within a clearly defined framework (e.g. players are not supposed to lie when asked what time it is). These borderline cases are interesting, but they do not undermine the importance of the distinction between indeterminacy and defeasibility. Moral principles can be highly indeterminate without being defeasible, and there can be cases where a principle is defeated even though we have no problem to see how it should be interpreted and implemented.

While we can make moral principles only less indeterminate, we might hope to turn defeasible into indefeasible principles by spelling out their exceptions. For example, one might change the principle 'Keep your promise' into 'Keep your promise unless breaking it is necessary to save a life'. However, it will quickly become clear that we will need to expand the list of exceptions. For example, we will need to account for immoral promises, such as the promise to kill an innocent person. There are likely to be many cases that we will not be able to anticipate. But even if it were theoretically possible to foresee and specify all the exceptions to our moral principles, these principles will be highly complex. It is highly doubtful whether we would be able to formulate and understand such a set of exceptionless principles, let alone learn and use them. In what follows I will, therefore, assume that most moral principles are defeasible. The defeasibility of moral principles takes different forms in theoretical and practical moral reasoning. I shall start my discussion with the latter.

Defeasibility in practical moral reasoning

The claim that moral principles are defeasible is often treated as synonymous with the claim that they have exceptions. These exceptions are then seen as posing a threat to principle-based ethics because they are taken to provide counterexamples to the universal generalizations stated by moral principles such as 'All lies are morally wrong' or 'Killing a person against her or his will is always impermissible'. Examples of lying which are morally neutral (e.g. when playing Diplomacy) or killings which we deem to be morally permissible (e.g. killing in self-defence) appear to refute these principles.[51] However, as it stands, this line of thought is flawed. First of all, it is important to note that to treat something as an exception to a given principle is not to treat it as a counter-example that refutes the principle. An exception is not a falsifying counterexample. What is usually meant by saying that there is a tension between principles and exceptions, is that principles which are stated as universal generalizations of the form 'All *F*s are *G*s' can have no exceptions, only counterexamples. If a principle says that every object or state of affairs that is *F* is also *G* and we find an object or state of affairs that is *F* and not *G*, the principle is refuted. So if a principle is exception-laden it cannot be phrased in the form of a strictly universal generalization. But when it comes to moral principles we need to say more than that.

The above line of thought rests on a theoretical conception of moral principles. It presupposes that it is the function of moral principles to make true statements about the world. When used as theoretical principles, moral principles are refuted if they fail to truly describe some sort of moral reality. Like the empirical principles in the sciences they are based on the observation of certain regularities. They are well founded if we have observed many positive instances of the principle, and no negative instances. If, like Dancy and his generalist critics, we think of moral principles as theoretical generalizations, 'particular cases [...] function as some sort of a test for moral principles'.[52] As noted before, I do not deny that moral principles fulfil important theoretical functions. They are used to assess and determine the moral status of particular actions, institutions or characters. I will say more about the exceptions to moral principles in theoretical reasoning in the next section. At this point, I want to stress that when used as practical principles, moral principles have 'world-to-word direction of fit'.[53] Instead of reflecting the world, the primary function of practical principles is to change it. They are used to change, guide or control the behaviour of agents with decision-making capacities. A look at the wider category of plans and policies is illuminating in this context. A policy such as 'Fasten your seatbelt when driving in a car' does not make a statement about the world, but is used to steer the behaviour of agents within this world. Understood as long-term commitments, moral principles do not purport to make true statements about the world, their purpose is to steer and mould it. A case of permissible lying, for example, is not an exception to the principle 'Do not lie', in the same sense that a black swan is a counterexample to the universal generalization 'All swans are white'.

However, this does not mean that practical principles are indefeasible. Michael Bratman makes this point very clear. When I intend to buckle up when driving in a car, go to the dentist every six months, or not make important decisions after a long and stressful day, I do not intend so to act *no matter what*. I am not committed to buckling up in certain emergency situations, or going to the dentist in the event of an earthquake.[54] We might try to build all these qualifications into the specification of our practical principle, but Bratman rightly points out that in most cases this task seems hopeless as long as we avoid trivial specifications like 'unless the circumstances make so acting inappropriate'.[55] Instead, what we should do is to recognize that there is an inevitable defeasibility in almost all practical principles. There can be circumstances in which we will need to block the application of a practical principle to a particular case. Blocking the use of a principle is not the same as abandoning or revising it. Bratman explains that 'the defeasibility of general policies makes it possible to block the application of the policy to the particular case without abandoning the policy'.[56] For example, in an emergency I do not give up my general policy of buckling up, but I might still block its application to my particular case and not bother with my seatbelt.[57] Understood as long-term commitments, moral principles are not refuted or abandoned if we cannot act on them in a particular situation. I do not abandon my principle of promise-keeping if I have to break a promise in order to save a life in a particular situation, I only block its application to that particular case. The same holds true for lying when playing the game Diplomacy. Strictly speaking, it is not the moral principle itself that is defeasible, but the enactment of the principle in a particular case. A principle whose enactment is blocked in a particular case is not defeated in the sense of being abandoned.

Bratman points out that a good plan is 'a plan for the world I find myself in'.[58] If I live in a country where the majority of cars have no seatbelts, it will be very difficult for me to adhere to my policy of buckling up. What does this mean for moral principles? An agent who finds herself in a world in which she constantly has to break her promises cannot live by the principle 'Do not break your promises'. However, long-term plans and personal policies are something that agents are committed to and whose fulfilment is important to them. This is especially true for moral principles. Good moral agents will, therefore, not abandon their principles easily, and will try to change the world so that they can live in accordance with them. A moral agent who lives in a society in which she constantly has to lie and break promises, for example, will try to change this society or leave it. The same is true for many non-moral principles: an agent who is committed to a policy of buckling up will try to only drive in cars which are equipped with seatbelts.

Moreover, since failing to act in accordance with a practical principle on too many occasions will at some point effectively undermine it, an agent who is committed to the principle will be careful about when to block it. The absence of blocking the enactment of a practical principle in a particular case has to be the 'default'. An agent might block her policy of buckling up when rushing someone to hospital, but not when she is late for work. Good moral agents will be especially careful about blocking moral principles. In this context Thomas Hill points out that making an exception here and there may not at first force a moral agent to rethink her position. However, after a while she may well wonder how she can continue to make what seem on each occasion justifiable exceptions without having, in effect, abandoned her principles. As Hill puts it, 'ships with too many holes sink, and principles with too many gaps no longer function as principles'.[59] Stressing the fact that moral principles should not be blocked carelessly is not enough to solve this problem. More needs to be said about the circumstances under which the enactment of a moral principle in a particular case is appropriately blocked.

There are two different kinds of cases in which the enactment of a moral principle might be blocked. The first are cases like lying when playing the game Diplomacy or not promoting a person's happiness if it is based on the sadistic pleasure the person takes in someone else's misery. The practical principles of caring about other people's happiness and not lying do not extend to these cases. They were never supposed to govern them. A non-moral example is helpful to illustrate this point. If I adopt a principle of eating at least five portions of fruit or vegetables a day, for example, I do not intend this principle to extend to cases where I have stomach flu or where I am violently seasick. In these cases I do not block the principle because of a more important policy or project. The principle was never supposed to extend to cases where eating fruit and vegetables will have a negative impact on my health. We could try to avoid this form of defeasibility by making our practical principles more specific. Instead of adopting a principle of eating five portions of fruit or vegetables a day we could adopt a principle of doing so unless it has a negative impact on our health. Instead of adopting the principle 'Do not lie' we could adopt the principle 'Do not lie, unless you are playing the game Diplomacy'. However, trying to spell out all the cases which a practical principle is not supposed to govern would render most of these principles unmanageably long. What is more, practical principles are supposed to guide us in a world that can change in ways we are unable to foresee. It is impossible to anticipate all eventualities. Moral agents are, therefore, well advised to adhere to the more general, defeasible version of the principles and block their enactment in the exceptional cases. We should not cherish – not even as an ideal – the conception of a set of indefeasible, exceptionless moral principles.

The second kind of cases in which we have to block the enactment of a moral principle to a particular case are more common, and also more serious. These are cases where we cannot avoid hurting someone's feelings by telling the truth or breaking a promise to save a life. In such cases the enactment of two or more of our moral principles are in conflict with each other, and, therefore, we have to block one or more of them. The problem here is not that the principles do not extend to the exceptional case, but that we cannot act on all of them in that particular case. Due to the particular circumstances in which the moral agent finds herself, the principles are incapable of joint instantiation. In contrast to cases like lying when playing Diplomacy, the blocked principle does not lose its normative force and leaves 'remainders' or 'residues'.[60] That is, although we cannot act on the blocked principle, it nevertheless calls for an appropriate response. For example, we might be required to apologize for breaking a promise, confess to a necessary lie afterwards, feel regret or even remorse for harming someone, etc.

A plurality of practical principles can conflict intrinsically or contingently.[61] Principles that conflict intrinsically can never be simultaneously instantiated. Attempts to adopt such a set of principles will constantly produce genuine and irresolvable conflicts. For example, we cannot live both by a principle of thinking for ourselves and a principle of always deferring to the judgement of others. But the attempt to enact a plurality of practical principles does not need to lead to conflicts. Principles that do not conflict intrinsically are consistent and can be jointly instantiated in at least some circumstances. However, such principles may nevertheless give rise to contingent conflicts: telling the truth will sometimes (but not always) hurt somebody, and saving a life can sometimes (but not always) require a lie. It does not even take a plurality of principles to generate such contingent conflicts: saving a life will sometimes cost another, and a principle of respect for life can sometimes lead to conflicts.[62] Think for example of cases where a doctor has to decide between saving the life of a mother and saving the life of her unborn child. These contingent conflicts are conflicts not between principles but between ways of living up to the principles in particular circumstances.[63] That is, they are conflicts not between the act-types prescribed by moral principles but conflicts between particular tokens of these act-types. Recall that moral principles prescribe, permit, forbid, recommend or condemn certain act-*types*. When we implement moral principles in a particular situation we have to perform act-*tokens* of these *types*, which may be incompatible with some act-tokens of other types. But these contingent conflicts do not show that a plurality of principles *must* lead to conflicts.

By adopting a set of moral principles an agent accepts certain obligations.[64] I have argued that there can be circumstances where the enactment of a moral principle in a particular case is appropriately blocked. But this does not mean that moral principles are merely rules of thumb or rough practical guides which we expect and allow people to ignore when they see fit. Practical moral principles are long-term commitments which bind agents with necessity. Since moral agents should not be required to do the impossible, it is important that the conflicts they face are the result of their particular, contingent circumstances, and not a necessary consequence of being subject to, or adopting, a plurality of moral principles. That is, it must not be the case that a set of principles of obligations could never be jointly satisfied. Fairness demands that there is no intrinsic conflict between, say, a principle of keeping one's promises and a principle of beneficence. Moral conflicts cannot be intrinsic.

However, this does not mean that there will be no serious moral conflicts. By making a particular promise to a particular person in a particular situation, a moral agent might find herself in a serious conflict between keeping this promise and helping someone in need. In many cases the conflict will be due to a prior wrongdoing or failure of the agent herself. She might have been able to avoid the conflict, for example, if she had thought more carefully about the consequences of making and keeping a particular promise. In other contexts, the circumstances that lead to a particular conflict may be beyond the agent's control. Unjust institutions and the wrongdoings of others can place moral agents in situations of serious conflict. Knowing that these conflicts are contingent is important for moral agents because it means that they can try to change the world so that their principles become jointly satisfiable. Deliberation about how to avoid violations of one's moral obligations would be futile if the value conflicts leading to these violations were always and necessarily unavoidable. It would mean that however hard moral agents try to fulfil their duties, and however much they try to change the world they are living in to avoid moral conflicts, their attempts will be doomed to failure.

Given the contingency of conflicts between moral principles, it is not only the case that moral agents *can* try to change the particular circumstances in which they find themselves and which lead to the conflict, they often have an obligation to do so. In cases of moral conflict the blocked principle leaves a remainder. The demands of the blocked principle have to be acknowledged. In some cases this might include renegotiating or ending some relationship that leads to conflict, or changing certain institutional structures or features of one's environment to prevent such conflicts from recurring. Moreover, it is important to remember that in their capacity as practical principles moral principles function as long-term commitments. Long-term commitments structure the way in which we live our lives. Consider the following example of taking on a non-moral commitment. Someone who plans to become a professional athlete, for example, will lead her life in a certain way. She will schedule her work and social life around her training, follow a particular diet, might move to another city with better training opportunities, etc. An agent who follows a certain long-term plan will try to structure her life and world in a way that allows her to accomplish the plan. Plans concerning ends embed sub-plans concerning means and preliminary steps. Forming and pursuing these sub-plans is a necessary part of carrying out our long-term plans successfully. If an agent claims to have a long-term plan but does nothing to implement it, we may eventually conclude that she has a wish rather than a plan. The same holds true for following moral principles. By adopting a set of moral principles an agent commits herself to live her life in a certain way. She will try to structure her life and world in a way that allows her to jointly satisfy all of her moral principles. Moral principles do not only require that agents seek to enact certain act-types, they also require the moral agent to think about the means and circumstances necessary for the joint fulfilment of these principles. A principle of nonmaleficence and a principle of truthfulness imply a duty actively to avoid situations in which we have to lie in order to prevent serious harm or in which we have to harm someone by telling the truth. For example, we might have an obligation to avoid involvement in dubious projects or to try working towards more just institutions. Fulfilling a moral principle is thus not only, or even primarily, a matter of performing a particular act-token in a particular situation, but of living and thinking in a certain way. Understood in this sense, the obligations that moral principles impose are indefeasible and do not conflict. They bind moral agents with necessity. Moral principles can bind with necessity because they are consistent. They can be jointly instantiated in at least some circumstances and they require moral agents to try ensuring that these circumstances obtain. Contingent conflicts can arise at the level of act-tokens when agents try to act on moral principles in a particular case. Practical moral principles are defeasible in the sense that in such cases of conflict their enactment in a particular case might be appropriately blocked. As I pointed out earlier, blocking a principle is not the same as revising or abandoning it.

Are there also cases in which we should reconsider or even abandon one of our moral principles? A look at the way in which we deal with non-moral practical principles and plans is again illuminating in this context. In an emergency situation I do not reconsider or abandon my principle of fastening the seatbelt when driving a car, I merely block its enactment in this particular case. However, faced with new information about seatbelts I might reconsider and even abandon my principle concerning their use.[65] Similarly, I might abandon my principle of eating five portions of fruits and vegetables a day if I learn that three portions would have the same beneficial effect. A good commitment is consistent with my beliefs about the world.[66] Moral principles should be consistent with our moral (and non-moral) beliefs. We take the enactment of the practical principle 'Do not lie' to be appropriately blocked in certain circumstances because we believe that not all lies are *pro tanto* wrong. There is thus a link between the defeasibility of moral principles in practical reasoning and their defeasibility as principles in theoretical reasoning. Let us now look at the defeasibility of moral principles in theoretical reasoning.

Defeasibility in theoretical moral reasoning

Moral principles take a stance with regard to the moral status of certain act-types. Used as theoretical principles they tell us, for example, that a certain act-type is morally wrong. The problem is that there can be cases where particular tokens of this act-type might seem actually morally right. So how can we judge a particular act of, say, lying to be morally right and at the same time insist on the truth of a principle according to which lying is morally wrong? In some contexts lying is morally wrong, but in others it is not. The natural answer to this problem is to say that moral principles are exception-laden. In their capacity as theoretical principles, moral principles purport to make true general statements about the world. If most of these statements are exception-laden, moral principles cannot take the form of strict generalizations. Luckily, moral principles are not the only principles which fail to provide universal generalizations. Most of the generalizations discovered in the special sciences like biology, economics or psychology are not exceptionless. Some authors claim that even the principles of fundamental physics are exception-laden.[67] This provides defenders of exception-laden moral principles with a good basis for a companions in guilt argument. If we have – and indeed make frequent use of – exception-laden generalizations in the sciences, moral principles should not be abandoned on the grounds of their exception-ladenness, either. It seems to be no more problematic to appeal to exception-laden principles in ethics than in, say, biology.[68] However, what exactly does it mean to say that the principles employed in theoretical moral reasoning are exception-laden? In order to answer this question it is helpful to have a closer look at how exceptions are dealt with in the sciences.

In the sciences exception-laden principles are usually introduced by drawing a distinction between strict generalizations that hold for all cases and *ceteris paribus* generalizations that hold other things being equal. While strict generalizations are contradicted by a single counterinstance, *ceteris paribus* generalizations allow for exceptions. Instead of 'All F's are G's' they take the form 'All F's are G's, *all else being equal*'. However, despite their widespread use, the status of *ceteris paribus* principles in the sciences is controversial. It proves difficult to spell out exactly what it means to say that all F's are G's, *all else being equal*. To say that all F's are G's, *except those that are not,* is unhelpful. For this reason, many authors argue that *ceteris paribus* clauses render law-like statements vacuous unless such clauses can be explicitly reformulated as antecedents of strict universalizations that face no counterinstances.[69] According to this view, scientific laws can be incomplete, but not exception-laden. It has to be at least in principle possible to complete the antecedents of these laws, or they will not qualify as laws. To refute these critics, defenders of the possibility of exception-laden scientific laws have to provide a non-vacuous account of the *ceteris paribus* clause.

Peter Lipton has offered a promising account of *ceteris paribus* laws in the sciences. Lipton argues that they should be conceived of as incomplete descriptions, i.e. universal generalizations with incomplete antecedents.[70] He points out that even if *ceteris paribus* laws could, in principle, be converted into exceptionless generalizations by listing all the possible forms of interference, this would not convert them into strict laws. The generalizations would be only contingently true. They would be only contingently true because the absence of disturbing factors depends heavily on accidental conditions.[71] This fits well with the status of supervenience-functions in the particularist/generalist debate. In the first chapter I pointed out that there is a wide consensus among particularists and generalists that supervenience-functions do not qualify as moral principles because they contain all sorts of irrelevancies and contingencies. There is a further reason for not conceiving of moral principles as incomplete, but theoretically completable, universal generalizations. In Chapters One and Two, I showed that if we want to take the context-sensitivity of the moral relevance and polarity of act-descriptions seriously, we should not deny that this context-sensitivity at least sometimes transcends codifiability. It is overly optimistic to assume that we could codify all the conditions under which an act-type is morally relevant – and in which way it is relevant – in finite and manageable terms. Since it is impossible to spell out their various exceptions, theoretical moral principles are hedged by a *ceteris paribus* clause. Moral principles tell us, for instance, that *other things being equal* we should not lie or cause harm. As in the case of *ceteris paribus* laws in the sciences, we should not understand moral *ceteris paribus* principles as incomplete, but theoretically completable, versions of universal generalizations. However, how exactly should we understand the *ceteris paribus* qualifier?

Lipton understands *ceteris paribus* laws in dispositional terms. He holds that they refer to stable dispositions such as 'glass is breakable'. To say that glass breaks when dropped, *ceteris paribus*, means that glass is fragile and that this feature is not readily lost.[72] Instead of seeing *ceteris paribus* laws as descriptions of what happens when there are no interfering forces, Lipton suggests that we see *ceteris paribus* laws as descriptions of one force that is present even in situations where many other forces are in play, and even if there is no situation where the first force acts alone. Furthermore, Lipton emphasizes that the fact that a disposition manifests itself in one situation does not in general provide evidence that it will manifest itself in another.[73] He also points out that the stability of dispositions is a matter of degree and that some dispositions are more stable than others.[74]

On the face of it, Lipton's account seems to offer a good basis for explaining the exception-ladenness of moral principles in theoretical reasoning. To begin with, the fact that a disposition which manifests itself in one situation does not in general provide evidence that it will manifest itself in another, appears to fit well with the need for context-sensitivity in moral reasoning. In Chapter One, I pointed out that whether, and in what ways, an act-description is morally relevant depends on the particular context in which the action occurs or, put more metaphorically, on the whole story that we want to tell about the situation. Lipton's remark that some dispositions are more stable than others also accords well with what we seem to observe in the moral realm. Some moral principles are less defeasible than others. For example, there seem to be fewer cases of permissible killings of human beings than of permissible lying. There thus appear to be helpful parallels between Lipton's account of *ceteris paribus* laws and some of the things we want to say about moral principles. However, Lipton's account cannot accommodate the whole spectrum of the defeasibility of theoretical moral principles. According to Lipton, *ceteris paribus* laws 'describe dispositions or forces that are stably present whether or not all things are equal'.[75] His account of *ceteris paribus* laws thus presupposes that the disposition or force specified by a given law is present even if other things are not equal.[76] Translated into the moral realm, this would mean that while the force of a moral principle can be outweighed by another moral principle, and as a result fail to manifest itself in a particular situation, moral principles cannot lose their force entirely. That is, we would need to understand the principle 'Breaking a promise is wrong, *ceteris paribus*' as saying that breaking a promise is always a moral minus. There will be situations in which breaking a promise is the right thing to do *all things considered*, e.g. when breaking the promise is necessary to save a life. But if we follow Lipton's account, even in such cases breaking a promise remains a moral minus. Lipton's account allows for defeasibility at the *overall* or *all things considered* level, but not for defeasibility at the *contributory* level. It can accommodate the kind of defeasibility we find in Ross' theory of *prima facie* duties, but it fails to account for the cases that particularists like Dancy tend to bring forward. In the scenarios particularists usually sketch, a given action is supposed to count as a moral minus or as morally neutral even though our principle tells us that actions of this type generally have a positive moral valence, and vice versa. The principle 'Promoting pleasure is morally valuable', for example, might be thought to be defeasible in this sense. Promoting pleasure is a moral minus if the pleasure is sadistic. In order to clarify the distinction between the two forms of defeasibility, I will use the terminology of act-descriptions which I introduced in Chapter One.

The task of theoretical moral reasoning is to determine the moral status of particular actions, institutions or agents. Assume that we try to determine the moral status of a particular action by subsuming it under a given principle. An action x is subsumed by a generalization G in virtue of having a description under which it corresponds to the act-type specified by G. As I pointed out in Chapter One, it is widely accepted that an action can be described in numerous different ways. Since an action can have multiple descriptions it may be subsumed under several moral generalizations. So x may be subsumed by a distinct generalization G as well, in virtue of having a description under which it corresponds to the act-type specified by G. For example, an action may be the breaking of a promise as well as the saving of a life. For this reason, we cannot determine the moral status of a particular action by simply subsuming it under a given principle. The fact that a particular action falls under a given principle, because it can be described so as to correspond to the act-type specified in the principle, does not determine the moral status of that particular act-token. Moral principles tell us that certain act-descriptions are morally relevant and relevant in a certain way, other things being equal. The principle 'Breaking a promise is morally wrong', for example, tells us that, other things being equal, the fact that an action can be correctly described as breaking a promise is morally relevant, and relevant in a negative sense. There are two different kinds of ways in which things can fail to be equal. In the case of defeasibility at the overall level, the act-description that the principle picks out is relevant, and relevant in the way the principle states, but the principle does not fix the overall moral status of the action. This happens if the action also falls under another, more relevant, act-description. The action may be morally wrong in virtue of being the breaking of a promise, but morally right in virtue of being the saving of a life. The latter act-description is more relevant, and thus determines the overall status of the action. However, the fact that the action is also the breaking of a promise should nevertheless figure in our deliberation about the moral status of the action. The action would have been morally better if the promise had been kept. In the case of defeasibility at the contributory level, the act-description that the principle picks out is irrelevant (although applicable) to the moral status of the particular action or relevant in the opposite way.

While it is widely accepted that moral principles are defeasible when it comes to determining the overall moral status of an action, the possibility of defeasibility at the contributory level is more controversial. Whether or not one thinks that moral principles are defeasible at the contributory level will depend on whether one finds plausible the examples which particularists bring forward. This in turn will depend on one's first-order theory about the content of moral principles. The fact that promoting pleasure counts as a moral minus when it is the sadist's pleasure in his victim's suffering, for example, will be relevant only if one believes that there is a principle to the effect that pleasure is morally valuable. In the absence of a belief in the truth of the principle, one will obviously remain unconvinced by the example. If anything, the example will confirm one's belief in the falsehood of the principle and the first-order ethics that contains it. The example does nothing to show that the principles of one's favoured first-order ethics are defeasible in the same way. This is especially so because the range of examples that particularists offer for defeasibility at the contributory level is highly restricted. As far as I am aware, the only example given for a case where something that is designated as a moral plus by a principle turns out to be a moral minus is the case of sadistic pleasure which I have referred to many times in this book. An example offered for the opposite case is the principle 'Pain is bad'. One might argue that this principle is defeated at the contributory level when the pain is constitutive of athletic accomplishment. It makes the accomplishment difficult and thereby more valuable. Examples brought forward for cases where an act-description that the principle picks out as morally relevant fails to be relevant include lying while playing Diplomacy and returning a book to someone who has stolen it from the library.[77] Generalists could deal with these examples, and hence with the problem of defeasibility at the contributory level, by simply denying the truth of the moral principles in question. This is not an unreasonable thing to do. The fact that up to now particularists have referred to the same restricted range of examples over and over again suggests that they will quickly run out of counterexamples when challenged. Moreover, there are many first-order ethics which do not contain principles about the goodness of promoting pleasure, the badness of pain, the wrongness of lying as such and the rightness of returning what has been borrowed. However, since I aim to be as neutral as possible with regard to different first-order moral theories, I want to leave open the possibility of defeasibility at the contributory level. As noted, Lipton's account is not helpful in this context because it assumes that *ceteris paribus* laws describe dispositions or forces which are present even when things are not equal.

So how should we understand the *ceteris paribus* qualifier attached to theoretical moral principles? A look at another account of *ceteris paribus* laws in the sciences is helpful in this context. Paul Pietroski and Georges Rey argue that *ceteris paribus* clauses 'are "cheques" written on the banks of independent theories, their substance and warrant deriving from the substance and warrant of those theories, which determine whether the cheque can be cashed'.[78] These cheques represent a 'promise' to the effect that all abnormal instances can be explained by citing factors independent of that law. If the promise cannot be kept, the cheque was no good to begin with. That is, the apparent counterexample is a genuine one, and the putative law is false. According to Pietroski and Rey, *ceteris paribus* laws 'carry a plethora of explanatory commitments'.[79] I contend that the same is true with regard to the principles employed in theoretical moral reasoning. An action which falls under the act-description 'breaking a promise' but which we nevertheless judge to be morally permissible needs to be explained. The principle 'Breaking promises is wrong, *ceteris paribus*' demands an explanation of why breaking the promise is morally permissible in the particular situation at hand. That is, we need to be able to explain why other things are not equal in that particular case in independent terms. In their capacity as theoretical principles, moral principles entail what Barbara Herman calls a 'deliberative commitment'.[80] If, in virtue of having a certain description, a particular action falls under a given principle, the moral agent is committed to take the principle into account when deliberating about the moral status of the action. In cases where the principle fails to determine the moral status of the action, the agent needs to be able to explain why. This explanation will at least implicitly refer to other moral principles and in that sense be independent of the defeated principle. For example, the fact that breaking the promise was the right thing to do overall might be explained by pointing out that it was necessary to save a life.

The task of discovering whether one principle is more important to the assessment of the moral status of an action than another is aided by the fact that some moral principles are less defeasible than others. Moral principles share this feature with other *ceteris paribus* principles. Earlier, I pointed out that according to Lipton some dispositions are more stable than others. The fact that different *ceteris paribus* principles have different degrees of stability opens up the possibility of a default theory that establishes certain default priority relations which hold between different *ceteris paribus* or default principles.[81] For instance, the principle of nonmaleficence could be said to have a default priority over the principle of beneficence. This priority relation holds only by default because there may be cases where the expected benefits outweigh the harm and where the principle of beneficence might thus have priority. It is, therefore, not possible to establish a strict ranking of moral principles. However, default priority relations nevertheless provide moral agents with a useful framework for assessing the moral status of particular actions, institutions or characters. This is not to deny that deciding whether, and if so why, a moral principle is defeated in a particular case can be a difficult and controversial task. I will say more about how defeasible moral principles figure in theoretical reasoning in the next section. My aim in this section was to show that the *ceteris paribus* qualifier attached to moral principles in their theoretical capacity is not vacuous. The *ceteris paribus* qualifier carries with it an explanatory commitment.

I want to stress a final point with regard to the defeasibility of both theoretical and practical moral principles. Allowing moral principles to be defeasible raises the suspicion that they are just rules of thumb that can be ignored and abandoned when we see fit. It is, therefore, important to be clear about the differences between rules of thumb and the form of moral principles I defended earlier. According to my account, moral principles are defeasible, but they are far from being mere rules of thumb. Rules of thumb are external, intellectual tools. They are useful generalizations of our past moral experience. In this context G. E. Moore, for instance, conceives of moral principles as probabilistic generalizations that provide us with knowledge about which kinds of actions will, under certain given circumstances, generally produce better effects than others.[82] Act-utilitarians in particular recommend rules of thumb as a convenient and reliable substitute for doing utility calculations anew in routine situations. Rules of thumb are heuristics that are supposed to point us towards the action with the optimal outcome.[83] They are mere time- and thought-saving devices.[84] Rules of thumb function as second-best strategies. Advocates of rules of thumb hold that it is only because of our lack of time, our limited cognitive abilities and our liability to biases and special pleading that we need to rely on these rules. Martha Nussbaum summarizes this idea nicely:

> When there is no time to formulate a full concrete decision, scrutinizing all the features of the case at hand, it is better to follow a good summary rule than to make a hasty and inadequate concrete choice. Furthermore, rules give constancy and stability in situations in which bias and passion might distort judgment. Rules are necessary because we are not always good judges; if we really were operating ethically as well as we should, we would not have the same need for them.[85]

In contrast to such rules of thumb, moral principles are not mere intellectual tools that we could dispense with if we were better moral judges. I have argued that we should think of moral principles as internalized long-term commitments. In the case of practical moral reasoning, these commitments structure the way in which we live our lives. A good moral agent will try to structure her life and world in a way that allows her to jointly satisfy all of her principles. In cases where she is unable to act on all of her principles, and as a result has to block one or more of them, the blocked principles leave a remainder. Rules of thumb leave no remainders. They are tools that can, and maybe should, be ignored if we can do without them. Furthermore, it is plausible to assume that there will be some principles that a good moral judge will treat as sacrosanct, i.e. indefeasible. Earlier I mentioned the principle 'Do not torture' as a possible candidate for an indefeasible moral principle. Used as theoretical principles, moral principles carry with them a deliberative commitment. If a particular action falls under a given principle, we are committed to take the principle into account when deliberating about the moral status of the action, and if the principle fails to determine the moral status of the action, we need to be able to explain why. With regard to rules of thumb, things are the other way around: we need to explain why we should rely on a rule of thumb when deliberating about the moral status of a particular action. Since rules of thumb are second-best strategies, an agent using these strategies has to be able to explain why she does not use the best strategy. Moral principles as I defended them in this chapter are not rules of thumb.

The purpose of this and the previous section was to explain how the generality of moral principles is compatible with the need for context-sensitivity. I argued that moral principles can be context-sensitive in virtue of their indeterminacy and their defeasibility. Having explored and defined these two central features of the nature of moral principles, I now need to say more about their roles in moral thought and action. However, one thing should be clear already: indeterminate and defeasible principles do not apply themselves. Whatever roles principles play in morality, they will need to play this role in conjunction with a capacity of judgement. This leads to the second part of the particularist challenge: why do moral principles need to be supplemented, but are not supplanted by judgement? Why do we need moral principles? The next two sections set out to answer this question by offering an account of the roles of moral principles with regard to the activity and capacity of moral judgement.

Moral principles and the activity of moral judgement

The term moral judgement can refer to three distinguishable things. First, it can refer to the *capacity* to judge whether a given object of moral assessment (an action, person, institution or state of affairs) is of a certain moral kind (right or wrong, virtuous or vicious, just or unjust, etc.) and how to act in the light of this insight. This capacity of moral judgement is sometimes referred to as moral discernment, moral sensitivity or moral wisdom. Second, the term moral judgement can describe the exercise of the capacity of judgement, that is, the *activity* of judging an action, person, institution or state of affairs. The activity of moral judgement is sometimes described as moral deliberation or moral reasoning.[86] Third, 'moral judgement' can designate the *product* of the activity of moral judgement. Understood in this sense moral judgements might alternatively be called moral verdicts. Thus, the term 'judgement' can refer to the ability to judge, the activity of judging and the product of this activity.

Corresponding to these three meanings of moral judgement, there are three main categories of questions. The first category of questions concerns the capacity of moral judgement and asks how we should conceive of this capacity and its development. Jean Piaget and Lawrence Kohlberg's work on the moral development of children falls within this category. More recently, research in cognitive neuroscience has explored 'where' moral judgement takes place; that is, which brain areas are involved when we make moral judgements.[87] A related, but much older, question is in what kind of psychological state we are when we make moral judgements. While cognitivists argue that the state of moral judgement is best characterized as a state of belief, non-cognitivists hold that moral judgements express non-cognitive attitudes similar to emotions, desires, approval or disapproval. Questions about the state of moral judgement are closely linked to questions about the moral motivation of an agent rendering a judgement. These are important and interesting questions, but they are not the concern of this book. I am concerned with moral judgement as a capacity in two respects. First, in the previous section it became clear that moral principles of the form I defend need to be supplemented by moral judgement. Second, in 'Moral principles and the capacity of moral judgement' (pp. 188–209), I will argue that the capacity of moral judgement itself is essentially principle-based. My claim is that the person of good moral judgement is best understood as a person of principle.

The second group of questions concerns the activity of moral judgement. How do we judge particular actions, institutions and characters? And what happens once we believe that the action, institution or agent with which we deal is of a certain kind? How do we judge what to do in a particular situation and how do we decide how to do it? In this section I will distinguish and describe the different roles which moral principles play in these activities.

The third category of questions concerns moral judgement understood as the product of the activity of moral judgement and its justificatory status. The activity of moral judgement should result in moral verdicts and actions that are justified. Under what conditions is an agent justified in making a moral judgement? A judgement that is justified cannot be arbitrary. It is, therefore, natural to think that in order for a moral judgement to be justified, it has to be in accordance with a moral rule or principle. However, this line of argument leads to a number of problems and needs refinement. Particularists will object that a moral judgement is justified if it is reached through an acceptable process and that this process need not, or should not, be principle-based. I will discuss the justificatory role of moral principles in connection with the activity of judgement.

So what is the role of principles in the activity of moral judgement? One might think that this is a question for the psychological laboratory, rather than the philosophical armchair. There is a fast-growing number of empirical moral psychologists, and one might think that they are better suited than traditional moral philosophers to tackle questions about moral judgement and the roles of moral principles.[88] However, the projects pursued in recent empirical moral psychology differ significantly from the project pursued in this book and in debates about moral particularism more generally. In contrast to the empirical work done by moral psychologists, the model of moral reasoning and moral judgement offered in this and the next section is essentially normative. I argue that moral reasoning and moral judgement *ought* to be principle-based. But more needs to be said here. It would be futile to make normative claims about how we should reason and act as moral agents if it were empirically impossible for human beings to reason and act in that way. The principle-based model of moral reasoning and judgement I propose therefore has to be at least empirically possible. It has to meet what might be called the requirement of 'minimal psychological realism': the development, decision processing, behaviour and character presupposed by the model have to be possible for creatures like us.[89] I claim that we can reason and act in the principle-based ways I describe. However, it is also plausible to assume that more than one model of moral reasoning and judgement is empirically possible and that the requirement of minimal psychological realism by itself is hence not sufficient to decide between alternative models.[90] The question of which model of moral judgement to promote therefore cannot be settled in the psychological laboratory.

Most particularists offer a similar mix of conceptual, normative and descriptive claims. Dancy's thesis that moral thought and judgement does not depend on a suitable supply of moral principles, for example, is not an empirical thesis. Dancy explicitly acknowledges that '[p]eople do "have" principles, and [that] they do [...] appeal to them in making their own decisions and in judging the actions of others'.[91] His claim is that we can and should do without moral principles. In what follows I will argue for the opposite claim, namely that moral thought and judgement can and should be principle-based. Empirical findings will be relevant only insofar as it should be at least empirically possible for us as human beings to reason and act in accordance with the proposed principle-based model of moral reasoning and judgement.

Before presenting my own account of principle-based moral reasoning, I will discuss two influential alternative models: the subsumptive model and the option-choice model of moral reasoning.

The subsumptive model

According to the subsumptive model, moral reasoning proceeds by way of subsuming particular cases calling for moral evaluation under general moral principles. On this model we approach a new case with a set of principles, and then decide the case by deciding which of those principles the case falls under. A piece of reasoning counts as sound or justified if it subsumes the case under the correct principle. Moral justification would thus consist in the subsumption of particular instances under general rules or principles. According to this view, what makes it right to apply a moral concept to a given object of moral assessment is a rule for doing so. A person will be epistemically warranted in applying a certain moral concept if this application is rule-governed. It does not take long to see that this model of moral reasoning is flawed. As Kant pointed out, 'judgement cannot always be given yet another rule by which to direct its subsumption (for this would go on to infinity)'.[92] Since the decision of whether to apply or follow a certain principle or rule cannot, on pain of regress, always be guided by yet another 'meta-rule', there has to be a form of moral reasoning that goes beyond the application of rules. If this form of reasoning is ever justified, it cannot be on grounds of following a rule or principle.

A further deficiency of the subsumptive model is that it fails to account for *practical* reasoning. The subsumptive model fits only *theoretical* reasoning, i.e. reasoning *that* a certain action, institution or agent is of a certain kind or falls under a certain description. Practical reasoning is reasoning about what to do once we believe that the action, institution or agent with which we deal is of a certain kind. In the case of practical reasoning it does not make sense to speak of the task of judgement as the subsumption of a particular action under a general principle, because the agent has yet to decide how to act.[93]

But even if we focus solely on theoretical moral reasoning the subsumptive model is problematic. It is ill suited to account for the defeasibility of moral principles. In the previous section, I argued that when used as theoretical principles we can think of moral principles as being hedged by a *ceteris paribus* clause. If moral principles are *ceteris paribus* principles, then the fact that a given action can be subsumed under a certain principle does not determine the moral status of the action. We might be dealing with a case where other things are not equal, and where the principle is, therefore, defeated at the overall or even the contributory level.

The option-choice model

According to another popular model, moral reasoning is a process of choosing between a set of possible options, courses of action, reasons or principles. In order to determine the overall moral status of an action we have to balance the weights of the relevant considerations against each other. In the second chapter I discussed this option-choice model as one way in which Dancy and his generalist critics could try to remodel reasoning about what to do as a form of theoretical reasoning and thereby escape the charge of ignoring a central aspect of moral reasoning. We saw that the option-choice model construes options as act-types whose normative status can be determined in the same manner in which we determine whether something is, or is not, the case. According to the option-choice model, reasoning about what to do is thus just another form of theoretical reasoning. I argued that despite this apparent advantage, Dancy and his generalist critics are well advised not to adopt the option-choice model. Since the option-choice model is, at least implicitly, presupposed by a number of metaethical and first-order moral theories, it is worth looking at it in more detail. It is taken for granted by consequentialists, and phrased in terms of choices between different 'reasons for action' the model is also employed by many contemporary metaethicists. In what follows, I will show that despite its initial appeal, the option-choice model raises epistemological and ethical problems which give us good reasons to look for an alternative model of practical reasoning.

According to the option-choice model, reasoning about what to do is a matter of picking and choosing from an already specified range of options. As I pointed out in the second chapter, one problem with this view is that in most situations we are not able to compile a finite list of all the options open to us, because there will simply be too many such options and our time and mental capacities are limited. At this point the problems of defenders of the option-choice model mirror those of simple act-consequentialists – with the notable exception that act-consequentialism is hardly ever proposed as a decision-procedure. The charge of epistemological over-demandingness is a standard objection against consequentialism. It is widely accepted, even among consequentialists themselves, that act-consequentialism is unworkable as a decision-procedure. Bentham, for instance, remarked that act-utilitarianism cannot, and should not, 'be strictly pursued previously to every moral judgement'.[94] It is simply impossible for us to predict and compare the utility of all the options open to us in any given moment. Consequentialists have suggested various ways of dealing with this problem. One possibility is to argue that agents are not required to select the best option, but only an option that is 'good enough'. That is, defenders of the option-choice model could switch from a maximizing to a satisficing approach. We have already encountered this approach as a possible answer to the problem of value incomparability in 'Indeterminacy' (pp. 118–38). The satisficing model offers a solution for the problem of making a choice in cases where an enormous number of alternatives are to be compared. Instead of trying to achieve the best outcome, the agent is asked to settle on the first satisfactory alternative she comes across. I pointed out that while satisficing might work well for many non-moral decisions, its use is highly controversial in the moral realm. When we are concerned with avoiding harm, establishing justice or helping those in need, settling on the first satisfactory alternative is often not good enough.

Satisficing is, of course, only one of the answers consequentialists have given in response to the epistemological challenge the option-choice model raises. Another way of restricting the option-range an agent is supposed to take into account in practical deliberation is to focus on the likely consequences of an action or the consequences an agent can reasonably be expected to foresee.[95] What these suggestions have in common is a failure to take seriously the fact that decisions about what options should be on the list can itself require serious deliberation. This is not to deny that there can be situations where the options an agent faces are clear and limited. In the same way in which it is possible to construct cases in which act-consequentialism is a feasible decision-procedure, there are cases in which the option-choice model can be made to work. However, it is an illusion to assume that reasoning about what to do is always, or even predominantly, a matter of picking the right option from a given finite list.

At the end of the second part of this book I pointed out that depicting practical reasoning as a matter of picking and choosing from an already specified range of options is not only epistemologically but also ethically dubious. It is morally misleading because it suggests that we need not worry about which options are options worth considering. Like the charge of epistemological over-demandingness, the charge of moral defectiveness is common in discussions of consequentialism. Take the well-known 'organ harvest' scenario, where a surgeon could kill an innocent, healthy individual, who happens to visit someone in hospital, to harvest her organs and transplant them into five patients, thereby saving five lives.[96] Most people's response to this scenario is that harvesting the organs of innocent visitors (or other patients) is not an option and should not enter into the surgeon's (or anyone's) deliberation. This example illustrates that it is neither possible, nor desirable, to avoid going normative in fixing the range of options to be taken into consideration in practical deliberation.

It is not only consequentialists who are confronted with these problems. The problems of epistemological over-demandingness and moral defectiveness are rooted in the general option-choice model employed by consequentialists. Many theories that avail themselves of the seemingly innocuous terminology of 'reasons for action' presuppose the same model, and accordingly have to deal with the same problems. It is now common for philosophers of action and metaethicists to speak of practical deliberation as a matter of weighing different reasons for action, where reasons for action are understood as considerations that count in favour or against performing a particular action.[97] According to this picture, there is a variety of courses of actions in any given situation that we might choose to perform in that situation. Each of these options will normally have some features that give rise to reasons in favour of adopting it and some features that give rise to reasons speaking against the option. In addition, each of these reasons has a metaphorical weight or strength attached to it, corresponding to how heavily it counts in favour of or against adopting a particular option. Practical reasoning is then depicted as a process of weighing reasons. However, before we can weigh our reasons for and against a particular option we need to specify these reasons. The problem is that in most cases there will be a vast array of reasons for or against performing a particular action. Moreover, there will be various reasons to perform or refrain from numerous alternative courses of action. The number of possible reasons will depend on one's particular theory of reasons. Moral particularists, for instance, hold that anything whatever might provide a reason if the circumstances are suitable.[98] As Margaret Little remarks:

[A]ny feature may assume moral significance, from shoelace colour to the day of the week: after all, against a rich enough story, there are cases in which the change from Tuesday to Wednesday makes all the difference.[99]

Given time constraints and our limited mental capacities, it is difficult to see how we could ever successfully accomplish the task of practical reasoning in the light of such an incomprehensibly large number of possible reasons for action.[100] We can call this the 'too many reasons' problem.[101] There are broadly three strategies for dealing with this problem.

The first strategy is to concede that the number of possible reasons might be incomprehensibly large, but argue that many of these reasons will usually be irrelevant or of negligible weight and, therefore, need not be taken into account.[102] However, rather than solving the 'too many reasons' problem, this strategy merely shifts it to a higher level of practical reasoning. The agent now has to make normative judgements about the relevance of various possible reasons for action and in doing so she will have to take account of an incomprehensibly large number of reasons. One might argue that knowing which reasons are relevant is simply a matter of intuition or practical wisdom: we do not need to identify and deliberate about all the possible reasons for action in order to know which are the relevant ones. Yet, even if one finds this answer epistemologically convincing, it is, as the option-choice model more generally, morally misleading insofar as it suggests that we do not need to worry about questions of normative relevance in practical deliberation. As I pointed out earlier, discerning which options or reasons are relevant is an essential, and often difficult, task in practical deliberation.

The second strategy for dealing with the 'too many reasons' problem is to simply insist that the number of considerations that can function as reasons is limited.[103] However, while this might move practical reasoning according to the option-choice model within the realm of the humanly possible, it does not tell us how we reason about what our reasons are. Agents deliberate about their reasons for action. They think about what reasons they have to perform a particular action, and whether their reasons are good or bad reasons. The option-choice model does not capture this central evaluative element of practical deliberation.

The third strategy for reducing the amount of possible reasons for action to a manageable number is to adopt a broadly Humean theory of reasons. According to the Humean theory of reasons, reasons for actions are closely linked to an agent's desires. An agent cannot have a reason to perform an action if that action does not serve some of her desires. That is, there has to be a 'promotion relation' between an agent's reasons for action and her desires.[104] Since an agent's desires are arguably finite in number, and since it is reasonable to assume that most agents have a good grasp of what they desire, one might think that this approach avoids the epistemological problems of the option-choice model. However, whether a limited number of desires implies a limited number of reasons depends on how strong one takes the promotion relation between reasons and desires to be. On the strongest reading of the promotion relation, an agent has a reason to perform a particular action if, and only if, the action is a necessary means to the fulfilment of some of her desires. While this would reduce the number of reasons an agent has to take into account in practical deliberation, it seems unreasonably strong. There seem to be many cases where we think that an agent has a normative reason to perform a particular action because it is likely to contribute to the attainment of some end she desires, even though the action is neither necessary nor sufficient to the attainment of that end. Someone who wants to lose body weight, for example, has a reason not to order cake for dessert even though not ordering the cake is neither necessary nor sufficient for attaining this aim. According to the weak reading of the promotion relation, an agent has a reason to perform a particular action if, and only if, the action increases the likelihood of the fulfilment of one of the agent's desires.[105] On the face of it this seems more plausible than the strong reading of the promotion relation. Yet, understood as implying only a weak promotion relation, the Humean theory of reasons does nothing to solve the 'too many reasons' problem. If anything, it makes matters worse. In this context Mark Schroeder, a defender of the Humean theory of reasons and the weak promotion relation, concedes that the list of possible reasons for action is virtually endless. According to Schroeder, you have a reason to eat your car to get your daily allowance of iron, for example, provided that you have a desire to get at least the recommended allowance of iron.[106]

One might think that although a shift to the Humean theory of reasons does not help to decrease the number of possible reasons for action, it significantly decreases the epistemic costs associated with a large number of reasons. Reasons to eat one's car will not, and need not, figure in agents' practical deliberation. Instead, rational agents will naturally focus on reasons for actions that promise to best satisfy their strongest desires. The main problem with this reply is that it will generate normative reasons of the wrong kind. For example, an agent with a strong desire to torture other human beings will have a strong normative reason to do so. This seems wrong. Similarly, it seems plausible to argue that an agent has strong normative reasons to refrain from torture, to help others, or to eat healthy even if she lacks the corresponding desires. This is a familiar objection against the Humean theory of reasons and its defenders have offered different replies. One way to reply is to switch from an agent's actual desires to her informed or ideal desires and argue that this will generate the right kind of reasons.[107] Another reply is to deny that the weight or strength of an agent's reasons for action has to correspond to the strength of her desires.

If the weight of a reason in deliberation is not proportional to the strength of the desire, the Humean can argue that an agent's reason to, say, torture others is of negligible weight and hence ought not to figure in her deliberation.[108] I do not want to take a stance on the plausibility of either of these replies. The crucial point is that both require a level of normative deliberation that cannot be captured by the option-choice model itself. The option-choice model does not tell us how the agent accomplishes the task of practical deliberation about which desires to develop, modify or reject, or how much normative weight to place on her desires. Consequently, it is at best incomplete.

So far I have been concerned exclusively with the epistemological and moral problems of specifying the range of options the option-choice model tells us to assess and decide from. But even if we bracket these problems and take the option-range to be fixed, it is hard to see how the model could provide a cogent model of practical reasoning. It proves extremely difficult to spell out the idea of weighing options, or so I shall argue next.

According to the option-choice model, practical deliberation is a process of choosing between a set of options. This is usually described as a process of weighing one's options or reasons for action. In order to determine what one ought to do *all things considered* the agent has to balance the weights of her various options against each other. However, agents are not kitchen scales and any weight that their options, reasons or principles might have can only be metaphorical. The weighing metaphor needs to be spelled out. Consider, for example, David Brink's weighing conception of moral reasoning:

> To determine all-things-considered obligations we must do *moral factor addition*. It is not essential to the factor addition model that we always be able to assign precise numerical values to the various moral forces present in a situation. What is important is that the moral status of an act *sans phrase* results from adding the moral forces, positive and negative, contributed by the various morally relevant factors; the act with the highest moral total is all-things-considered obligatory.[109]

Brink's weighing conception assumes that, given the values of the individual options, the function which determines the overall moral status of a particular act is an additive one. That is, the status of the act is determined by adding up the separate positive and negative effects of the various options. However, in most cases we cannot, and do not, simply add up the value of individual options. It is plausible to assume that the interplay of different options is too complicated to be adequately captured in additive terms. In this context Shelly Kagan remarks that the overall moral status of an action might not be the result of adding, but rather of multiplying some of the moral factors, and adding the rest.[110] Similarly, John Broome acknowledges that the function governing the combination of moral factors 'may be a complicated function'.[111] But both Kagan and Broome nevertheless assume that the combinations of moral factors can be captured in the form of *a* function. In the first chapter we saw that particularists like Dancy deny that there is any finitely specifiable combinatorial function: additive, multiplicative or otherwise. I am inclined to agree with particularists on this point: the normative landscape seems to be too complex to be captured in a finite weighing function that limited beings like us would be able to formulate and understand.

What is more, the possibility of such a function presupposes the commensurability and comparability of values. In order for there to be a combinatorial function, the value of the various options, reasons or principles need to be comparable and measurable on a single scale of units of value. In cases where the items to be weighed are incommensurable or incomparable the model is useless. One might hope to at least evade the problem of incommensurability by conceiving of the weighing process as comparative or ordinal rather than cardinal. We can compare and rank different options, reasons or principles without assigning them anything like an exact weight. When we weigh our reasons for and against an option in a particular situation we do not normally seem to assign exact weights to these reasons, nor do we need a calculus to compare our different options. However, in order to provide a model of moral reasoning it is not enough to say that reasons lend some kind of weight to conclusions and that these weights are assembled somehow. The weighing metaphor itself does little to illuminate the process of moral reasoning. It does not tell the agent how to compare and balance her various options in moral deliberation. The weighing model is thus in serious danger of being either overly epistemologically demanding or uninformative.

These epistemological problems have, of course, not gone unnoticed by defenders of the weighing conception and there might be solutions to at least some of them. The option-choice model is nearly always embedded within broader theoretical frameworks that make various additional metaphysical, episte-mological and normative claims. It is reasonable to assume that these additional theoretical claims offer at least some answers to the epistemological problems raised above. However, the very fact that the option-choice model is in need of such external support provides good reasons to look for an alternative model of moral reasoning. This is especially so because conceiving of moral reasoning as a process of weighing options, reasons or principles is not only epistemologically but also morally problematic. It suggests that all moral reasoning is a matter of deciding between conflicting bearers of value. Instead of encouraging agents to act in a way that does justice to all of their different values and requirements, it urges them to decide between them. Moral reasoning is portrayed as a process of bargaining and compromise. Agents who are accustomed to thinking in terms of weighing are likely to give up prematurely. Since for them moral reasoning is a constant process of picking and choosing, they will see conflicts between options even in cases where the options are actually compatible. It might lead agents to view moral conflicts as irresolvable even when they are not. On the weighing model agents will be likely to reason about which of their moral duties are weightier and which ones are less so, and can therefore be neglected, instead of focusing their attention on figuring out how to jointly satisfy their duties. They will reason about how to weigh the option of telling a lie against the option of being cruel, for example, instead of thinking about how to convey the truth in the kindest way possible. On a more fundamental level, the weighing metaphor suggests that all moral requirements can be outweighed and are thus never absolute. It encourages agents to look upon moral requirements as something less than strict requirements.

Given that neither the subsumptive nor the weighing model provides a satisfactory model of moral reasoning, how are we to conceive of moral reasoning?

Moral reasoning as default reasoning

The term 'reasoning' describes ways of moving from one thought to another thought or action. Theoretical reasoning moves from thought to thought, while the aim of practical reasoning is action. Reasoning about what to do in a particular situation needs to be preceded by the appreciation that a particular action, institution or agent is of a certain kind or falls under a certain description. We need to recognize that something is, say, unjust before we can start to think about how to deal with this injustice. Theoretical moral reasoning is in this sense prior to practical moral reasoning. However, the account of reasoning with defeasible moral principles that I will sketch below applies to theoretical as well as practical reasoning, and I will use examples from both forms of reasoning. I will say more about the implementation of moral principles, and hence the specific structures of practical moral reasoning, shortly.

All models of moral as well as non-moral reasoning should account for the fact that sound reasoning does not allow for arbitrary moves. Agents who reason soundly neither introduce assumptions arbitrarily, nor do they move from one point to another arbitrarily.[112] A move is arbitrary if there is no satisfactory justification for making it. What counts as a satisfactory justification is regulated by certain standards. Reasoning is movement in thought that is non-arbitrary and thus justifiable with regard to some standards. These standards can guide the *form* or the *content* of a piece of reasoning. They regulate what counts as a justifiable transition from one thought to another. An example of an important *formal* standard when it comes to accessing a piece of reasoning is consistency. A person who claims that both *p* and not-*p*, violates one of the basic formal standards of sound reasoning. We aim to think and act consistently, and we criticize others and ourselves for failing to do so. Standards concerning the *content* of a piece of reasoning are less straightforward. This is at least partly due to the fact that what counts as a justifiable transition from one thought to another will depend crucially on the context in which the reasoning takes place. That a joke is funny and will make others laugh is a good justification to tell the joke at a party, but will not be an acceptable justification in the context of a funeral. This context-sensitivity means that most standards regarding the content of a piece of reasoning are defeasible. Most reasoning is reasoning by default.

In order to explain the notion of default reasoning, it is helpful to start with a non-moral case. John F. Horty gives the following example.[113] If we are told that Tweety is a bird, it would be natural for us to conclude that Tweety is able to fly. Our everyday reasoning is governed by a general default according to which birds, as a rule, are able to fly. There is a default rule of the form $A \rightarrow B$ that allows us to conclude B, by default, whenever it has been established that A. So if A stands for the statement that Tweety is a bird, and B for the statement that Tweety can fly, then $A \rightarrow B$ is the rule that allows us to conclude that Tweety can fly, by default, once it has been establishes that Tweety is a bird. This particular default is an instance of the general default: $Bird(x) \rightarrow Fly(x)$. The rule justifies us to move from 'Tweety is a bird' to 'Tweety can fly'. But this justification is defeasible. Once we learn that Tweety is a penguin, an ostrich or another flightless bird, that it had its wings clipped, is ill, etc., we should withdraw our initial judgement. The same holds true for practical reasoning. Consider the following example of a piece of instrumental reasoning. If my end is to have an espresso, a suitable means might be going to a particular café, but I will retract my decision when I learn that the café is closed due to refurbishment. Instrumental reasoning is default reasoning: an apparently satisfactory instrumental inference can be defeated by adding further premises.[114]

Moral reasoning is best understood as following the same pattern. Like all forms of reasoning, moral reasoning consists of ways of moving from one thought to another thought or action that are non-arbitrary and thus justifiable. Moral principles provide standards for moving from one thought to another thought. Consider the following example of practical reasoning. After holding a number of job interviews, a staff manager thinks about which of the candidates she should hire for the job. She reasons that she should give candidate B the position because it is her best friend's son. Her reasoning is morally flawed. Given that we agree on some principle of fairness or equal opportunity, nepotism is not a morally acceptable reason for favouring one applicant over another. Similarly, someone who thinks that she ought to give to charity and who reasons that the most effective way of fulfilling this obligation is to murder her rich uncle and appropriate his assets, violates the principle 'Do not kill human beings'. Although she starts off with some good moral intentions and although her instrumental reasoning is correct, her moral reasoning is seriously flawed. It picks out a morally unacceptable means to a (morally worthy) end. However, like most forms of reasoning, moral reasoning is reasoning by default. Thus, while violating the principle of consistency automatically disqualifies a piece of reasoning as unsound, an agent might be reasoning morally correctly despite apparently violating a moral principle. The majority of moral principles are default principles. The standards they provide are defeasible. If an agent is told that an action involves lying, for example, she is justified in concluding that the action is morally wrong. But in a situation where lying is necessary to save a life, for example, the principle 'Lying is wrong' is defeated and hence does not justify us in concluding that the action is wrong. Similarly, if we learn that a person killed someone we conclude, by default, that this was morally wrong. Our conclusion is justified by a default principle that proscribes killing. But if we then learn that the person acted in self-defence, we should reconsider our conclusion. Default principles mark inferential relations which hold by default and which guide our moral reasoning. The default principle that killing is wrong marks an inferential relation between killing and wrongness. Once we learn that an action involves killing we can conclude that it is wrong, *other things being equal*. In 'Defeasibility' (pp. 138–56), I argued that the *ceteris paribus* qualifier attached to theoretical moral principles carries with it an explanatory commitment. In cases where a principle is defeated, we need to be able to explain why other things are not equal. That is, we will need to be able to show that the principle is defeated by another moral principle. To adopt a moral principle is to assume a deliberative commitment. We are committed to take certain general moral considerations into account when we deliberate. Most of the standards which moral principles provide are defeasible, but they cannot be disregarded without justification. For example, a principle of fairness or equal opportunity will tell an agent that the fact that the applicant is her best friend's son is rarely, if ever, a justification for giving him the job. If we decide to violate a default principle we need to be able to justify our breach of the principle to others and ourselves.

The conception of moral reasoning as reasoning by default is based on ground that is common between generalists and particularists. Particularists like Dancy concede that '[moral] competence requires knowledge of the default'.[115] Although particularists believe that moral considerations are uncodifiably context-dependent, they acknowledge that some considerations possess a reasonably stable moral valence. For instance, they acknowledge that lying 'normally' or 'generally' has a negative moral valence. The fact that something is a lie provides a default reason. According to Dancy, a default reason 'is a consideration which is reason-giving unless something prevents it from being so'.[116] He points out that default reasons are features that 'may be set up to be reasons, in advance as it were, although it is always possible for them on occasions to fail to give us the reasons they are set up to give'.[117] Given that particularists want to claim that they can offer a workable moral epistemology, the possibility of defaults is crucial. For – as Dancy puts it – the possibility of default reasons 'palliates the sort of pure variabilism that threatens to turn value judgement into mere guesswork'.[118] However, what particularists want to deny is that default reasons are moral principles. But knowledge of the default is general moral knowledge. If we have knowledge of default reasons our moral knowledge cannot be restricted to particular cases. By means of default reasons the moral judge possesses knowledge about how certain considerations function in general, *other things being equal*. It is moral principles that provide us with default reasons. Dancy himself points out that a default reason is 'something that the competent judge can bring to the new situation; one is not reduced to starting from scratch again each time'.[119] He even remarks that in virtue of default reasons 'rationality has something *rule-like* to work from'.[120]

So far I have offered a general account of how we reason with defeasible moral principles. In the next section I shall say more about how we can act on or implement defeasible moral principles. Much of our everyday reasoning is practical reasoning about what to do. People reason about their career choices and about whether or not to have children, they think about how to help a friend in distress, how to make the world a better place and, more mundanely, about how to spend their holidays and whether to have dessert or not. How can, and how should, we reach decisions about what to do in such cases? In what follows I will argue that practical reasoning is best understood as reasoning about the joint enactment of one's practical principles.

Moral principles and practical reasoning

The principle-based model of practical reasoning I propose starts with the observation that practical reasoning does not take place in a void: agents do not enter practical deliberation empty-handedly. Rather, decisions about what to do in a particular situation are made against the background of a web of commitments. When reasoning about how to spend her holidays, for example, an agent might be governed by a commitment to live in an environmentally friendly way, and thus avoid long air journeys; or, she might have a commitment to attain the maximal value for money and so travel during off-season. Among an agent's commitments practical principles play an especially important role in practical reasoning. The principles I have in mind here are not just any practical principles: they are the principles the agent endorses as *her* principles. The agent does not merely act in accordance with the principle, but takes a pro-attitude towards the act-type prescribed by the principles and forms a standing intention to act in certain ways in the future. The principles I take to be central to practical reasoning are what Kant called 'maxims', that is, an agent's subjective principles of action.[121] To say that these principles are 'subjective' is not to say that one and the same principle cannot be adopted by many different agents at different times, in different circumstances. Most practical principles are acquired through socialization and in many, if not most, cases there will be no exact point in an agent's life where she consciously decides to adopt a particular principle. However, this notwithstanding, practical principles are more than mere habits. The agent endorses the principle as her principle. Practical principles so understood are a subcategory of an agent's commitments. Forming or adopting a practical principle is taking up a commitment. In contrast to other commitments, such as the commitment to fulfil a particular plan, practical principles like 'Do not drink and drive' or 'Do not lie' are perpetually in force. They are perpetually in force because no matter how often we fulfil these commitments, they still commit us to future fulfilments.[122]

In order to fulfil the commitment to a practical principle an agent has to act on the principle. In 'Indeterminacy' (pp. 118–38), we saw that practical principles, including moral principles, are indeterminate in implementation. Since practical principles prescribe, forbid, recommend or condemn certain act-*types*, and since an act-type can be instantiated by various different act-tokens, practical principles necessarily underdetermine action. Practical principles need to be implemented or enacted. How do we implement practical principles? That is, how do we decide which act-token to perform? In this context a remark Kant made with regard to the enactment of imperfect duties is illuminating. According to Kant, we must not weigh one moral duty against another, but rather 'limit one maxim of duty by another'.[123] O'Neill has shown that this task of limiting one maxim by another provides a cogent answer to the question of how to enact practical principles. In what follows I will build on O'Neill's work without buying into any substantial Kantian doctrines. The idea of limiting one practical principle by another is a helpful one independently of a Kantian framework.

O'Neill draws attention to the fact that we usually adopt and are bound by a plurality of practical principles. We do not just think about how to enact, say, a principle of beneficence. When deliberating about what to do, we are looking for ways of being beneficent without being unjust, of being just without being indifferent to the special needs of particular persons, of avoiding injury without lying, and so on.[124] And it is not only moral principles that enter our deliberation. We are looking for a way of being beneficent without ignoring our own needs and non-moral projects. When we reason about how to implement a practical principle, we thus reason about how to implement this principle alongside our various other principles and commitments. The fact that we are bound by a plurality of principles helps, rather than complicates, practical reasoning. In that sense reasoning about what to do is similar to solving an equation; just as certain equations can be solved only because we know a sufficient number of constraints, certain questions about how we ought to act are more easily resolvable if we take account of the constraints of multiple practical principles.[125]

Understood in this way, practical reasoning is a matter of finding an act that meets the plurality of our various commitments by limiting the enactment of one principle by the enactment of another. Practical reasoning is the search for actions that fulfil our various moral and non-moral commitments. Each of our commitments can place restrictions on what means are admissible for the fulfilment of one or more of our other commitments. The multiple demands of our various moral and non-moral principles narrow the scope of practical deliberation to a limited set of possible act-tokens.

However, sometimes it is impossible to find an act-token that jointly satisfies the multiple demands of our various principles. There are cases in which we cannot avoid hurting someone's feelings by telling the truth or breaking a promise to save a life. Such conflicts are a common experience. I take it to be uncontroversial that severe conflicts between an agent's practical principles undermine effective agency. This is not to say that effective agency requires absolute consistency. In this context David Wong points out that sometimes there is no more effective alternative for an agent than to have aspects of her identity – including certain long-term commitments – that conflict to some degree. Such conflicted identities may seem appropriate, for instance, in a complex society in which individuals must perform roles that make very different demands on them. Wong cites the example of India where traditional communities and household structures coexist with new industrial enterprises.[126] He argues that '[t]o some extent, people can mitigate the conflict between different aspects of identity by contextualising their operation – by limiting their ramification to certain domains'.[127] Agents can have, and live in accordance with, a number of *mutually independent* systems of plans and principles. And even when these systems of plans and principles cannot easily be delimited in their ramification and are, therefore, liable to conflict, 'it may be better to live with a limited degree of conflict than to fail to have those aspects of identity needed to navigate in different domains of action'.[128] Indeed many agents live quite happily and successfully divided against themselves. However, this does not change the fact that in order to be successful in their actions agents must have a certain degree of consistency among their various plans and principles. One can acknowledge that effective agency requires a certain level of consistency between an agent's practical principles without subscribing to any strong Kantian consistency requirements. Due to the importance of consistency for successful action, reasoning about what to do cannot merely be a matter of deliberating about how to enact a particular principle or set of principles in a particular situation. We also need to reason about which commitments to adopt and retain in the first place.

The fact that we cannot act in accordance with all our principles in a particular case indicates that we need to reconsider some of our commitments, or try to change some aspects of the world we are living in, to prevent such conflicts from reoccurring. To say that practical deliberation takes place against the background of a set of pre-existing commitments does not mean that agents cannot question these commitments in the process of thinking about what to do. In failing jointly to enact her principles in a particular situation, an agent might realize that her system of commitments is internally inconsistent or inconsistent with the world she is living in. Having identified this inconsistency the agent can try to resolve it and thereby increase her chances of successful action.

Moral principles can play a special role in this context. Conflicts between non-moral principles often do not come to light because the principles are usually limited to certain domains of an agent's life. For example, a doctor who adheres to a policy of washing her hands before and after contact with each patient will normally not wash her hands whenever she shakes hands with someone in her private life. Similarly, a person might have a strict policy of punctuality in her professional life, but care little about being on time when it comes to private parties. If the domains of the principles are mutually independent, an agent might live happily and successfully in accordance with a set of inconsistent practical principles. However, conflicts involving moral principles cannot be avoided by limiting their ramification to certain domains. There is widespread agreement among moral philosophers of various persuasions that a good moral agent will stay committed to and try to enact her moral principles in all areas of her life. She will not treat her principle of honesty or justice, for example, as something that she values and tries to implement in her private life, but which she brackets as soon as she enters the business world. Doing so would show a misunderstanding of what moral principles are. The fundamental position of moral principles among an agent's practical principles is constitutive of moral principles. Unlike principles of business etiquette or profit maximization, moral principles are widely believed to apply to all areas of an agent's life. A good moral agent will not abandon her moral principles in favour of her non-moral commitments. She will abandon or alter the non-moral commitments that conflict with her moral principles. Moral principles thus do not only structure the agent's deliberation about what to do in a particular situation, but also her reasoning about what kinds of aims, plans and projects to adopt or retain.

This means that although there are some occasions – such as moral dilemmas – where agents engage in explicit *moral* reasoning, the reasoning of good agents is always guided by their moral commitments. A good moral agent will not reason about how to fulfil her non-moral commitments without taking any moral considerations into account in order then, on occasion, to engage in moral reasoning about whether her non-moral commitments and the means to fulfil them are morally permissible. If a good moral judge reasons about what to do, her moral principles will prevent her from adopting certain ends and means. She does not engage in a process of prudential reasoning and only afterwards reasons about whether her ends and means are morally permissible. A good moral agent has internalized her moral commitments in such a way that certain thoughts will not even cross her mind. If she wants to pursue a certain career, for instance, and reasons that the best way to further her career would be to get a particular post but that this post is currently not vacant, it would not even cross her mind to lie or murder to get it. The moral agent does not need to engage in a separate course of reasoning in order to find out what is the morally right thing to do in this case.

Practical reasoning, as I characterized it, is not mono-linear. That is, practical reasoning usually does not start with a commitment to a single end and then, by thinking about the necessary means to achieve this end, conclude in a particular action or intention. Rather, in reasoning about what to do, the agent is moving back and forth between her various commitments and the possible means to fulfil them. An agent's commitments, and in particular her moral commitments, will mark certain means as problematic and rule out other means altogether. A failure to find admissible means for fulfilling a certain commitment might lead the agent to abandon this commitment or to reconsider her overall set of commitments. This is not a process of weighing one's practical principles against each other, but of limiting the enactment of one principle by the enactment of one's other principles. In cases of persistent conflicts between the principles it is a matter of reconsidering one's principles in light of one's overall set of commitments. The agent works towards a certain level of consistency between her various commitments in order to increase her chances of successful action.

Thus understood, practical reasoning resembles a web rather than a linear chain of syllogisms.

So I propose that we conceive of practical reasoning as reasoning about how simultaneously to enact a plurality of moral and non-moral commitments. We enter practical deliberation with a set of commitments. Practical principles function as long-term commitments, i.e. commitments that are perpetually in force. Because practical principles prescribe act-types and not act-tokens they underdetermine action. In reasoning about what to do we are looking for an act-token that jointly satisfies the demands of our various moral and non-moral principles. The principles limit the means available for each other's enactment. Due to their universal scope, the limits on permissible means imposed by moral principles are particularly powerful, and this characteristic gives them a special role in structuring our practical deliberation. Moral principles do not only structure our reasoning about what to do in a particular situation, but also our reasoning about which non-moral principles, plans and ends to commit to in the first place.

The principle-based model of practical reasoning I propose avoids both the epistemological and the moral difficulties of the option-choice model. Consider again the example of an agent trying to do her weekly grocery shopping. We saw that in most situations we are not able to compile a finite list of all the options open to us, because there will simply be too many such options and our time and mental capacities are limited. When compiling her shopping list, or when thinking about what to buy while walking through the aisles of the supermarket, the agent will not list all of her options and then choose among them. Following the model of practical reasoning outlined above, she will approach the question of what to buy with a pre-existing set of commitments. The agent might be on a limited budget, for example, and thus make it her principle to spend as little as possible on groceries. At the same time, she might be committed to ensuring that she and her family have a healthy and well-balanced diet. When thinking about what to buy the agent's primary concern will be to find a way of meeting these two aims. Many options will not even cross her mind. A vegetarian normally will not check what is on offer in the meat section and someone who is committed to buying only fair-trade products will focus on those products. Thus, in most cases we should not, and indeed cannot, check all of the options open to us in a particular situation. Rather we try to fulfil our various commitments.

This is not to deny that we sometimes decide what to do by choosing among options. We *do* specify and compare options. However, what I want to deny is that reasoning about what to do is generally best understood as a matter of specifying a list of options available to us and then choosing one of them by means of some sort of criteria. Practical reasoning does not start with thinking about options. It starts with a web of commitments – including the long-term commitments practical principles present – and its primary aim is the joint enactment of these commitments. Thinking of practical reasoning in this way helps to show how limited beings like us manage to decide what to do. Our practical principles limit what we consider as options in the first place. Practical principles determine which options are relevant options. They impose a screen of admissibility on options. Moreover, the options themselves are not possible courses of action open to us in a particular situation *simpliciter*, but options about how to fulfil our various commitments in that particular situation. We do not specify an array of options available to us in a particular situation and then narrow them down by determining whether or not each accords with our moral and non-moral principles. According to the model of practical reasoning I outlined above, things are the other way round. Practical reasoning is reasoning about how simultaneously to enact a plurality of practical principles. We approach a particular situation with a set of practical principles and then search for an act-token that fulfils these principles. The principles limit the means available for each other's enactment. That is, they limit the options. This principle-based model of practical deliberation offers a simpler, and more realistic, explanation of the process of deliberation about what to do than the option-choice model.

Moreover, in contrast to the option-choice model, the principle-based model of practical reasoning does not presuppose the comparability of values. We can perform an action that promotes both aesthetic enjoyment and justice (e.g. return a stolen picture to a museum), even though the justice and the aesthetic enjoyment produced by the action might be incomparable. According to the principle-based model, practical reasoning is not a process of weighing different values *against each other*, but of interpreting and enacting these values in a way that allows us to fulfil them *together*. A defender of the option-choice model might object that this misses the point. If we are in a situation where promoting justice and aesthetic enjoyment can be fulfilled by the same action, we do not need to compare and decide between them. Incomparability only becomes a problem if an agent's options are incompatible. According to proponents of the option-choice model, the interesting and difficult cases are those where an agent's options are incompatible. Indeed, conflicts between values that are hard to resolve seem to be common. Happiness can conflict with knowledge, mercy with justice, economic equality with liberty, and so on. However, as I pointed out earlier, the principle-based model of practical reasoning does not deny the possibility of such conflicts. Allowing moral principles to be defeasible does not undermine their central role in guiding action. If we cannot act in accordance with all of our moral principles in a particular situation, the enactment of one or more of the principles needs to be blocked. However, a commitment to a set of moral principles not only involves the commitment to act in certain ways in particular situations, it also involves a commitment to change the world and plan one's life in such a way that the moral principles can be jointly implemented. If we have to block one or more of our moral principles in a particular case, this shows us that we need to reconsider some of our non-moral plans and commitments, or even try to change the world, in order to prevent such moral conflicts from reoccurring. So although the blocked principles do not guide our action in the particular case, they guide our reasoning about what aims, plans and projects to adopt or retain. Moral conflicts serve as an indicator that an agent's system of commitments requires revision in order to increase her chances of successful action. In failing to jointly enact her moral principles in a particular situation, a moral agent might realize that her system of intentions is internally inconsistent or inconsistent with the world she is living in. Having identified this inconsistency the agent can try to resolve it and thereby increase her chances of successful action. As I showed earlier in this chapter, the option-choice model is misleading because it suggests that all practical reasoning is a matter of deciding between conflicting bearers of value. Instead of encouraging the moral agent to look for an action that would allow her to fulfil her different commitments, it urges her to decide between them. She will see conflicts between values even in cases where they are actually compatible, because her focus lies on weighing values rather than thinking about how best to enact them.

One of the most commonly cited grounds for comparison indeterminacy and value incompatibility is the plurality and diversity of values. To some extent this is misleading because, as we saw in 'Indeterminacy' (pp. 118–38), comparison indeterminacy and value incompatibility can obtain between different bearers of the same value as well as between different bearers of different values. The question of whether there can be any value conflicts is therefore independent of the question of whether there is one single, all-encompassing value or a plurality of values. A plurality of values does not necessarily lead to conflicts and opting for a monistic value system is no safeguard against conflicts. However, it is nevertheless plausible to assume that value pluralism increases the likelihood of value incomparability and incompatibility. In the context of practical deliberation this apparent disadvantage of accepting value pluralism turns out to be an advantage. The fact that we adopt and are bound by a plurality of principles helps, rather than complicates, practical reasoning. The multiple demands of our various moral and non-moral principles narrow the scope of practical deliberation to a limited set of possible act-tokens. Each of our moral principles can place restrictions on what means are admissible for the fulfilment of one or more of our other moral and non-moral principles. Practical reasoning is a search for actions that jointly fulfil our various moral and non-moral commitments. This search only has prospects of success if it is not the case that our commitments are never jointly satisfiable. In 'Defeasibility' (pp. 138–56), I argued that for basic reasons of fairness the conflicts between moral principles can only be contingent. Due to this contingency of moral conflicts, we can hope to change our non-moral commitments and our world so that our practical principles become jointly satisfiable.

A critic might still doubt whether on closer inspection the principle-based model really fares any better than some of the more refined versions of the option-choice model. We saw that one might hope to evade the problem of specifying a relevant option-range by understanding options in terms of reasons for action and adopt a broadly Humean theory of reasons. According to Humeans, an agent's relevant option-range is constituted by her desires. As I noted earlier, one serious and well-known problem with this approach is that it is likely to generate the wrong kind of reasons. Some of an agent's desires will single out options as relevant or good options that we are inclined to consider irrelevant or bad. Likewise, an agent will disregard normatively relevant options if she lacks the corresponding desires. On the principle-based model an agent's relevant option-range is constituted by her long-term commitments, that is, her practical principles. Clearly, not all commitments an agent might have are good commitments. The principle-based model thus seems to suffer from the very same problem as the Humean version of the option-choice model: an agent who commits herself to bad practical principles will regard irrelevant or bad options as relevant or good options, and vice versa. As in the case of desire-based practical deliberation, there seems to be little we can say to such an agent. But this objection is misguided. We can see why by getting clearer about the difference between desiring something and committing oneself to something.

There is no contradiction in disapproving of something one desires because an agent does not need to identify with, or endorse, her desires. As autonomous agents we are not simply pushed around by our desires; we can decide whether or not we take a particular desire to be a reason to do something. In contrast to desiring, committing oneself to something implies a value judgement. Committing oneself to a practical principle is an act of endorsement. The agent approves of the principle, and by making it *her* principle identifies with it. This does not mean that agents never commit themselves to particular projects or general principles which, on reflection, they do not entirely endorse. We sometimes embark on projects whose value we doubt and we act on principles that we have not scrutinized properly. However, what is important is that adopting a commitment inevitably implies a value judgement, whether or not the agent explicitly accepts that judgement or fully understands it. By committing herself to something the agent opens herself to critical assessment in a way that she does not by merely desiring something. The only form of critical assessment that desire-based practical deliberation allows for is means-end assessment: agents can be criticized for inconsistencies between means and ends. Commitments add an extra layer of normative judgements which opens practical deliberation to critical normative assessment: agents can be criticized for adopting bad commitments.

At this point one might worry that while the principle-based model of practical reasoning allows us to criticize ourselves and others for adopting bad commitments, it does not help us to choose better commitments. Earlier in this chapter I argued that the option-choice model does not tell us how we accomplish the task of deciding which reasons for action are relevant or good reasons. One might think that the principle-based model falls foul of the same objection. It does not seem to guide an agent's reasoning about which commitments are good commitments.

In addressing this worry, it is important to distinguish the demand for a model of practical reasoning that guides an agent's reasoning about which commitments are good commitments from a demand for a metaethical account that explains what makes a commitment a good commitment. The principle-based model meets the first demand, but not the second. That is, it offers an account of practical reasoning, but not a complete metaethics or first-order moral theory. It is, however, compatible with a number such theories, including Kantian ethics, Aristotelian ethics and different versions of moral realism. On the principled-based model, it is the fact that conflicting commitments undermine effective agency that forces agents to reason about which commitments to adopt and retain. The more consistent an agent's system of commitments is, the smaller are the chances of conflicts between them, and the better are her chances that she will be able to jointly satisfy her various commitments at any given time. Accordingly, one important criterion for the assessment of a practical principle is whether or not it is consistent with an agent's overall system of commitments. For Kantians, and other moral theorists with a strong belief in the importance of consistency and rationality, this might be sufficient to distinguish good commitments from bad ones.[129] However, since it seems that an agent's overall system of commitments can be internally consistent and yet misguided, many will doubt that consistency alone is enough. Fortunately, the principle-based model has more to offer. An agent's commitments have to take account of the world around her in order to guide her well. An agent will try to change and mould the world in order to fulfil her commitments, but the world can only be changed so much. We are unable to change the laws of physics or certain basic facts about human nature. Good practical principles take account of these facts. For example, a principle according to which we are required to help each and every human being that is in need is not a good principle to adopt because it ignores the fact that our time, energy and external resources are limited.[130] The same holds true for non-moral commitments. Committing myself to being in London at 4 p.m., for instance, is not a good commitment if it is physically impossible for me to get there by that time. Whether something is a good practical principle will be context- and agent-dependent. However, due to our common human nature we share a large proportion of commitments, and given some general facts about human flourishing, there will be some general facts about what kind of practical principles are good principles. Especially for defenders of Aristotelian ethics this will provide a promising basis for the development of a substantial moral theory.[131] Yet even moral realists, according to whom the deciding criteria for the normative assessment of practical principles will be external to an agent's set of commitments, can adopt the principle-based model of practical reasoning developed above. For realists the search for consistency within a set of commitments, as well as these commitments and the world, will be a way of tracking or detecting the truth rather than constituting it. Such a realist will bring her commitments in accordance with each other and the world in the hope that doing so will bring her closer to the truth about which commitments are morally good.[132] This is compatible with the principle-based model of practical reasoning because the model is neutral with regard to metaphysical questions about what makes a commitment a morally good commitment. Instead, it offers resources to develop an account of moral reasoning about the ethical status of agents' commitments.

A critic with particularist inclinations might protest that most of what I have said in this section simply misses the point because it mischaracterizes the activity of moral judgement. I have assumed that the activity of moral judgement is a conscious process of theoretical and practical reasoning which, if successful, issues in propositional knowledge. By contrast, particularists like Dancy often claim that moral knowledge is 'more like knowledge-how than like knowledge-that'.[133] For many particularists moral knowledge is a skill of discernment, 'a way of seeing, a way of being sensitive to the moral facts'.[134] They could thus argue that the activity of moral judgement is not principle-based because it does not follow the conscious reasoning processes I described in this chapter. This objection needs to be taken seriously. There is some plausibility in the claim that we can know how to perform morally right acts without having many, if any, beliefs about which acts are morally right or about what makes them morally right. Moreover, we seem to at least sometimes make moral judgements in the blink of an eye. When turning the corner of a street and encountering someone who has fallen over, for example, we can see at once that we should offer to help. It seems that we do not need to infer this judgement from the principle that we have a duty to help those whom we find in distress. We 'just see' what response the situation calls for. So what can generalists say about such immediate 'snap' judgement?

Snap judgements

Particularists often emphasize Aristotle's remark that 'judgement depends on perception'.[135] By describing moral judgement in perceptual terms, particularists sometimes give the impression that all moral judging is something done in the blink of an eye. A good moral judge is able to see which features of a situation are morally relevant and what course of action they prompt. She 'just sees' what is the right thing to do. Particularists like Dancy insist that all moral judgement is noninferential.[136] They have recently been joined by some moral psychologists. According Jonathan Haidt, for example, there is empirical evidence for the thesis that moral judgements are typically caused by moral intuitions that are 'a kind of cognition but [...] not a kind of reasoning'.[137]

It is important to distinguish descriptive questions concerning the psychological process of moral judgement from normative questions about the justification of the outcome of this process. Most moral psychologists are well aware of this distinction. Haidt, for instance, points out that his claim about reasoning being rarely the direct cause of moral judgement 'is a descriptive claim, about how moral judgments are actually made [...] [and] not a normative or prescriptive claim, about how moral judgments ought to be made'.[138] He acknowledges that what I dubbed snap judgements can lead to suboptimal and even disastrous moral decisions.[139] I contend that in order to justify her snap judgements, a moral agent needs to be able at least partly to formulate the principle on which she takes her action or verdict to be based. She will need to be capable of illustrating and explaining her judgement in terms of similar cases, examples or analogies.[140] This means that she has to abstract from the particular action or verdict and to show in what respects it is similar to, or different from, other cases. This requires the ability to see that something particular is of a general kind. When asked to justify a snap judgement, we will describe the case as, say, a case where someone needed help or where someone was harmed. We thereby implicitly or explicitly evoke moral principles. We describe an act-token as being of a certain type, and we take a stance with regard to this type of action. This is not to deny that snap judgements are often based on a gut feeling; something may 'just feel' wrong or we may 'sense' that something is unjust. Such feelings are a good reason for further enquiry. However, if after careful deliberation we are still not able to say more than that, neither others nor we ourselves ought to take our judgement to be justified. Especially with snap judgements, it will often be enough to describe the situation to get others to 'see' it the way we do. Others will agree with our evaluation of a particular situation if the described act-type falls within the shared, stable part of the moral concepts employed by our moral principles. Moral principles provide us with a tool of abstraction that is necessary for moral justification.

This quest for moral justification shows that although know-how constitutes an important part of morality, it is not the only kind of knowledge which is important. When it comes to serious moral problems we want to have justified beliefs about them. Moral knowledge is a matter of knowledge-that as much as a matter of knowledge-how. In spite of their emphasis on knowledge-how, particularists do not deny this. Most particularists aspire to a form of moral realism. We have seen that they speak of moral properties, moral truths and moral facts, of features that make actions right and wrong, etc. The debate between generalists and particularist takes place against the background assumption that there are moral truths and that we can have true beliefs about them. Especially in situations of moral conflict and disagreement we do not only want to claim that our moral beliefs are true, but we also want to be able to justify them. Thus, generalists and particularists agree that even though the traditional analysis of knowledge as justified true belief might be neither sufficient nor necessary, truth and justification remain an essential part of moral epistemology.

Apart from being a necessary element of moral justification, principles fulfil another important function in snap judgement. Intuitive, immediate judgement is of the utmost importance in situations that require quick action; sometimes every second counts. But a snap judgement can also seriously mislead us. It can be the source of wrong and harmful decisions and actions. Because it happens quickly and largely unconsciously, snap judgement is easily distorted by biases of one sort or another.[141] Trying to formulate the underlying principle of our verdict or action can help us to uncover and outweigh these biases. Or we might realize that things are actually much more complicated than we initially thought and qualify our verdict. Moreover, adopting or recalling certain principles – e.g. principles concerning discrimination on the basis of race or gender – can make us more aware of the danger of biases and lead us to judge more carefully in situations to which these principles might apply.

In addition, it is important to note that cases where we apparently 'just see' what is morally required might nevertheless involve inferences from general moral principles. The inferences which we draw in such cases might be so obvious and happen so quickly that they escape our conscious attention. One sign of this might be that if our behaviour is challenged we are disposed to justify it by reference to a moral principle, and to criticize our own and other people's deviation from it. The distinction between processes that are under direct control and those that are not cuts across any distinction between inferential rule-based processes and other processes.[142]

Furthermore, acting on a principle need not be conceived of as an inferential process. Take grammatical rules for example. In ordinary speech native speakers follow grammatical rules automatically and effortlessly. When asked to articulate the rules they might be unable to do so or, if they try to think about them consciously, find this confusing. Nonetheless there are rules at work that determine what counts as a well-formed sentence. This suggests that rules and principles do not always function as premises of inferential reasoning or as abstract intellectual tools that we employ consciously. In the next section I will argue that, understood as internalized long-term commitments, moral principles can shape our moral character and sensitivity and are, as such, constitutive of the capacity of moral judgement. Thus, on my account the person of good moral judgement – the person who often 'just sees' what is the right thing to do – is a person of principle.

Moral principles and the capacity of moral judgement

Moral generalists are often accused of ignoring the importance of the capacity of moral judgement. At the forefront of those who have attacked traditional principle-based ethics for their alleged failure to account for moral judgement are contemporary virtue ethicists with their focus on practical wisdom or phronesis.[143] Many virtue ethicists hold that '[g]iving priority to the general loses us the ethical value of surprise, contextuality, and particularity'.[144] They complain that 'moral philosophy's customary focus on action-guiding rules and principles [...] [has] masked the importance of moral perception to a full and adequate depiction of moral agency'.[145]

Many of those who accuse traditional generalists of ignoring the importance of judgement base their criticism on an overly demanding conception of what moral principles are and what they can accomplish. In the first chapter I pointed out that many particularists think of moral principles as purely mechanical decision-procedures that can be applied without any insight, imagination or judgement. Charles Larmore, for instance, asserts that Kantians and utilitarians have been at one 'in seeking a fully explicit decision procedure for settling moral questions'.[146] He claims that as a result 'they have missed the central role of moral judgement'.[147] I also showed that McDowell, McNaughton and Dancy make similar accusations. McNaughton assumes that the aim of traditional principled ethics is to find 'a set of rules which could be applied by anyone, whatever their sensitivity or experience, to discover the right answer'.[148] He then argues that moral judgement 'cannot be replicated by the use of a decision procedure which could be grasped by someone who had no appreciation of what was at stake'.[149] Similarly, McDowell points out that there are cases 'in which a mechanical application of the rules would strike one as wrong'.[150]

But these are claims that no sensible generalist would deny. Generalists should and can agree with particularists like McNaughton that moral principles are 'no substitute for a sensitive and detailed examination of each individual case'.[151] Neither utilitarians nor Kantians, for example, think of moral principles as purely mechanical decision-procedures. In this context John Stuart Mill remarked that there 'is no difficulty in proving any ethical standard whatever to work ill, if we suppose universal idiocy to be conjoined with it'.[152] Moral agents need to be able to identify options and predict and calculate their likely consequences in order to apply the principle of utility. According to Mill, even the process of weighing pleasure against pain is a matter of judgement that cannot be replicated by the use of a mechanical decision-procedure:

> What is there to decide whether a particular pleasure is worth purchasing at the cost of a particular pain, except the feelings and judgements of the experienced? [153]

Similarly, Brad Hooker emphasizes that '[r]ule-consequentialists are as aware as anyone that figuring out whether a rule applies can require not merely attention to detail, but also sensitivity, imagination, interpretation, and judgement'.[154] Hare remarked that to ask for a moral algorithm is 'to ask for a way of escaping from the labour of moral thought'.[155] Kantians are equally keen to stress the importance of judgement. Kant himself pointed out that we can have no algorithm for judgement, since every application of a rule would itself need supplementing with further rules.[156] O'Neill argues that moral principles do not provide us with an 'autopilot for life' and that '[j]udgement is always needed in using or following – and in flouting – rules or principles'.[157] Contractualists like Thomas M. Scanlon emphasize that moral principles 'leave wide room for interpretation and judgement'.[158]

So given that most generalists acknowledge that moral principles do not apply themselves and that in following them judgement is always needed, why do so many of their critics conceive of moral principles as mechanical decision-procedures? The thought seems to be that by acknowledging the importance of moral judgement one diminishes, and even calls into question, the importance of moral principles. So – the argument might go – either moral principles function like algorithms that can be applied mechanically without any insight, imagination and judgement, or they are of no importance at all. If we need moral judgement to apply and follow moral principles, why should we not use this faculty to judge particular moral cases directly? In the first chapter we saw that this is exactly what particularists suggest we should do. They argue that moral judgement not merely *supplements* but *supplants* principles. Particularists insist that we can, and should, make moral decisions on a case-by-case basis without any principles. According to particularists, moral principles are made redundant by judgement.[159] In order to address this challenge generalists have to provide an account of the nature of moral judgement, and the relation between moral judgement and moral principles. So far they have neglected this point.

Although generalists stress the importance of moral judgement, they have disappointingly little to say about it. They give the impression that moral judgement is a mysterious faculty about which we can say little more than that it needs to be somehow added to our knowledge of moral principles. Particularists are right to complain that this is unsatisfactory. In what follows, I will argue that the capacity of moral judgement is best conceived of not as something that supplements moral principles but rather as something that is itself principle-based. The aim is to show that, contrary to the claims made by particularists and other critics of principle-based ethics, generalists have the resources to develop a convincing theory of moral judgement.

Principle-based moral judgement

Although particularists frequently accuse generalists of ignoring the importance of judgement, they themselves have little to say about what it is for a person to have a capacity for moral judgement. Larmore, for instance, remarks:

> Although we can understand [...] what kinds of situations call for moral judgement, the kinds of tasks which it is to accomplish, and the preconditions for its acquisition, there is very little positive we can say about the nature of moral judgement itself [...]. We appear able to say only what judgement is *not*, and not what it *is*.[160]

Similarly, Benedict Smith claims that 'judgement resists an explicit characterization'[161] and Dancy writes:

> [O]ur account of the person on whom we can rely to make sound moral judgements is not very long. Such a person is someone who gets it right case by case. To be consistently successful, we need to have a broad range of sensitivities, so that no relevant feature escapes us, and we do not mistake its relevance either. But that is all there is to say on the matter. To have the relevant sensitivities just is to be able to get things right case by case.[162]

This is not very helpful. We need to know what kinds of sensibilities are required for sound moral judgement and how we can develop these sensibilities. Both particularists and generalists will agree that a person of good moral judgement possesses sensitivity, experience and discernment. A person of moral judgement is sensitive to needs of others and the details of the situations she finds herself confronted with. She is good at recognizing what has to be done and what is the best way of doing it. These are qualities that a good moral agent – a person of moral character – aims to cultivate. How considerate and sensitive people are to the needs of others, how carefully they examine the details of a particular case and think about what to do, depends crucially on their character. The capacity of moral judgement is thus closely linked to what kind of person we are. The basis of an individual's moral character is normally formed in childhood through socialization and moral education. Again, this is something that is uncontroversial between generalists and particularists. Some particularists are even prepared to concede that moral principles can provide useful pedagogic tools and they might thus be willing to acknowledge that moral principles are important for the development of an agent's character.[163] However, particularists are keen to emphasize that once we have reached moral maturity we will not need these principles any more. According to particularists, moral principles can play an important part in the moral education of children, but only 'as "moral training wheels" that have to be discarded in maturity'.[164] By contrast, I argue that, properly understood, moral principles are essential not only for the moral novice but also for the morally experienced person.

An individual will typically challenge and qualify at least some of her moral principles as she grows older, gains life experience and reflects on moral questions. She will endorse them as *her* principles and they will become a part of her moral character. I claim that during a successful process of individual moral development moral principles change from being external pedagogic tools and precepts to internal long-term commitments. The agent does no longer act merely in accordance with the principle, but takes a pro-attitude towards the act-type prescribed by the principle and forms a standing intention to act in certain ways in the future. Earlier I argued that moral principles form an important subcategory of an agent's commitments. Forming or adopting a moral principle is taking up a commitment. Like all practical principles, moral principles function as *long-term* commitments. In contrast to other commitments, such as the commitment to fulfil a particular plan or the commitment to fulfil a particular promise, long-term commitments like 'Do not drink and drive' or 'Do not break your promises' are perpetually in force. They are perpetually in force because no matter how often we fulfil these commitments, they still commit us to future fulfilments.[165] In what follows, I will show that understood as internalized long-term commitments, moral principles play two central roles in the constitution of an agent's character. First, moral principles shape an agent's moral sensibilities and, second, moral principles are crucial for an agent's identity and unity over time. Let me start with the first point.

In 'Defeasibility' (pp. 138–56), I pointed out that long-term commitments structure the way we live our lives. Someone who plans to become a professional athlete, for example, will lead her life in a certain way. She will schedule her social life around her training, follow a particular diet, move to another city with better training opportunities, etc. Plans concerning ends embed sub-plans concerning means and preliminary steps. Forming and pursuing these sub-plans is a necessary part of carrying out our long-term plans successfully. The same holds true for moral principles. By adopting a set of moral principles an agent commits herself to live her life in a certain way. She will try to structure her life and world in a way that allows her to jointly satisfy her moral principles. Moral principles do not only require that agents seek to enact certain act-types, they also require them to think about the means and circumstances necessary for the joint fulfilment of the principles. By structuring her life and world in a way that allows her to jointly satisfy her moral principles, an agent will improve her moral sensibilities. Over time she will become more sensitive to the needs of others and the details of the situations with which she finds herself confronted. That undertaking certain commitments shapes an agent's experience and improves her sensibilities is a common phenomenon. An entrepreneur committed to make lucrative investments, for example, might recognize a promising business idea in something that few others would take seriously. Parents committed to the security of their toddler will see hazards where others just see an open bottle of detergent, plug sockets, or a staircase. An experienced salesman who is committed to a good sales performance can sometimes see what a customer wants, and how much he is prepared to spend, at the moment the person walks into the shop. In all these cases trying to live up to their particular commitments leads agents to develop and cultivate special sensibilities. By adopting and internalizing moral principles as long-term commitments moral agents develop and cultivate their moral sensibilities.[166]

This way of understanding moral principles helps to answer the concern that by focusing on general moral principles we overlook the details of the particular situations we are confronted with. Many particularists argue that moral principles are not only made redundant by moral judgement, but they also distort our judgement. In this context Dancy claims that 'generalism is the cause of many bad moral decisions [because] [...] [it] encourages a tendency not to look hard enough at the details of the case before one'.[167] It is said that thinking in terms of moral principles blunts moral sensibilities. Particularists believe that it leads to people 'sticking to their principles', rather than being sensitive to what is called for in the particular case.[168] I argue that the opposite is the case. Trying to live in accordance with their various moral and non-moral principles helps moral agents to become more sensitive to the needs of others and details of the situations with which they find themselves confronted. As a result a good moral judge will sometimes be able to 'just see' what is the right thing to do.

Understanding moral principles as long-term commitments which form our moral sensitivity also helps to deal with the phenomenon of snap judgements discussed in the previous section. We saw that many particularists insist that moral knowledge is not propositional knowledge of moral principles, but rather a skill of discernment. They argue that the aim of moral upbringing should not be conformity with a set of moral principles, 'but to see situations in a special light, as constituting reasons for action'.[169] According to particularists, a good moral judge is able to see which features of a situation are morally relevant and what course of action they prompt. I agree that a good moral judge will at least sometimes be able to see what is the right thing to do without having to infer this judgement from any moral principles. However, particularists are wrong to take this ability to 'just see' what is the right thing to do as evidence for the alleged redundancy of moral principles. The acquirement of a rich set of moral sensibilities does not render an agent's moral principles superfluous. Let me illustrate this point with one of the non-moral examples mentioned above. An experienced entrepreneur will not abandon her principle of making lucrative investments because she can 'just see' whether or not something is a lucrative business idea. That would be absurd. The same holds true for the moral case. Understood as long-term commitments, moral principles are practical principles. As explained earlier in the book, practical principles have world-to-word direction of fit. The primary function of practical principles is not to describe and assess the world, but to change, guide and control the behaviour of agents with decision-making capacities.[170] An agent needs to have a grasp of the world around her in order to change it. She needs to be in the possession a rich set of sensibilities to fulfil her practical principles. Being able to 'just see' that someone needs help thus does not render the principle of beneficence superfluous. On the contrary, it is a sign of the agent's ability to fulfil or implement the principle.

A similar point can be made with regard to our emotional responses or reactions to certain actions or situations. Sometimes we seem to 'just feel' that an action is right or wrong. We often feel anger, for example, when we experience injustice. Particularists might view these cases as evidence for their claim that moral verdicts do not need to be principle-based.[171] However, according to the model of principle-based judgement proposed here, emotional reactions to certain actions or situations are a sign of an agent's strong commitment to her moral principles and aid the successful fulfilment of these principles. Once internalized, moral principles become emotionally charged.[172] By adopting a set of moral principles an agent commits herself to live her life in a certain way and the development of her moral sensibilities helps her to live up to these commitments. Particularists are mistaken to assume that 'one cannot *both* follow a moral principle *and* have one's behaviour arise from a moral reaction'.[173] Adopting a set of moral principles as internal long-term commitments facilitates the development of a rich set of moral sensibilities and these sensibilities in turn facilitate the successful enactment of one's moral principles. The relation between moral principles and moral sensibilities is one of mutual facilitation. This is not to say that being committed to a set of moral principles is the same as having moral judgement. The capacity of moral judgement is a complex aggregate of various sensibilities. The commitment to a set of moral principles leads agents to develop and refine these sensibilities. It leads agents to develop and refine their moral sensibilities because these sensibilities are necessary for the fulfilment of their moral commitments, that is, the successful enactment of their moral principles. By committing herself to a set of moral principles an agent also commits herself to the means necessary for the fulfilment of this commitment, and the development of her moral sensibilities is an essential part of these means.

So far I have argued that in trying to fulfil moral principles understood as internalized long-term commitments an agent gains experience and develops her moral sensibilities. However, an agent could not develop and cultivate her moral sensibilities, and hence her capacity of judgement, without conceiving of herself as an agent, i.e. as having a certain identity and unity over time. This leads me to the second central role which moral principles play in the constitution of an agent's character. I contend that as internalized long-term commitments moral principles are essential for an agent's identity and unity over time. I will emphasize two connections between moral principles and an agent's identity, but I do not claim that these are the only connections. First, moral principles can provide forward-looking psychological connections between an agent's present self and her future self. These psychological connections support the agent's identity over time. Adopting a set of moral principles means taking on certain long-term commitments, and to take on a long-term commitment is to form a standing intention to act in certain ways in possible future situations. As internalized long-term commitments, moral principles thus give rise to a psychological connection between an agent's present intentions and the future execution of these intentions. For example, by adopting a principle of honesty an agent commits her future self to be truthful and to avoid situations where she cannot fulfil this commitment. Secondly, moral principles are crucial to an agent's identity because they provide her with a way to construct and understand herself as a certain person. Recent work in moral psychology confirms this point. Jesse Prinz, for instance, remarks that by internalizing moral principles '[m]orality becomes a central part of our self-conceptions'.[174] According to Prinz, '[w]e identify with moral rules, and we like to affiliate with people whose values are similar to our own'.[175] Moral principles offer an individual a way to define herself as a person with certain principles.[176] For example, someone might understand herself as a person who keeps her promises, values honesty and is passionate about working towards what she believes to be a fairer society. Moreover, such an agent will be likely to prefer socializing with people who share her moral principles and the principles in question might form part of a group identity.

Moral principles are not the only long-term commitments that help to form an agent's identity and unity over time.[177] However, I want to argue that moral principles have a special place among an agent's long-term commitments and thus a special importance for her identity and unity over time. Many non-moral commitments are restricted to certain domains of an agent's life. According to the model of principle-based judgement defended here, the domain of moral principles is not restricted in this sense. In 'Defeasibility' (pp. 138–56), I argued that a good moral agent will stay committed to and try to enact her moral principles in all areas of her life. This is not to deny that different contexts often require different responses and forms of conduct. The demands of justice, for example, are likely to be different depending on whether the agent is acting, say, as the recruitment officer of a company or choosing Christmas presents for her niece and nephew. Similarly, the requirements of honesty might be different in private life and in the business world. Withholding certain information and creating false expectations might – in some situations and to some extent – be as appropriate in the business world as it is when playing poker. Moral principles prescribe, forbid, recommend or condemn certain act-types, not act-tokens. When we follow moral principles we have to perform particular tokens of these act-types. In 'Indeterminacy' (pp. 118–38), we saw that moral principles underdetermine action because an act-type can be instantiated by various different act-tokens. Which act-token best implements the act-type specified by the principle will depend on the details of the particular situation in which we find ourselves. The indeterminacy of moral principles entails a need for context-sensitivity in the sense that their enactment must be sensitive to context.[178] The moral agent acquires this context-sensitivity in the process of trying to live up to her various moral principles. In the same way in which a salesman is likely to improve his ability to determine which customers and circumstances call for which sales tactic by trying to fulfil his commitment to a good sales performance, a moral agent will improve his ability to see which action or response is appropriate in which context by trying to fulfil his various moral commitments. What is important for the present purpose is that the fact that moral principles require context-sensitive enactment is consistent with them being binding across all domains of an agent's life. Moral principles might require different actions and responses in different contexts, but rather than undermining their universal bindingness this context-sensitivity is part of their successful enactment. As pointed out before, unlike principles of business etiquette or profit maximization, moral principles apply to all areas of an agent's life. Due to their universal bindingness moral principles help to form the core of a good agent's character, i.e. the part of a person's character that remains the same across the different areas of her life. Most people have to play various different roles in their daily life and they often have to act and think differently in order to fulfil these different roles adequately. Moral principles offer a way of unifying these various roles, or rather of building and retaining a sense of self that transcends them.

According to the conception of the capacity of moral judgement proposed here, moral principles and moral judgement are deeply intertwined. Instead of conceiving of moral judgement as a mysterious capacity that needs to be somehow added to moral principles, I suggest that we think of the capacity of judgement as being itself principle-based. The misguided dichotomy between principles and judgement stems from a misguided understanding of moral principles as tools that help us to arrive at the right moral verdict or act in the morally right way. Thinking of moral principles as tools leads one to think of them as something that is separate from the capacity of judgement. It suggests that moral principles are something that needs to be supplemented by judgement. Being in possession of a set of tools is of little use if one does not know how to use them. It requires experience and judgement to use tools. Moreover, some tools are useful only for the novice and should be dispensed with once the person has mastered the skill in question. Moral principles are not like this. They are essential for the moral novice as well as for the moral expert. Moral principles function as internalized long-term commitments that form an agent's capacity for judgement rather than as tools that need to be supplemented by judgement.

This principle-based model of moral judgement fulfils the requirement of minimal psychological realism set out at the beginning of 'Moral principles and the activity of moral judgement' (pp. 156–88). People clearly adopt, and try to live up to, an array of long-term commitments, some of which are moral. Moreover, there are numerous examples from everyday life that show how trying to live up to a certain commitment shapes an agent's experience and improves her sensibilities. That people identify themselves through their commitments is an equally common phenomenon. It is thus realistic to assume that human beings can form a capacity of moral judgement in accordance with the proposed principle-based model.

Once it is acknowledged that the capacity of moral judgement is best understood as being inherently principle-based, the particularist's charge that moral judgement supplants rather than supplements moral principles does not get off the ground. The burden of proof is now shifted onto particularists. They have to offer a plausible account of moral judgement that does not rely on moral principles. What might such a particularist account of moral judgement look like? Earlier I pointed out that, according to particularists, a person of moral judgement 'just sees' which features of a situation are morally relevant and what course of action they prompt. According to Dancy, we develop this perceptual-like moral competence 'by developing a set of prototypes, clearest cases, or best examples'.[179] He argues that once we have a sufficient grasp of a range of prototypical cases we can conceive of less clear cases or less good examples in terms of their distance from the prototype or prototypes. Therefore, moral training does not need to rely on principles but can instead proceed by studying a range of morally significant situations and cases.[180] One serious difficulty particularists will have to address when developing this model of moral judgement is that in order to learn something from a particular situation we need to be able to see it as being of a general kind. An example or a case is always an example or a case *of something*. The knowledge that we acquire through paradigms, prototypes, clearest cases or best examples is *general* knowledge. A particular situation by itself will be of no use in learning a moral concept unless we are able to view it as an instance of a general type: a proto-*type*. As I pointed out in 'Indeterminacy' (pp. 118–38), this does not fit well with the particularist's claim that our basic moral knowledge is particular. According to the principle-based model of moral judgement outlined above, a good agent develops and cultivates her moral sensibilities by trying to live up to her various moral principles. Her moral commitments let her see particular situations in a certain light. They channel the agent's perception and make her see particular situations as being of a general kind. Particularists need to devise a plausible alternative explanation of how the agent knows what general features to look for in a particular situation and how this quest for general moral knowledge can be incorporated within a particularist theory. The challenge they face in this context is one of conceptual consistency, rather than empirical adequacy. Particularists have to explain how the fact that the knowledge we acquire through prototypical cases is general knowledge is compatible with their assumption that our basic moral knowledge is particular.

At this point at least some particularists might object that while the principle-based model of moral judgement developed above is plausible, it is not one that is only open to generalists. We saw that a number of particularists want to make room for moral principles understood as rules of thumb or heuristics and one might think that such rules are all one needs to make the proposed principle-based model of moral judgement work. But this is a mistake. Rules of thumb are intellectual tools. They are useful generalizations of our and other people's past moral experience. I have argued against thinking of moral principles as tools on the grounds that it leads one to think of them as something that is separate from the capacity of judgement. The model of moral judgement I propose is based on a notion of moral principles as internalized long-term commitments. At the end of 'Defeasibility' (pp. 138–56), I pointed out that rules of thumb are second-best strategies. It is only because of our lack of time, our limited cognitive abilities and our liability to biases and special pleading that we need to rely on these rules. Rules of thumb are like the automatic setting of a camera.[181] Many cameras come with a number of preset configurations that work well for standard photographic situations. For example, many cameras have a portrait setting for taking pictures of people indoors and a landscape setting for taking pictures of larger objects in broad daylight. These automatic settings make taking pictures easy. One does not need to worry about things like focus, aperture or shutter speed. However, while taking pictures with the automatic setting is very efficient, it is not flexible and is therefore likely to lead to bad results in non-standard situations. In unusual situations and when used by a good photographer, the manual mode of a camera will provide much better results. But the manual mode is not very efficient. It takes time, effort and expertise to take good photos with a manual camera. The decision of whether or not to base one's moral decisions on rules of thumb can be understood as being analogous to the decision of whether or not to use one's camera in the automatic rather than in the manual mode.

So what is the difference between moral principles understood as rules of thumb and moral principles understood as long-term commitments, and why is it relevant when thinking about the capacity of moral judgement? The central difference between rules of thumb and moral principles understood as long-term commitments lies in their respective success conditions. Good rules of thumb are rules that, although they can sometimes lead the agent astray when making moral judgements, produce correct moral judgements in the majority of cases. If an agent makes a moral judgement on the basis of a heuristic rule, and the judgement is correct, then the rule successfully tracked some truth. The analogy with the camera holds again. Artistic aspirations aside, the purpose of a camera is to produce an accurate representation of the world. Manufacturers add automatic settings to their cameras in order to increase the users' chances of achieving this goal. Moral principles understood as internalized long-term commitments do not track some independent correctness conditions. Rather, they determine their own success conditions. An agent makes the correct judgement or takes the right action if she successfully enacts her moral principles. She gets things wrong if she fails to live up to her moral commitments. This is the case for all of an agent's commitments. If an agent acts on a plan, for example, the plan does not track some independent conditions for what it is for the action to be successful. The action is successful if it successfully enacts the agent's plan. An agent who plans to take the 10 a.m. flight to

Frankfurt, for example, will count as having performed a successful action if she boards a plane to Frankfurt at 10 a.m. By contrast, good rules of thumb or heuristics can promote success in action, but they do not determine what qualifies as a successful action. As a rule of thumb, arriving at the airport at least an hour before departure will significantly increase the agent's chances of catching her flight, but the rule does not determine what it is for her action to be successful. Moreover, in the case of rules of thumb, being successful sometimes requires ignoring the rule and instead taking account of the particular context and circumstances one finds oneself in. For example, as a rule of thumb, speaking the truth is arguably more likely to maximize overall happiness than telling falsehoods, but there are situations in which an act-utilitarian will have to ignore this rule and tell a falsehood in order to maximize overall happiness. If an agent adopts a principle of honesty as a long-term commitment things are different. Successful action will be a matter of successfully enacting the principle alongside her other (moral and non-moral) commitments, and context-sensitivity is a necessary condition for their successful enactment.

This difference between moral principles and rules of thumb is crucial when it comes to moral judgement. I argued that a good agent forms her moral sensibilities by trying to live up to her various moral and non-moral commitments. The desire to fulfil her moral commitments leads her to become more sensitive to the needs of others and the details of the situations with which she find herself confronted. The development of a rich set of sensibilities is a necessary means for the successful fulfilment of one's moral commitments. If successful, the process of trying to live up to one's moral commitments will, therefore, inevitably lead to an improvement of one's moral sensibilities. By contrast, rules of thumb are, at best, an aid for agents who lack sufficient sensibilities. They do not prompt agents to develop them. Moreover, I have argued that moral principles have an identity-generating function which is crucial for the development of an agent's moral judgement. An agent could not develop and cultivate her capacity for judgement without conceiving of herself as an agent with a certain identity and unity over time. An agent is not like a camera which passively records the external world. Agents see the world through a grid of commitments and they try to change and mould the world in order to fulfil these commitments. I have argued that moral principles should be at the core of an agent's commitments. Rules of thumb, whose function it is to track some independent correctness conditions, cannot fulfil this identity-generating role. It is only as long-term commitments that moral principles become something through which an agent can actively shape the world, rather than passively mirror it. Of course, the agent also needs a reasonably accurate picture of the world around her to fulfil her commitments successfully. Otherwise she will constantly bump into objects and fall off edges. In order to fulfil her moral commitments successfully an agent needs to be in the possession of a multitude of facts about the world ranging from basic facts about the physical world, general facts about human nature, social and cultural facts about the society she is living in, to particular facts about the needs of the individuals with which she is interacting. However, it is the use she makes of these facts that constitutes her agency.[182] It is her commitments, and not her ability to track some independent correctness conditions, that make her an agent with a certain identity and unity over time. So it is only as long-term commitments, and not as rules of thumb or heuristics, that moral principles are something through which a person can construct and understand herself as an agent.

Particularists might protest that when they claim that moral thought and action should not, or cannot, be based on moral principles, often not mean moral principles understood as long-term commitments. In reply to this objection, it is important to recall that particularists often fail to do justice to the tradition of principled ethics. Throughout this book we have seen that particularists often base their criticisms on a misguided conception of the nature and roles of moral principles. There is no reason for generalists to accept this conception of moral principles mistakenly attributed to them. If it turns out that particularists are happy to acknowledge the importance of moral principles understood as long-term commitments, generalists should welcome this as a crucial step forward in the debate about the nature and roles of moral principles. It would mean that there is a conception of moral principles under which morality can, and should, be principle-based, and under which the charge that generalists cannot make sense of moral judgement is unjustified. Such an agreement would not render the conception of moral principles and the model of moral judgement presented here trivial or uncontroversial.

It worth noting that the line between proponents and opponents of the proposed model of moral judgement is likely to be orthogonal to the traditional divide between particularists and generalists. Some consequentialists, for example, will be likely to reject the conception of moral principles on which the model is based. I pointed out that, understood as internalized long-term commitments, moral principles do not track independent correctness conditions. The principles themselves determine what it is to act successfully. This conception of moral principles does not fit well with forms of consequentialism that separate the success conditions of moral action from what goes on in the agent's mind. According to act-utilitarians, for example, an action is right if it maximizes overall utility independently of whether or not the agent intended the action. Other consequentialist and deontologist ethics, including rule- and motive-consequentialism, will not have this problem.[183] Whether or not generalists are happy to adopt the model of moral judgement proposed in this chapter will thus depend to a large extent on their respective first-order theoretical moral stance. Although this book has followed particularists and their generalist critics in understanding the enquiry into the nature and roles of moral principles as a metaethical enquiry, this result should not be surprising. It seems naive to suppose that metaethical claims about the nature and roles of moral principles will have no implications for first-order moral theory, and vice versa. The current particularist/generalist debate is a metaethical debate between two more or less clearly defined camps. If what I have said here is correct, then this way of construing the debate oversimplifies matters. This does not mean that we cannot think about moral principles outside the confines of particular first-order moral theories. But it means that generalists need to think about the implications of their theories of moral principles for first-order ethics, and vice versa.

Moral judgement, principles and dilemmas

At the beginning of this chapter I pointed out that generalists acknowledge the importance of moral judgement for following and applying moral principles, but that they tend to have disappointingly little to say about the nature of moral judgement and the relation between judgement and principles. Particularists claim that moral judgement not merely supplements, but rather supplants, moral principles. They insist that we can, and should, make moral decisions on a case-by-case basis without relying on any principles. In order to answer the particularist challenge, generalists have to provide an account of the relation between moral principles and moral judgement that shows why we need moral principles. I propose that we think of moral principles as internalized long-term commitments that form our moral character and sensitivity, and, as such, constitute an essential part of the capacity of moral judgement. I have argued that the traditional polarization between moral principles and judgement is untenable because judgement draws essentially on principles. Moral generalists can thus not only acknowledge the importance of moral judgement, they also have the resources to develop a plausible theory of the capacity of moral judgement. This gives them an important advantage over moral particularists who, despite seeing themselves as the advocates of moral judgement, have so far failed to provide a plausible account of its nature and development.

In this final section I will put the principle-based account of moral judgement and reasoning developed in the previous sections to the test by considering situations in which principles are commonly thought to be of no use to moral agents, namely moral conflicts and dilemmas. The purpose of this section is illustrative.

Throughout this book we have seen that, contrary to the impression given by many particularists, traditional defenders of principled ethics do not believe in the possibility of an algorithmic moral decision-procedure. Generalists acknowledge that moral principles cannot be applied mechanically, that is, without any insight, imagination or judgement. However, many traditional generalists nevertheless aim at a complete moral decision-procedure, albeit not one which could be applied mechanically. This aim cannot be attained if there are irresolvable moral conflicts, i.e. moral dilemmas. A decision-procedure is a method of picking out one alternative as uniquely right in such a way that no incompatible alternative is right in the same way. A moral decision-procedure is complete if it picks out one uniquely right alternative from every morally relevant set of incompatible alternatives in every morally relevant situation.[184] A moral dilemma is a situation where at the same time: (1) there is a moral requirement for an agent to adopt each of two alternatives; (2) neither moral requirement is overridden in any morally relevant way; (3) the agent cannot adopt both alternatives together; and (4) the agent can adopt each alternative separately.[185] The possibility of such genuine moral dilemmas renders the quest for a complete moral decision-procedure futile. Most traditional generalists therefore deny the existence of genuine moral dilemmas and try to show that these dilemmas are merely apparent. Mill, for instance, holds that the principle of utility provides a common standard through which any apparent moral conflict can be resolved.[186] Hare hopes to solve the problem of moral dilemmas by distinguishing between two levels of moral thinking:

> Those who say, roundly, that there can just be irresoluble conflicts of duties are always those who have confined their thinking about morality to the intuitive level. At this level the conflicts are indeed irresoluble; but at the critical level there is a requirement that we resolve the conflict, unless we are to confess that our thinking has been incomplete. We are not thinking critically if we just say 'There is a conflict of duties; I ought to do A, and I ought to do B, and I can't do both'. But at the intuitive level it is perfectly permissible to say this.[187]

Similarly, Herman wants to account for our experience of moral dilemmas, but she insists that there are 'procedures of deliberation'[188] by which all moral dilemmas can, in principle at least, be resolved. Alan Donagan argues that whenever an apparent dilemma is discovered this shows only that the moral theory as so far developed is defective and needs further revision until the dilemma is avoided.[189] Other authors deny the possibility of moral dilemmas on grounds of conceptual considerations, rather than any particular moral theory.[190] It is not the purpose of this section to discuss these different arguments. Although I believe that generalists should not deny the possibility of genuine moral dilemmas, I do not want to argue for this point here. In what follows I will simply assume that moral dilemmas, as defined at the beginning of this section, are possible. What I want to point out is that even in a moral dilemma moral judgement can be essentially principle-based. In contrast to the widely held belief that moral principles are of no use in a genuinely dilemmatic situation, I will show that principles fulfil important functions in moral dilemmas.

The first thing to note is that in real life, situations do not come labelled as moral conflicts or dilemmas. In contrast to philosophical discussions of moral dilemmas, we are seldom faced with clearly defined cases. We need to have apprehended and assessed a situation before we can realize that we are faced with a difficult moral situation in which our moral principles pull in opposite directions. It is only after thoroughgoing reflection on this conflict that we might, in a further step, realize that we are in a genuine moral dilemma. The appreciation and assessment of a situation is a matter of theoretical moral judgement, i.e. reasoning *that* a certain action, institution or agent is of a certain kind or falls under a certain description. Moral principles have two main roles in this context. First, moral principles are crucial for the development and improvement of the capacity of moral judgement. In the previous section I argued that by adopting and internalizing moral principles as long-term commitments, moral agents develop and cultivate their moral sensibilities. These sensitivities are crucial for the detection of a moral dilemma.

The second function of moral principles in theoretical judgement is to channel our reasoning. Once we have realized that we are faced with a difficult situation that asks for moral reasoning, moral principles guide our moral appraisal and assessment. They serve to interrogate the situation. When we judge a particular situation we ask, for example, whether someone has been harmed or whether a person has spoken the truth. Even if it should turn out that in that particular case causing harm was not morally wrong or that lying was unavoidable, our moral principles nevertheless provided us with a helpful starting point for moral enquiry. But they do not only provide the starting point of moral reasoning. In 'Moral principles and the activity of moral judgement' (pp. 156–88), I showed that moral principles can provide standards for sound moral reasoning. Since most moral principles are default principles, moral reasoning is reasoning by default.

It is easy to underestimate how much reasoning can be required to realize that one is faced with a moral dilemma. If moral principles cannot be jointly enacted this will be because of the particular circumstances in which an individual finds herself. In order to decide whether the conflict is irresolvable we need to take the particulars of the individual's situation into account, e.g. the special historical circumstances and institutions under which she lives, her personal, professional and public responsibilities and so on. Take Jean-Paul Sartre's famous example of a young man who is torn between his responsibilities as a son and as a French citizen.[191] The man's mother is old, ill and cannot fend for herself. However, there may be many ways to arrange for the care of aging parents and the fact that the young man believes that he should stay at home and support his mother is due to his and her particular situation. The same is true for the man's civic responsibilities. It is only because his country is under occupation by the German army that he believes it his responsibility to join the resistance force. Whether there is a conflict and whether this conflict is irresolvable thus depends on the details of the case. Moral principles help us to interrogate the case and will reveal, for instance, the injustice of the occupation and the wrongfulness of the aims of the occupying force. As a consequence, the young man might realize he has not only a civic responsibility to defend his country, but a moral responsibility to fight against an unjust and dangerous regime. Moreover, moral principles will channel his reasoning. For instance, they will rule out certain options such as lying to his mother about his plan to join the resistance in order not to worry her. So although Sartre rightly stresses that 'no general code of ethics can tell you what you ought to do [in a moral dilemma]',[192] moral principles nevertheless play a crucial role in the assessment of the dilemma.

If after due deliberation we come to the conclusion that we are in a moral dilemma, we need to think about what to do. This is a matter of practical moral judgement. Having realized that there are different and, in the context, incompatible moral requirements, and that neither requirement is overridden in any morally relevant way, we need to decide on one course of action. If the conflicting moral requirements stem from more than one principle we will need to decide which principle to block. In a moral dilemma we are justified in choosing either of the incompatible alternatives since there are no moral grounds to prefer one alternative to the other. However, there will be a number of considerations to be taken into account when we think about *how* to make the decision and how to fulfil one of the requirements. For instance, in many cases flipping a coin in front of people whose lives are at stake in order to decide whom to rescue would arguably disrespect the seriousness of the case, and make the situation worse for those who are affected by the decision. We need to reason about how to implement the principle on which we have chosen to act. As I pointed out earlier, the fact that we are bound by a plurality of principles will help us to decide which act-token to perform in the particular situation.

A dilemmatic moral situation requires us to specify our options and find the right means to realize these options. Principles have a crucial role to play at this stage of moral reasoning insofar as they will mark certain options and means as morally dubious and rule out others altogether. Specifying options and searching for means to fulfil certain ends is an important step in the process of moral reasoning because it can often alter our ends or even our original assessment of the situation. If we realized, for instance, that we lack the means to fulfil either of two moral requirements, we are in a very unfortunate position, but not in a moral dilemma. For example, a doctor who realizes that she does not have the means to save any of her patients is in a terrible situation, but she does not face a moral dilemma. She does not need to choose between the patients because she cannot help any of them. We might also be lucky and find a way to fulfil both of the two, at first seemingly incompatible, moral requirements.

But even if the conflict proves to be irresolvable, moral reasoning does not stop with the decision for, and fulfilment of, one of the moral requirements. Once the action is taken we expect a good moral judge to behave and feel in a certain way. Consider the often-cited example of the identical twins whose lives are in jeopardy.[193] Through force of circumstance the agent can save only one of the children and there are no moral grounds for choosing one twin over the other. Having saved one of them, we would expect the agent to feel regret about the death of the other twin and to act accordingly, e.g. offer the relatives her condolences, attend the funeral and so on. To decide what kind of behaviour and actions are appropriate will require moral reasoning. Moreover, we will expect the moral agent to think about how to avoid similar dilemmas in the future. These intuitions are difficult to explain if one views moral principles as purely *external* moral requirements imposed on an agent. In a moral dilemma an agent will necessarily fail to fulfil one of the moral requirements and cannot be blamed for doing so. The agent will have done all she could do by fulfilling one of the requirements. The fact that she feels regret and even guilt when failing to fulfil one of the moral requirements is best explained by the assumption that moral principles function as long-term commitments which are adopted and internalized by moral agents. Moral principles influence our behaviour and feelings because they form an important part of our moral character. I have argued that moral principles are something through which a person can construct and understand herself as an agent. Virtue ethicists often accuse utilitarians and deontologists of being 'act-centred', that is, focusing entirely on the question 'Which is the right action, x or y?' and thereby ignoring the moral character of the agent.[194] In a moral dilemma a solely act-centred approach will not take us very far since an agent is justified in choosing to fulfil either of the incompatible requirements and will do the right thing as long as she fulfils one of them. By contrast, viewing moral principles as part of an agent's moral character allows us to shift the focus from the rightness of the act to the agent and what she should feel in, as well as after, a moral dilemma. Although moral principles do not provide us with a complete decision-procedure, they nevertheless play an essential role in guiding and channelling our moral judgement in cases of moral dilemmas.

Notes

1   Rosanna Keefe, *Theories of Vagueness* (Cambridge: Cambridge University Press, 2000), p. 6.

2   Keefe, *Theories of Vagueness*, p. 7.

3   Ibid., pp. 7–8.

4   See Bertrand Russell, 'Vagueness', *Australasian Journal of Psychology and Philosophy* 1 (1923), pp. 84–92; Michael Dummett, 'Wang's paradox', *Synthese* 30 (1975), pp. 301–24.

5   See Michael Tye, 'Vague objects', *Mind* 99 (1990), pp. 535–57; Terence Parsons and Peter Woodruff, 'Worldly indeterminacy of identity', *Proceedings of the Aristotelian Society* 95 (1995), pp. 171–91; Ken Akiba, 'Vagueness in the World', *Nous* 38 (2004), pp. 407–29.

6   See Timothy Williamson and Peter Simons, 'Vagueness and ignorance', *Proceedings of the Aristotelian Society, Supplementary Volumes* 66 (1992), pp. 145–77; James Cargile, 'The Sorites Paradox', *British Journal for the Philosophy of Science* 20 (1969), pp. 193–202.

7   See Keefe: *Theories of Vagueness*, p. 15.

8   Or rather, if the vagueness is 'merely' semantic – i.e. if it affects our natural language but not the objects and properties which we aim to describe with this language – then some moral questions will have no determinately true answers *expressible in natural language*.

9   R. Mark Sainsbury, 'Concepts without boundaries', in Rosanna Keefe and Peter Smith (eds), *Vagueness. A Reader* (Cambridge, MA: Harvard University Press, 1996), pp. 251–64, p. 251. I will follow Sainsbury in referring to the non-vague picture of concepts and categorization as the 'classical' picture. However, one may rightly wonder how 'classical' this picture actually is, and who defended it. The philosophical positions that come to mind are different forms of Aristotelian or Leibnizian essentialism, which have been minority views for a long time. In biology, essentialist definitions of species are obsolete since at least the time of Darwin.

10   Sainsbury, 'Concepts without boundaries', p. 258.

11   Ibid., p. 262.

12   Jonathan Dancy, 'Can the particularist learn the difference between right and wrong?', in K. Brinkmann (ed.), *The Proceedings of the Twentieth World Congress of Philosophy. Vol. 1 Ethics* (Bowling Green: Philosophy Documentation Center, 1999), pp. 59–72, p. 70.

13   Eleanor Rosch, 'Principles of categorization', in Eleanor Rosch and Barbara B. Lloyd (eds), *Cognition and Categorization* (New Jersey: Lawrence Erlbaum, 1978), pp. 27–48, p. 38.

14   See Jonathan Dancy, *Ethics Without Principles* (Oxford: Oxford University Press, 2004), p. 141: 'The basic reason-facts which we are to come to know are particular; their purview is initially restricted to the particular case. We need to be able to come to know these non-general facts, or to acquire justified beliefs about them; and our knowledge of them will be our basic normative knowledge.'

15   Russell, 'Vagueness', p. 87.

16   H. L. A. Hart, *The Concept of Law* (Oxford: Oxford University Press, 1961), pp. 121–34. I believe that it is possible to draw on Hart's notion of open-texture and his model of legal interpretation without accepting his legal positivism. By drawing an analogy with Hart's account of legal rules I do not wish to argue for anything analogous to legal positivism in ethics.

17   Hart, *The Concept of Law*, p. 144.

18   Ibid., p. 125.

19 Ibid.

20 Ibid., p. 135.

21 Ibid., p. 136.

22 Ibid., p. 123.

23 H. L. A. Hart, 'Positivism and the separation of law and morals', *Harvard Law Review* 71 (1958), pp. 593–629, p. 607.

24 Hart, *The Concept of Law*, pp. 125–7.

25 Things would be different if moral principles were given to us by some divine, infallible being. I acknowledge that the above argument and my conception of moral principles in general presuppose a robustly secular outlook.

26 At this point I follow B. Brix's interpretation of Hart's approach. See B. Brix, *Law, Language and Legal Determinacy* (Oxford: Clarendon Press, 1993), pp. 7–35.

27 See Hart, 'Positivism and the separation of law and morals', p. 124.

28 Brix, *Law, Language and Legal Determinacy*, p. 9.

29 See Linda Coleman and Paul Kay, 'Prototype semantics: The English word lie', *Language* 57 (1981), pp. 26–44.

30 This is not to suggest that 'bird' is an open-textured concept. The prototype theory of conceptual learning applies to different types of concepts. The concept 'bird' is arguably best understood as a natural-kind concept whose boundaries are fixed by some facts of nature. See Rosch, 'Principles of Categorization'.

31 See e.g. John L. Mackie, *Ethics. Inventing Right and Wrong* (London: Pelican Books, 1977), pp. 36–8.

32 I borrow this term from Russ Shafer-Landau, 'Ethical disagreement, ethical objectivism and moral indeterminacy', *Philosophy and Phenomenological Research* 54 (1994), pp. 331–44, 333.

33 Ruth Chang, 'Introduction', in Ruth Chang (ed.), *Incommensurability, Incomparability, and Practical Reason* (Cambridge, MA: Harvard University Press, 1997), pp. 1–34, pp. 1–2. Other authors use the term 'incommensurability' as synonymous with 'incomparability'. See for example J. Raz, *The Morality of Freedom* (Oxford: Oxford University Press, 1986), pp. 321–66.

34 Chang, 'Introduction', p. 4. Some authors who are concerned with moral indeterminacy talk about incommensurability rather than incomparability, – see Ronald Dworkin, *Justice for Hedgehogs*

(Cambridge, MA: Harvard University Press, 2011), pp. 88–9; Matthew Kramer, *Objectivity and the Rule of Law* (Cambridge: Cambridge University Press, 2007), pp. 220–4; Kramer, *Moral Realism as a Moral Doctrine* (Oxford: John Wiley & Sons, 2009), pp. 113–26.

35 See e.g. Raz, *The Morality of Freedom*, p. 322.

36 The example is taken from ibid., p. 332.

37 Chang, 'Introduction', p. 2.

38 See Derek Parfit, *Reasons and Persons* (Oxford: Oxford University Press, 1986), p. 431; James Griffin, *Well-Being: Its Meaning and Measurement* (Oxford: Oxford University Press, 1986), pp. 81, 96–8, p. 104; Thomas Hurka, *Perfectionism* (Oxford: Oxford University Press, 1993), p. 87.

39 See Chang, 'Introduction', pp. 23–7.

40 Ibid., p. 2.

41 See Herbert A. Simon, *Models of Man. Social and Rational. Mathematical essays on rational human behavior in a social setting* (London: Wiley, 1957). Also see Michael A. Slote, *Common-Sense Morality and Consequentialism* (London: Routledge, 1985).

42 The example is taken from Simon, *Models of Man*, pp. 246–7.

43 See Ben Bradley, 'Against satisfying consequentialism', *Utilitas* 18 (2006), pp. 97–108.

44 See James Griffin, 'Incommensurability: What's the problem?', in *Incommensurability, Incomparability, and Practical Reason*, pp. 35–51, p. 36.

45 Ibid., p. 37.

46 Indeterminacy in implementation is a necessary feature not only of practical principles, but of practical commitments in general. In this context Michael Bratman has stressed the 'characteristic incompleteness of plans' (Michael Bratman, 'Taking plans seriously', in Elijah Millgram [ed.], *Varieties of Practical Reason* [Cambridge: Cambridge University Press, 2001], pp. 203–19, p. 208). When initially formulated, plans often provide only a relatively general specification of some later mode of conduct. An agent who in the morning decides to go to the cinema, for example, does not settle at once on a complete plan for the evening. She may decide now to go to the cinema, and leave until later deliberation about which cinema to go to, which film to watch, how to buy tickets and how to reach the cinema. When she first decides to go to the cinema, the agent is aware that her plan is importantly

incomplete. She knows that she will need to specify her plans prior to the time of action. And even highly detailed plans will not normally specify what to do down to the most detailed, physical level (see ibid.).

47 In most cases more than one act-token will be appropriate.

48 Gerald C. MacCallum, 'Negative and positive freedom', *Philosophical Review* 76 (1967), pp. 312–34.

49 See Isaiah Berlin, 'Two concepts of liberty', in Isaiah Berlin, *Four Essays on Liberty* (Oxford: Oxford University Press, 1969), pp. 118–72.

50 See e.g. Philip Shenon, 'Senators clash with nominee over torture and limits of law', *New York Times*, 19 October 2007.

51 See for example Pekka Väyrynen, 'Moral generalism: Enjoy in moderation', *Ethics* 116 (2006), pp. 707–41, p. 725.

52 Jonathan Dancy, *Moral Reasons* (Oxford: Blackwell, 1993), p. 67.

53 See G. E. M. Anscombe, *Intention* (Cambridge, Mass.: Harvard University Press, 2000, first published 1957), pp. 56–7.

54 Michael Bratman, *Intention, Plans, and Practical Reason* (Stanford: Center for the Study of Language and Information 1999, first published 1987), p. 88.

55 Ibid., p. 89.

56 Ibid., p. 90.

57 Ibid., p. 89.

58 Ibid., p. 31.

59 Thomas E. Hill, Jr., 'Making exceptions without abandoning the principle: or how a Kantian might think about terrorism', in Thomas E. Hill, Jr., *Dignity and Practical Reason in Kant's Moral Theory* (New York: Cornell University Press, 1992), pp. 196–225, p. 200.

60 There is an extensive literature on moral remainders and the related 'dirty hands problem' which I cannot discuss here. For moral residues see Bernard Williams, 'Ethical consistency', *Proceeding of the Aristotelian Society, Supplementary Volumes* 39 (1965), pp. 103–24; Ruth Barcan Marcus, 'Moral dilemmas and consistency', *Journal of Philosophy* 77 (1980), pp. 121–36; Thomas E. Hill, Jr., 'Moral dilemmas, gaps, and residues: A Kantian perspective', in H. E. Mason (ed.), *Moral Dilemmas and Moral Theory* (Oxford: Oxford University Press, 1996), pp. 167–98. For the dirty hands problem see Michael Walzer, 'Political action: The

problem of dirty hands', *Philosophy and Public Affairs* 2 (1973), pp. 160–80; C. A. J. Coady and Onora O'Neill, 'Messy morality and the art of the possible', *Proceeding of the Aristotelian Society, Supplementary Volumes* 64 (1990), pp. 259–94.

61 See Onora O'Neill, *Towards Justice and Virtue. A constructive account of practical reasoning* (Cambridge: Cambridge University Press, 1996), pp. 158–61.

62 Ibid., p. 159.

63 Ibid.

64 Not all moral principles formulate duties and obligations; they can also express permissions, recommendations and warnings.

65 See Bratman, *Intention, Plans, and Practical Reason*, p. 89.

66 See ibid., p. 31.

67 See Nancy Cartwright, *How the Laws of Physics Lie* (Oxford: Clarendon Press, 1983).

68 See Paul M. Pietroski, 'Prima facie obligations, ceteris paribus laws in moral theory', *Ethics* 103 (1993), pp. 489–515, pp. 496–7.

69 See for example Stephen Schiffer, 'Ceteris paribus laws', *Mind* 100 (1991), pp. 1–17; John Earman and John Roberts, 'Ceteris paribus, there is no problem of provisos', *Synthese* 118 (1999), pp. 438–78.

70 Peter Lipton, 'All Else Being Equal', *Philosophy* 74 (1999), pp. 155–68, pp. 158–9.

71 Ibid., pp. 160–3.

72 Ibid., p. 164.

73 Ibid., pp. 164–5.

74 Ibid., pp. 163–6.

75 Ibid., p. 155.

76 Ibid., p. 166.

77 As I pointed out earlier, the example of lying when playing Diplomacy is problematic because it is unclear whether we are really dealing with a case of defeasibility, or rather with a case of indeterminacy.

78 Paul M. Pietroski and Georges Rey, 'When others things aren't equal: Saving ceteris paribus laws from vacuity', *British Journal of the Philosophy of Science* 46 (1995), pp. 81–110, p. 82.

79 Ibid., p. 81.

80 Barbara Herman, *The Practice of Moral Judgment* (Cambridge, Mass.: Harvard University Press, 1996), p. 178.

81 This idea can already be found in W. D. Ross, *The Right and the Good*, Philip Stratton-Lake (ed.) (Oxford: Oxford University Press, 2002, first published 1930), p. 22: '[T]he duty of non-maleficence is recognized as [...] prima facie more binding. We should not in general consider it justifiable to kill one person in order to keep another alive, or to steal from one in order to give alms to another.'

82 See G. E. Moore, *Principia Ethica*, rev. edn (Cambridge: Cambridge University Press, 1993), edited and with an introduction by Thomas Baldwin.

83 See John Stuart Mill, *Utilitarianism* (Oxford: Oxford University Press, 1998), Roger Crisp (ed.).

84 See R. M. Hare, *Moral Thinking: Its Levels, Method, and Point* (Oxford: Oxford University Press, 1981), p. 37; Edward F. McClennen, 'The rationality of being guided by rules', in Alfred R. Mele and Piers Rawling (eds), *The Oxford Handbook of Rationality* (Oxford: Oxford University Press, 2004), pp. 222–39. For a recent defence of this conception of moral principles see Frederick Schauer, *Playing by the Rules. A Philosophical Examination of Rule-Based Decision-Making in Law and in Life* (Oxford: Oxford University Press, 1991); Alan H. Goldman, *Practical Rules. When we need them and when we don't* (Cambridge: Cambridge University Press, 2002).

85 Martha C. Nussbaum, *The Fragility of Goodness. Luck and Ethics in Greek Tragedy and Philosophy*, rev. edn (Cambridge: Cambridge University Press, 2001), p. 304.

86 This is not to say that moral judgement is always a process of deliberation or reasoning. I will later discuss the possibility of intuitive, immediate 'snap' judgement.

87 See for example Joshua Greene and Jonathan Haidt, 'Where (and how) does moral judgement work', *Trends in Cognitive Sciences* 6 (2002), pp. 517–23.

88 See Jonathan Haidt, 'The emotional dog and its rational tail', *Psychological Review* 108 (2001), pp. 814–34; Greene and Haidt, 'Where (and how) does moral judgement work'; Shaun Nichols, *Sentimental Rules. On the Foundations of Moral Judgment* (Oxford: Oxford University Press, 2004); Jesse Prinz, *The Emotional Construction of Morals* (Oxford: Oxford University Press, 2007); Simone Schnall, Jonathan Haidt, Gerald L. Clore and Alexander H. Jordan, 'Disgust as embodied moral judgment', *Personality and Social Psychology Bulletin* 34 (2008), pp. 1096–1109; Ron Mallon and Shaun Nichols, 'Rules', in John

M. Doris and the Moral Psychology Research Group (eds), *The Moral Psychology Handbook* (Oxford: Oxford University Press 2010), pp. 297–320.

89 See Owen Flanagan, *Varieties of Moral Personality. Ethics and Psychological Realism* (Cambridge, MA: Harvard University Press, 1991), p. 32.

90 See ibid.

91 Dancy, *Ethics without Principles*, p. 2.

92 Immanuel Kant, *On the common saying: That may be correct in theory, but it is of no use in practice*, in Mary J. Gregor (ed.), *Immanuel Kant. Practical Philosophy* (Cambridge: Cambridge University Press, 1996), p. 279, Ak 8:275.

93 See Onora O'Neill, 'Instituting Principles: Between duty and action', in Mark Timmons (ed.), *Kant's Metaphysics of Morals: Interpretative Essays* (Oxford: Oxford University Press, 2002), pp. 331–47, p. 335.

94 Jeremy Bentham, *An Introduction to the Principles of Morals and Legislation*, J. H. Burns and H. L. A. Hart (eds) (Oxford: Oxford University Press, 1996, first published 1789), p. 40.

95 See Marcus G. Singer, 'Actual consequence utilitarianism', *Mind* 86 (1977), pp. 67–77; Joan C. Harsanyi, 'Bayesian decision theory and utilitarian ethics', *The American Economic Review* 68 (1978), pp. 223–8; Bart Gruzalski, 'Foreseeable consequence utilitarianism', *Australasian Journal of Philosophy* 59 (1981), pp. 163–76.

96 See Philippa Foot, 'Abortion and the doctrine of double effect', *Oxford Review* 5 (1967), pp. 28–41; Judith J. Thomson, 'Killing, letting die, and the trolley problem', *The Monist* 59 (1976), pp. 204–17.

97 See T. M. Scanlon, *What We Owe to Each Other* (Cambridge, MA: Harvard University Press 2000, first published 1998).

98 Dancy, *Ethics Without Principles*, p. 111.

99 Margaret Olivia Little, 'Moral generalities revisited', in Brad Hooker and Margaret Olivia Little (eds), *Moral Particularism* (Oxford: Oxford University Press, 2000), pp. 276–304, p. 291.

100 See Sean McKeever and Michael Ridge, *Principled Ethics. Generalism as a Regulative Ideal* (Oxford: Clarendon Press, 2006), pp. 115–37.

101 The 'too many reasons' problem is usually discussed in the context of Humean theories of reasons. See for example Mark Schroeder, *Slaves of the Passions* (Oxford: Oxford University Press, 2007),

pp. 84–102. However, as I shall show below, the Humean 'too many reasons' problem is a version of the more general problem that stems from the option-choice model.

102 See Schroeder, *Slaves of the Passions*, pp. 84–102, p. 123–45. Particularists have tried to solve the 'too many reasons' problem by introducing the notion of a default reason. See Dancy, *Ethics Without Principles*, pp. 112–13; 'Defending the Right', *Journal of Moral Philosophy* 4 (2007), pp. 85–98, pp. 88–92; McKeever and Ridge, *Principled Ethics*, pp. 46–57.

103 See McKeever and Ridge, *Principled Ethics*, pp. 113–76.

104 See Schroeder, *Slaves of the Passions*, pp. 103–22.

105 Ibid., p. 113.

106 Ibid., pp. 95–6.

107 See for example Harry Frankfurt, 'Freedom of the will and the concept of a person', *Journal of Philosophy* 68 (1971), pp. 5–20; Michael Smith, *The Moral Problem* (Oxford: Blackwell, 1994).

108 See Schroeder, *Slaves of the Passions*, pp. 123–45.

109 David O. Brink, 'Moral conflict and its structure', in H. E. Mason (ed.), *Moral Dilemmas and Moral Theory* (Oxford: Oxford University Press, 1996), pp. 102–26, p. 103.

110 Shelly Kagan, 'The Additive Fallacy', *Ethics* 99 (1988), pp. 5–31, p. 17.

111 John Broome, 'Reasons', in Jay Wallace, Philip Pettit, Samuel Scheffler and Michael Smith (eds), *Reasons and Values. Themes from the Philosophy of Joseph Raz* (Oxford: Oxford University Press, 2004), pp. 28–55, p. 37.

112 See Onora O'Neill, 'Four models of practical reasoning', in Onora O'Neill, *Bounds of Justice* (Cambridge: Cambridge University Press, 2000), pp. 11–28, p. 12.

113 John F. Horty, 'Reasons as Defaults', *Philosophers' Imprint* 7 (2007), pp. 1–28, p. 3.

114 See Elijah Millgram, 'Practical reasoning: The current state of play', in *Varieties of Practical Reasoning*, pp. 1–26, p. 7.

115 Dancy, *Ethics Without Principles*, p. 191.

116 Ibid., p. 112.

117 Ibid.

118 Ibid., p. 185.

119 Ibid., p. 185.

120 Ibid., emphasis added.

121 Immanuel Kant, *Groundwork of the Metaphysics of Morals*, in *Immanuel Kant. Practical Philosophy*, 4:421 footnote.

122 See J. David Velleman, *Practical Reflection* (Stanford: Center for the Study of Language and Information, 2007).

123 Kant, *The Metaphysics of Morals*, p. 521, Ak 6:390.

124 O'Neill, 'Instituting principles: Between duty and action', pp. 342–3.

125 Ibid., p. 343.

126 David B. Wong, *Natural Moralities. A Defense of Pluralistic Relativism* (Oxford: Oxford University, 2006), p. 128.

127 Ibid., pp. 128–9.

128 Ibid., p. 129.

129 See for example Christine Korsgaard, *The Sources of Normativity* (Cambridge: Cambridge University Press, 1996).

130 This does not mean that we could not adopt a similar principle as a moral *ideal*. We could commit ourselves to strive towards the ideal of being able to help all those in need. However, the above principle requires us to actually help all those in need, and we should not commit ourselves to doing something we know we cannot do.

131 See for example Nussbaum, *The Fragility of Goodness*.

132 See for example David O. Brink, *Moral Realism and the Foundations of Ethics* (Cambridge: Cambridge University Press, 1989).

133 Dancy, *Ethics Without Principles*, p. 142.

134 David McNaughton, *Moral Vision, An Introduction to Ethics* (Oxford: Wiley-Blackwell, 1988), p. 205.

135 Aristotle, *Nicomachean Ethics*, second edition, translated and introduced by Terence Irwin (Indianapolis: Hackett Publishing Company, 1999), 1109b.

136 Dancy, *Ethics Without Principles*, pp. 101–8.

137 Haidt, 'The emotional dog and its rational tail', p. 814.

138 Ibid. p. 815.

139 See ibid.

140 Particularists like Dancy seem to accept this. See Dancy, *Ethics Without Principles*, pp. 148–55.

141 Haidt and his colleagues found out that extraneous feelings of disgust induced, for example, by sitting at a dirty desk makes

moral judgment more severe. See Schnall, Haidt, Clore and Jordan, 'Disgust as embodied moral judgment'.

142 Mallon and Nichols, 'Rules', pp. 302–3.

143 See Anscombe, 'Modern moral philosophy'; Alasdair MacIntyre, *After Virtue*. More recently, virtue ethicists have acknowledged that traditional principled ethics such as utilitarianism and Kantian ethics can allow for the importance of moral judgement. However, they still insist that it was only with the emergence of virtue ethics that generalists started to recognize the need for judgement. See Rosalind Hursthouse, *On Virtue Ethics* (Oxford: Oxford University Press, 1999), p. 40.

144 Nussbaum, *The Fragility of Goodness*, p. 310.

145 Lawrence Blum, 'Moral perception and particularity', *Ethics* 101 (1991), pp. 701–25, p. 701.

146 Charles E. Larmore, *Patterns of Moral Complexity* (Cambridge: Cambridge University Press, 1987), p. 12.

147 Ibid.

148 McNaughton, *Moral Vision*, p. 199.

149 Ibid.

150 John McDowell, 'Virtue and reason', in John McDowell, *Mind, Value, and Reality*. Cambridge, MA: Harvard University Press, 1998, pp. 50–73, p. 58.

151 McNaughton, *Moral Vision*, p. 190.

152 Mill, *Utilitarianism*, p. 70.

153 Ibid., p. 11.

154 Brad Hooker, *Ideal Code, Real World. A rule-consequentialist theory of morality* (Oxford: Oxford University Press, 2000), p. 88.

155 Hare, *Moral Thinking*, p. 212)

156 Immanuel Kant, *The Critique of Pure Reason* (Cambridge: Cambridge University Press, 1998), Paul Guyer and Allen W. Wood (eds), pp. 267–8; *Kants Werke* (Berlin: Walter de Gruyter, 1904/11), vol. 3, A 132–133 / B 171–2.

157 O'Neill, *Towards Justice and Virtue*, p. 78.

158 Scanlon, *What We Owe to Each Other*, p. 199.

159 See Dancy, *Ethics Without Principles*, pp. 135–7; 'Ethical particularism and morally relevant properties', pp. 530–47; Andrew Gleeson, 'Moral particularism reconfigured', *Philosophical*

Investigations 30 (2007), pp. 363–80; McNaughton, *Moral Vision*, pp. 62, pp. 190–205.

160   Charles Larmore, 'Moral judgement', *The Review of Metaphysics* 35 (1981), pp. 275–96, p. 293.

161   Benedict Smith, *Particularism and the Space of Moral Reasons* (New York: Palgrave Macmillan, 2011), p. 99.

162   Dancy, *Moral Reasons*, p. 64.

163   See McNaughton, *Moral Vision*, pp. 202–3; Jay L. Garfield, 'Particularity and principle: The structure of moral knowledge', in Brad Hooker and Margaret Olivia Little (eds), *Moral Particularism* (Oxford: Oxford University Press, 2000), pp. 178–204, pp. 199–204.

164   Gleeson, 'Moral particularism reconfigured', p. 372.

165   Velleman, *Practical Reflection*, p. 307.

166   This is corroborated by recent empirical work in moral psychology. See Prinz, *The Emotional Construction of Morals*, p. 272.

167   Dancy, *Moral Reasons*, p. 64. See also Gleeson, 'Moral particularism reconfigured', pp. 369–70.

168   McNaughton, *Moral Vision*, p. 203.

169   See John McDowell, 'Are moral requirements hypothetical imperatives?', *Proceeding of the Aristotelian Society, Supplementary Volumes* 52 (1978), pp. 13–29, p. 21.

170   In the second chapter I showed that many particularists and their generalist interlocutors conceive of moral principles as descriptive, truth-apt and explanatory propositions. Thus understood moral principles are 'word-to-world' directed and it is much more difficult to see why the acquisition of a rich set of moral sensibilities would not render such principles superfluous.

171   Given their commitment to cognitivism some particularists might be uneasy about taking this route. See Dancy, *Ethics Without Principles*, pp. 140–1. For alternative views see Sabine Roeser, 'A particularist epistemology: Affectual intuitionism', *Acta Analytica* 21 (2006), pp. 33–44; Sabine A. Döring, 'Seeing what to do: Affective perception and rational motivation', *Dialectica* 61 (2007), pp. 363–94.

172   See Shaun Nichols, *Sentimental Rules. On the Foundations of Moral Judgment* (Oxford: Oxford University Press, 2004); Prinz, *The Emotional Construction of Morals*.

173   Gleeson, 'Moral particularism reconfigured', p. 370.

174 Prinz, *The Emotional Construction of Morals*, p. 306.

175 Ibid., pp. 306–7.

176 This is a thought that can also be found in Kant's moral philosophy and has recently been developed by Christine Korsgaard. According to Korsgaard, 'the principles of practical reason are principles by means of which we constitute ourselves as unified agents' (*Self-Constitution. Agency, Identity, and Integrity* [Oxford: Oxford University Press, 2009], p. 25. Also see Christine Korsgaard, 'Personal identity and the unity of agency: A Kantian response to Parfit', in Christine Korsgaard, *Creating the Kingdom of Ends* [Cambridge: Cambridge University Press, 1996], pp. 363–97). I do not mean to commit myself to the details of Korsgaard's account here. In particular, Korsgaard's rationalist approach makes it difficult to account for the emotional component of principle-based moral judgement I alluded to earlier.

177 See Michael Bratman, 'Reflection, planning and temporally extended agency', in Michael Bratman, *Structure of Agency* (Oxford: Oxford University Press, 2007); Velleman, *Practical Reflection*.

178 Earlier in the book we saw that when particularists insist that moral principles are incompatible with context-sensitivity they usually have a different form of context-sensitivity in mind. They are concerned about cases where a particular act-token seems permissible even though there is a moral principle according to which actions of this type are forbidden. I offered an account of the defeasibility of moral principles in pages 138–56.

179 Dancy, 'Can the particularist learn the difference between right and wrong?', p. 70.

180 See ibid.

181 I borrow this analogy from Joshua Greene. See Joshua Greene, 'Beyond point-and-shoot morality: Why cognitive (neuro)science matters for ethics', *Ethics* (forthcoming). I do not mean to commit myself to any of the details of Greene's account. In particular, I do not subscribe to his view that moral heuristics are constituted by deontological principles, while the criterion of moral rightness is consequentialist.

182 This does not mean that an agent's understanding of these facts is divorced from, or prior to, what it is to be an agent. I argued that undertaking a commitment shapes an agent's experiences and sensibilities. An agent might be unable to fully understand certain

social and cultural facts about a society, for example, unless she has certain commitments such as a commitment for the welfare of some members of that society or a commitment to social justice. Our commitments shape who we are and how we see the world.

183 See Brad Hooker, *Ideal Code, Real World. A rule-consequentialist theory of morality* (Oxford: Oxford University Press, 2000); Robert M. Adams, 'Motive utilitarianism', *Journal of Philosophy* 73 (1976), pp. 467–81.

184 Walter Sinnott-Armstrong, *Moral Dilemmas* (Oxford: Oxford University Press, 1988), pp. 183–4.

185 Ibid., p. 29.

186 Mill, *Utilitarianism*.

187 Hare, *Moral Thinking*, p. 26.

188 Herman, *The Practice of Moral Judgment*, p. 173.

189 Alan Donagan, 'Consistency in rationalist moral systems', *The Journal of Philosophy* 81 (1984), pp. 291–309; 'Moral dilemmas, genuine and spurious: a comparative anatomy', *Ethics* 104 (1993), pp. 7–21.

190 See for example John Searle, 'Prima-facie obligations', in John Searle, *Philosophical Subjects: Essays presented to P. F. Strawson* (Oxford: Oxford University Press, 1980), pp. 238–59; Philippa Foot, 'Moral realism and moral dilemma', *Journal of Philosophy* 80 (1983), pp. 379–98; Judith J. Thomson, *The Realm of Rights* (Cambridge, MA: Harvard University Press, 1990); Brink: 'Moral conflict and its structure'.

191 Jean-Paul Sartre, *Existentialism is a Humanism* (New Haven: Yale University Press, 2007), John Kulka (ed.), trans. Carol Macomber, pp. 30–3.

192 Ibid., p. 33.

193 See Marcus, 'Moral dilemmas and consistency', p. 125.

194 See Hursthouse, *On Virtue Ethics*, pp. 47–8. However, Hursthouse acknowledges that utilitarians and deontologists can, and sometimes do, account for questions of moral character.

Conclusion

The current debate between moral particularists and moral generalists is notoriously obscure. Newcomers to the debate are usually puzzled by the plethora of terminology thrown at them and wonder what all the talk about holism, atomism, contributory reasons, default reasons, resultance bases or right- and wrong-making features is about. In Chapter One, I identified two main sources of confusion in the current particularist/generalist debate. First, I showed that particularists fail to specify their understanding of moral principles and principled ethics. Second, I pointed out that current particularists and their generalist interlocutors conflate the debate about the nature and roles of moral principles with a debate about the nature of moral reasons. I argued that these two debates should be kept apart. To some philosophers, clarifying and solving the problems of the current particularist/ generalist debate might not seem worth the trouble. They might view the problems as further evidence that particularism is an incoherent position that can be dismissed without further ado. I have shown that this response is mistaken. Suitably rephrased, particularism poses a serious challenge to defenders of principled ethics. The challenge is to show how particular moral judgements can – and why they should – be based on general moral principles. Generalists need to answer two important questions: how can moral principles accommodate the need for context-sensitivity, and why are principles necessary for moral thought and action? These are questions that generalists would have to address even if there were no particularists attacking their position. The fact that moral philosophy is dominated by principled approaches is no proof that morality is best understood in terms of principles. The widespread belief in, and reliance on, moral principles needs to be justified. In the absence of such a justification, the traditional link between morality and principles is little more than an unjustified prejudice. The central aim of this book has been to develop such a justification.

While initially many refused to take particularism seriously, over the last few years more and more moral philosophers have come to see the need to fend off the particularists' attack. Especially Dancy's theory has provoked an array of critical replies. Chapter Two of this book discussed the theories of Dancy's most prominent generalist critics, namely McKeever and Ridge's 'generalism as a regulative ideal', Väyrynen's theory of hedged moral principles, and Lance and Little's theory of defeasible generalizations. None of these theories stood up to scrutiny. In addition to various internal problems, these theories share one crucial deficiency: they disregard the practical use of moral principles. I have argued that by construing moral principles as exclusively theoretical principles, Dancy's generalist critics overlook the importance of practical reasoning, and the roles that moral principles play when we think about what to do. Dancy's generalist critics base their theories on an impoverished picture of moral reasoning. As a result, they fail to show how moral action can, and why it should, be based on moral principles. In contrast to Dancy's generalist critics, I have assigned moral principles a central role in practical reasoning.

The account of the nature and roles of moral principles I presented in Chapter Three of the book differs from the ones brought forward by Dancy's generalist critics in many respects. However, I am in agreement with Dancy's generalist critics on one important point. Like them, I have approached the question of how morality can, and why it should, be principle-based without any prior first-order theoretical commitments. It is important to stress that this does not mean that the account of moral principles I have defended in this book has no implications for first-order ethics. Dancy's generalist critics give the impression that a metaethical defence of moral principles can be entirely neutral with regard to first-order moral theories. But it is an illusion to assume that metaethical claims about the nature and roles of moral principles will have no implications for first-order moral theory. For example,

I have suggested that there is an irreducible plurality of defeasible moral principles. One cannot defend an irreducible plurality of defeasible moral principles on the metaethical level and at the same time be a traditional utilitarian on the first-order level. Moreover, I have argued against a conception of moral principles as rules of thumb. In particular, act-utilitarians tend to think of moral principles like 'Do not lie' as mere time- and thought-saving devices. First-order ethics that imply such an instrumental justification of moral principles are in conflict with the account of moral principles I presented in the third chapter of this book. In contrast to rules of thumb, moral principles as I construed them are far from being second-best strategies. According to my conception, moral principles are essential to a person's moral character and sensibility as well as her self-conception. That metaethical accounts of the nature and roles of moral principles have such implications for first-order ethics is not a problem. It does not mean that generalists can think about and defend moral principles only within the boundaries of a specific first-order moral theory. What it means is that metaethical generalists should reflect on the implications of their model of moral principles for first-order moral theories. Doing so is likely to help us decide between competing first-order moral theories. An ethical system that accords well with our chosen metaethical account of moral principles will be more plausible than one that does not. Examining the implication of the model of moral principles defended in this book for specific first-order moral theories promises to be fruitful, but goes beyond the scope of this book. The purpose of this book has been to defend the importance of moral principles at the same fundamental level at which particularists like Dancy purport to attack it.

I have defended the importance of moral principles by offering an account of their nature and roles in moral thought and action. In the third chapter of the book I showed that moral principles can accommodate the need for context-sensitivity in virtue of their indeterminacy and their defeasibility. Moreover, I argued that moral principles are constitutive of the capacity as well as the activity of moral judgement. Where does this leave the current debate between particularists and generalists? The authors of the debate tend to phrase their questions in absolute terms. Their central question is: are there moral principles? My answer is: it depends. It depends on one's conception of the nature and roles of moral principles. I have argued that it is implausible to think that there are exceptionless moral principles that can be applied without any insight, imagination or judgement. There are no moral algorithms. However, there are moral principles that function as internalized long-term commitments, and that due to their indeterminacy and defeasibility allow for context-sensitive use. What this shows is that there is no point in discussing whether or not ethics can and should be principled without having first reached an understanding of the nature and roles of moral principles. The current particularist/generalist debate needs to focus on the central question of what moral principles are and what roles they can play in moral thought and action. The primary question should no longer be whether someone is a particularist or generalist, but what form and function of principles he or she defends and opposes. The result would be a debate with fewer labels and fewer misunderstandings.

Having specified the nature and roles of moral principles, we can now also address the worries raised in the introduction of the book. There I asked how the complexity and diversity of moral and political life could possibly be captured in a finite set of principles. The answer lies in the indeterminacy of moral principles. Moral principles apply non-controversially only to those cases that lie at the stable core of the concepts they contain. In other cases they need to be interpreted. I argued that due to this indeterminacy, moral principles possess a flexibility that is crucial when we are confronted with new and challenging moral questions. Their indeterminate nature allows moral principles to be reasonably interpreted when they are applied to situations and problems that we did not foresee, or could not have foreseen, when we formulated or adopted the principles. Moreover, I have argued that since moral principles abstract away from the individual features of prototypical cases, they are flexible and adaptable in a way that a list of paradigms, prototypes, clearest cases and best examples is not. Moral principles can meet the diverse and ever-changing demands of moral and political life because they do not specify a definite set of cases to which they apply.

A further concern I raised in the introduction was that by focusing on general moral principles, we overlook the details of the particular situations we are confronted with. In the third chapter of the book I argued that the opposite is the case. Moral principles form and sharpen an agent's moral sensitivity. I claimed that by adopting and internalizing moral principles as long-term commitments moral agents develop and cultivate their moral sensibilities. Trying to live in accordance with their various moral and non-moral principles will help moral agents to become more sensitive to the needs of others and details of the situations with which they find themselves confronted.

Another common worry with regard to moral principles that I mentioned in the introduction is that they prescribe uniform action where we need to distinguish between the particular needs of particular individuals. Again, this worry is based on a misunderstanding of the nature of moral principles. Moral principles prescribe, forbid, recommend or condemn certain act-types, not act-tokens. They need, therefore, to be enacted or implemented. I pointed out that which act-token best implements the act-type specified by the principle depends on the details of the particular situation in which we find ourselves. The particular needs of the individuals involved in the situation are a crucial part of these context-dependent considerations.

The final sceptical concern I brought up in the introduction was that the good moral person is a person of empathy, sensibility, judgement and virtue, rather than a person of principle. In the third chapter of this book I showed that this is a false dichotomy. The person of good moral character and judgement *is* a person of principle.

It is important to be clear about what this book claims to have accomplished. This book defends the importance of moral principles by offering an account of their nature and roles in moral thought and action. However, I am far from claiming that this account of moral principles is in any way complete. This book offers a defence of moral principles, not a complete account of their nature and roles. For example, I have said nothing about the potential roles that moral principles might play in ensuring the stability of a society.[1] But even with regard to the roles of principles in moral reasoning – an issue to which I have devoted considerable space – more remains to be said. In this context one point is especially noteworthy. In this book, I have been concerned exclusively with the judgements and actions of *individual* moral agents. But moral reasoning is not a solitary endeavour. Further research is needed to see how the notion of moral principles and the framework of principle-based moral judgement developed in this book can be extended to *collective* moral reasoning. The term '*collective* moral reasoning' can be understood as referring either to a collective entity engaging in moral reasoning or to the collective reasoning process of a group of individuals. Understood in the first sense, collective reasoning raises interesting questions about corporate agency and corporate responsibility, in particular whether a corporation should be viewed as a moral agent. Would it be helpful if a corporation conceived of itself as a person of principle? How can moral principles guide and shape corporations? These are challenging and controversial questions. Understood in the second sense, collective moral reasoning raises questions of how we can reason morally *with one another*. One central problem when we reason with one another is moral disagreement. In this book, I have argued that moral principles apply non-controversially only to those cases that lie at the stable core of the concepts they contain. This offers an explanation for the phenomenon of moral disagreement since it leaves us with many cases in which the interpretation of moral principles will be a matter of controversy. Moreover, it is plausible to assume that what counts as a prototypical instance of a moral concept is at least to some extent culturally relative. This promises to be illuminating with regard to the phenomenon of cross-cultural moral disagreement. I believe that the account of moral principles developed in this book provides a fruitful starting point for further enquiry into the nature of moral reasoning.

This book showed that morality can, and should, be principled. But rather than putting an end to debates about principled ethics, it has opened up various new questions regarding the nature and roles of moral principles. Once one situates the rather narrow and self-contained debate between current particularists and generalists into a wider context, it becomes clear that questions about moral principles are crucial to the understanding of morality as well as the broader topic of practical reasoning. The history of moral philosophy has largely been a history of moral principles, and rightly so.

Note

1 Brad Hooker, for instance, argues that one of the main functions of moral principles is to increase the probability of conformity with certain mutually beneficial practices. See Brad Hooker, 'Moral particularism: Wrong and bad', in Brad Hooker and Margaret Olivia Little (eds), *Moral Particularism* (Oxford: Oxford University Press, 2000), pp. 1–22.

BIBLIOGRAPHY

Adams, R. M., 'Motive utilitarianism', *Journal of Philosophy* 73 (1976), pp. 467–81.

Akiba, K., 'Vagueness in the world', *Nous* 38 (2004), pp. 407–29.

Anscombe, G. E. M., 'Modern moral philosophy', *Philosophy* 33 (1958), pp. 1–19.

—*Intention*. Cambridge, MA: Harvard University Press, 2000, first published 1957.

Aristotle, *Nicomachean Ethics*, 2nd edn, translated and introduced by Terence Irwin. Indianapolis: Hackett Publishing Company, 1999.

Arras, J. D., 'Getting down to cases: the revival of casuistry in bioethics', *Journal of Medicine and Philosophy* 16 (1991), pp. 29–51.

Austin, J. L., 'A plea for excuses', in J. L. Austin, *Philosophical Papers*. Oxford: Oxford University Press, 1961, pp. 121–52.

Baier, A., 'Doing without moral theory?', in A. Baier, *Postures of the Mind. Essays on Mind and Morals*. London: Taylor & Francis, 1985, pp. 228–45.

Beauchamp, T. L. and J. F. Childress, *Principles of Biomedical Ethics*, 5th edn. Oxford: Oxford University Press, 2001.

Beauchamp, T. L. and D. DeGrazia, 'Principles and principlism', in G. Khushf (ed.), *Handbook of Bioethics*. Dordrecht: Springer, 2004, pp. 55–74.

Bedau, H. A., *Making Moral Choices. Three exercises in moral casuistry*. Oxford: Oxford University Press, 1997.

Bennett, J., 'Morality and consequences', in S. McMurrin (ed.), *The Tanner Lectures on Human Values*, vol. 2. Cambridge: Cambridge University Press 1981, pp. 45–116.

Bentham, J., *An Introduction to the Principles of Morals and Legislation*, J. H. Burns and H. L. A. Hart (eds). Oxford: Oxford University Press, 1996, first published 1789.

Berker, S., 'Particular reasons', *Ethics* 118 (2007), pp. 109–39.

Berlin, I., 'Two concepts of liberty', in I. Berlin, *Four Essays on Liberty*. Oxford: Oxford University Press, 1969, pp. 118–72.

Blum, L., 'Moral perception and particularity', *Ethics* 101 (1991),
    pp. 701–25.
—*Moral Perception and Particularity*, Cambridge: Cambridge University
    Press, 1994.
Boyd, R. N., 'How to be a moral realist', in G. Sayre-McCord (ed.),
    Essays on Moral Realism. New York: Cornell University Press, 1988,
    pp. 181–228.
Bradley, B., 'Against satisfying consequentialism.' *Utilitas* 18 (2006),
    pp. 97–108.
Bratman, M., *Intention, Plans, and Practical Reason*. Stanford: Center
    for the Study of Language and Information 1999, first published
    1987.
—'Taking plans seriously', in E. Millgram, *Varieties of Practical Reason*.
    Cambridge: Cambridge University Press, 2001, pp. 203–19.
—'Reflection, planning and temporally extended agency', in
    M. Bratman, *Structure of Agency*. Oxford: Oxford University Press,
    2007.
Brink, D. O., *Moral Realism and the Foundations of Ethics*. Cambridge:
    Cambridge University Press, 1989.
—'Moral conflict and its structure', in H. E. Mason (ed.), *Moral
    Dilemmas and Moral Theory*. Oxford: Oxford University Press, 1996,
    pp. 102–26.
Brix, B., *Law, Language and Legal Determinacy*. Oxford: Clarendon
    Press, 1993, pp. 7–35.
Broome, J., 'Reasons', in J. Wallace, P. Pettit, S. Scheffler and M. Smith
    (eds), *Reasons and Values. Themes from the Philosophy of Joseph
    Raz*. Oxford: Oxford University Press, 2004, pp. 28–55.
Cargile, J., 'The Sorites Paradox', *British Journal for the Philosophy of
    Science* 20 (1969), pp. 193–202.
Cartwright, N., *How the Laws of Physics Lie*. Oxford: Clarendon Press,
    1983.
Chang, R., 'Introduction', in R. Chang (ed.), *Incommensurability,
    Incomparability, and Practical Reason*. Cambridge, MA: Harvard
    University Press, 1997), pp. 1–34.
Cicero, M. T., *On Obligations. Translated with an introduction and
    notes by P. G. Walsh*. Oxford: Oxford University Press, 2011.
Coady, C. A. J. and O. O'Neill, 'Messy morality and the art of the
    possible', *Proceeding of the Aristotelian Society, Supplementary
    Volumes* 64 (1990), pp. 259–94.
Coleman, L. and P. Kay, 'Prototype semantics: the English word lie',
    Language 57 (1981), pp. 26–44.
Copp, D., 'Explanation and justification in ethics', *Ethics* 100 (1990),
    pp. 237–58.

Crisp, R., 'Particularizing particularism', in B. Hooker and M. O. Little (eds), *Moral Particularism*. Oxford: Oxford University Press, 2000, pp. 23–47.

—'Ethics without reasons?', *Journal of Moral Philosophy* 4 (2007), pp. 40–9.

Cullity, G., 'Particularism and presumptive reasons', *Proceeding of the Aristotelian Society, Supplementary Volumes* 76 (2002), pp. 169–90.

Cullity, G. and R. Holton, 'Particularism and moral theory', *Proceedings of the Aristotelian Society, Supplementary Volumes* 76 (2002), pp. 169–209.

Dancy, J., 'On moral properties', *Mind* 90 (1981), pp. 367–85.

—'Intuitionism in meta-epistemology', *Philosophical Studies* 42 (1982), pp. 395–408.

—'Ethical particularism and morally relevant properties', *Mind* 92 (1983), pp. 530–47.

—'The role of imaginary cases in ethics', *Pacific Philosophical Quarterly* 66 (1985), pp. 141–53.

—'Holism in the theory of reasons', *Cogito* 6 (1992), pp. 136–38.

—*Moral Reasons*. Oxford: Blackwell, 1993.

—'Can the particularist learn the difference between right and wrong?', in K. Brinkmann (ed.), *The Proceedings of the Twentieth World Congress of Philosophy. Vol. 1 Ethics*. Bowling Green: Philosophy Documentation Center, 1999, pp. 59–72.

—*Ethics Without Principles*. Oxford: Oxford University Press, 2004.

—'Enticing reasons', in J. Wallace, P. Pettit, S. Scheffler and M. Smith (eds), *Reasons and Values. Themes from the Philosophy of Joseph Raz*. Oxford: Oxford University Press, 2004, pp. 91–118.

—'What do reasons do?', in T. Horgan and M. Timmons (eds), *Metaethics After Moore*. Oxford: Oxford University Press, 2006, pp. 39–59.

—'When reasons don't rhyme', *The Philosopher's Magazine* 37 (2007), pp. 19–24.

—'An unprincipled morality', in R. Shafer-Landau (ed.), *Ethical Theory. An Anthology*. Oxford: Oxford University Press, 2007, pp. 771–74.

—'Defending the right', *Journal of Moral Philosophy* 4 (2007), pp. 85–98.

—'Review: Sean McKeever and Michael Ridge, principled ethics: Generalism as a regulative ideal. Oxford: Clarendon press, 2006', *Mind* 116 (2007), pp. 462–7.

—'Moral particularism', in E. N. Zalta (ed.), *The Stanford Encyclopedia of Philosophy* (Fall 2013 Edition), http://plato. stanford.edu/archives/fall2013/entries/moral-particularism/ [accessed 5 January 2014].

Davidson, D., 'The logical form of action sentences', in D. Davidson, *Essays on Actions and Events*, 2nd edn. Oxford: Oxford University Press, 2001, pp. 105–22.

—'The individuation of events,' in D. Davidson, *Essays on Actions and Events*. Oxford: Oxford University Press, 2001, pp. 163–80.

Donagan, A., *The Theory of Morality*. Chicago: University of Chicago Press, 1977.

—'Consistency in rationalist moral systems', *The Journal of Philosophy* 81 (1984), pp. 291–309.

—'Moral dilemmas, genuine and spurious: a comparative anatomy', *Ethics* 104 (1993), pp. 7–21.

Döring, S. A., 'Seeing what to do: affective perception and rational motivation', *Dialectica* 61 (2007), pp. 363–94.

Dummett, M., 'Wang's paradox', *Synthese* 30 (1975), pp. 301–24.

Dworkin, R., *Taking Rights Seriously*. Cambridge, Mass.: Harvard University Press, 1977.

—*Justice for Hedgehogs*. Cambridge Mass.: Harvard University Press, 2011.

Earman, J. and J. Roberts, 'Ceteris Paribus, there is no problem of provisos', *Synthese* 118 (1999), pp. 438–78.

Flanagan, O., *Varieties of Moral Personality. Ethics and Psychological Realism*. Cambridge, Mass.: Harvard University Press, 1991.

Foot, P., 'Abortion and the doctrine of double effect', *Oxford Review* 5 (1967), pp. 28–41.

—'The problem of abortion and the doctrine of the double effect', in P. Foot, *Virtues and Vices and Other Essays in Moral Philosophy*. Oxford: Oxford University Press, 1978, pp. 19–32.

—'Moral realism and moral dilemma', *Journal of Philosophy* 80 (1983), pp. 379–98.

Frankfurt, H., 'Freedom of the will and the concept of a person', *Journal of Philosophy* 68 (1971), pp. 5–20.

Frazier, R. L., 'Moral relevance and ceteris paribus principles', *Ratio* 8 (1995), pp. 113–27.

Garfield, J. L., 'Particularity and principle: the structure of moral knowledge', in B. Hooker and M. O. Little (eds), *Moral Particularism*. Oxford: Oxford University Press, 2000, pp. 178–204.

Gert, B., *The Moral Rules. A New Rational Foundation For Morality*. New York: Harper & Row, 1973.

Gibbard, A., *Wise Choices, Apt Feelings. A Theory of Normative Judgment*. Oxford: Oxford University Press, 1990.

Gilligan, C., *In a Different Voice. Psychological Theory and Women's Development*. Cambridge, MA: Harvard University Press, 1982.

Gleeson, A., 'Moral particularism reconfigured', *Philosophical Investigations* 30 (2007), pp. 363–80.

Goldman, A. H., *Practical Rules. When we need them and when we don't*. Cambridge: Cambridge University Press, 2002.

Greene, J., 'Beyond point-and-shoot morality: why cognitive (neuro) science matters for ethics', *Ethics* (forthcoming).

Greene, J. and J. Haidt, 'Where (and how) does moral judgement work?', *Trends in Cognitive Sciences* 6 (2002), pp. 517–23.

Griffin, J., *Well-Being: Its Meaning and Measurement*. Oxford: Oxford University Press, 1986.

—'Incommensurability: what's the problem?', in R. Chang, *Incommensurability, Incomparability, and Practical Reason*. Cambridge, Mass.: Harvard University Press, 1997, pp. 35–51.

Gruzalski, B., 'Foreseeable consequence utilitarianism', *Australasian Journal of Philosophy* 59 (1981), pp. 163–76.

Haidt, J., 'The emotional dog and its rational tail', *Psychological Review* 108 (2001), pp. 814–34.

Hare, R. M., *Freedom and Reason*. Oxford: Oxford University Press, 1963.

—*Moral Thinking: Its Levels, Method, and Point*. Oxford: Oxford University Press, 1981.

—'Principles', in R. M. Hare, *Essays in Ethical Theory*. Oxford: Oxford University Press, 1989.

Harman, G., *Change in View. Principles of Reasoning*. Cambridge, MA: Harvard University Press, 1986.

—'Moral particularism and transduction', *Philosophical Issues* 14 (2005), pp. 44–55.

Harsanyi, J. C., 'Bayesian decision theory and utilitarian ethics', *The American Economic Review* 68 (1978), pp. 223–8.

Hart, H. L. A., 'Positivism and the separation of law and morals', *Harvard Law Review* 71 (1958), pp. 593–629.

—*The Concept of Law*, Oxford: Oxford University Press, 1961.

Herman, B., *The Practice of Moral Judgment*. Cambridge, MA: Harvard University Press, 1996.

Hill, T. E. Jr., 'Making exceptions without abandoning the principle: or how a Kantian might think about terrorism', in T. E. Hill Jr., *Dignity and Practical Reason in Kant's Moral Theory*. New York: Cornell University Press, 1992, pp. 196–225.

—'Moral dilemmas, gaps, and residues: a Kantian perspective', in H. E. Mason (ed.), *Moral Dilemmas and Moral Theory*. Oxford: Oxford University Press, 1996, pp. 167–98.

Hooker, B., *Ideal Code, Real World. A Rule-Consequentialist Theory of Morality*. Oxford: Oxford University Press, 2000.

—'Moral particularism: wrong and bad', in B. Hooker and M. O. Little, *Moral Particularism*. Oxford: Oxford University Press, 2000, pp. 1–22.

Horkheimer, M. and T. W. Adorno, *Dialectic of Enlightenment.*
Philosophical Fragments, G. Schmid Noerr (ed.), trans. E. Jephcott.
Stanford: Stanford University Press, 2002.

Horty, J. F., 'Reasons as defaults', *Philosophers' Imprint* 7 (2007),
pp. 1–28.

Hurka, T., *Perfectionism.* Oxford: Oxford University Press, 1993.

Hursthouse, R., *On Virtue Ethics.* Oxford: Oxford University Press,
1999.

Jackson, F., P. Pettit and M. Smith, 'Ethical particularism and patterns',
in B. Hooker and M. O. Little (eds), *Moral Particularism.* Oxford:
Oxford University Press, 2000, pp. 79–99.

Jonsen, A. R., 'Casuistry: an alternative or complement to principles?',
Kennedy Institute of Ethics Journal 5 (1995), pp. 237–51.

Jonsen, A. R. and S. Toulmin, *The Abuse of Casuistry. A History and
Moral Reasoning.* Berkeley: University of California Press, 1989.

Kagan, S., *The Limits of Morality.* Oxford: Oxford University Press,
1989.

—'The Additive Fallacy', *Ethics* 99 (1988), pp. 5–31.

Kamm, F. M., *Morality, Mortality,* vol. 2. Oxford: Oxford University
Press, 1996.

—*Intricate Ethics. Rights, Responsibilities, and Permissible Harms.*
Oxford: Oxford University Press, 2007.

Kant, I., *Groundwork of the Metaphysics of Morals*, in M. J. Gregor
(ed.), *Immanuel Kant. Practical Philosophy.* Cambridge: Cambridge
University Press, 1996.

—*On the common saying: That may be correct in theory, but it is of
no use in practice*, in M. J. Gregor (ed.), *Immanuel Kant. Practical
Philosophy.* Cambridge: Cambridge University Press, 1996.

Keefe, R., *Theories of Vagueness.* Cambridge: Cambridge University
Press, 2000.

Kirchin, S., 'Particularism, generalism and the counting argument',
European Journal of Philosophy 11 (2003), pp. 54–71.

—'Particularism and default valency', *Journal of Moral Philosophy* 4
(2007), pp. 16–32.

Korsgaard, C., *The Sources of Normativity.* Cambridge University Press,
1996.

—'Personal identity and the unity of agency: a Kantian response to
Parfit', in C. Korsgaard, *Creating the Kingdom of Ends.* Cambridge:
Cambridge University Press, 1996, pp. 363–97.

—*Self-Constitution. Agency, Identity, and Integrity.* Oxford: Oxford
University Press, 2009.

Kramer, M., *Objectivity and the Rule of Law.* Cambridge: Cambridge
University Press, 2007.

—*Moral Realism as a Moral Doctrine*. Oxford: John Wiley & Sons, 2009, pp. 113–26.

Lance, M. N. and M. O. Little, 'Defeasibility and the normative grasp of context', *Erkenntnis* 61 (2004), pp. 435–55.

—'Particularism and antitheory', in D. Copp (ed.), *The Oxford Handbook of Ethical Theory*. Oxford: Oxford University Press, 2006, pp. 567–94.

—'Where the laws are', in R. Shafer-Landau (ed.), *Oxford Studies in Metaethics*. Oxford: Oxford University Press, 2007, pp. 149–71.

—'From particularism to defeasibility in ethics', in M. N. Lance, M. Potrc, and V. Strahovnik (eds), *Challenging Moral Particularism. Routledge Studies in Ethics and Moral Theory*. New York: Routledge, 2008, pp. 53–74.

Larmore, C. E., 'Moral judgement', *The Review of Metaphysics* 35 (1981), pp. 275–96.

—*Patterns of Moral Complexity*. Cambridge: Cambridge University Press, 1987.

Lind, A. and J. Brännmark, 'Particularism in question: an interview with Jonathan Dancy', *Theoria* 74 (2008), pp. 3–17.

Lipton, P., 'All else being equal', *Philosophy* 74 (1999), pp. 155–68.

Little, M. O., 'Moral generalities revisited', in B. Hooker and M. O. Little (eds), *Moral Particularism*. Oxford: Oxford University Press, 2000, pp. 276–304.

MacCallum, G. C., 'Negative and positive freedom', *Philosophical Review* 76 (1967), pp. 312–34.

MacIntyre, A., *After Virtue*. Notre Dame: University of Notre Dame Press, 1981.

Mackie, J. L., *Ethics. Inventing Right and Wrong*. London: Pelican Books, 1977, pp. 36–8.

Mallon, R. and S. Nichols, 'Rules', in J. M. Doris and the Moral Psychology Research Group (eds), *The Moral Psychology Handbook*. Oxford: Oxford University Press, 2010, pp. 297–320.

Marcus, R. B., 'Moral dilemmas and consistency', *Journal of Philosophy* 77 (1980), pp. 121–36.

McClennen, E. F., 'The rationality of being guided by rules', in A. R. Mele and P. Rawling (eds), *The Oxford Handbook of Rationality*. Oxford: Oxford University Press, 2004, pp. 222–39.

McDowell, J., 'Are moral requirements hypothetical imperatives?', *Proceeding of the Aristotelian Society, Supplementary Volumes* 52 (1978), pp. 13–29.

—'Comments on "Some rational aspects of incontinence"', *Southern Journal of Philosophy* 27 (1988), pp. 89–102.

—'Virtue and reason' in J. McDowell, *Mind, Value, and Reality*.
  Cambridge, MA: Harvard University Press, 1998, pp. 50–73.
—'Values and secondary qualities', in J. McDowell, *Mind, Value and
  Reality*. Cambridge, MA: Harvard University Press, 1998, pp. 131–50.
McKeever, S. and M. Ridge, *Principled Ethics. Generalism as a
  Regulative Ideal*. Oxford: Clarendon Press, 2006.
—'Preempting principles: recent debates in moral particularism',
  Philosophy Compass 3/6 (2008), pp. 1177–92.
McNaughton, D., *Moral Vision. An Introduction to Ethics*. Oxford:
  Wiley-Blackwell, 1988.
—'An unconnected heap of duties?', *The Philosophical Quarterly* 46
  (1996), pp. 433–47.
McNaughton, D. and P. Rawling, 'Unprincipled ethics', in B. Hooker and
  M. O. Little (eds), *Moral Particularism*. Oxford: Oxford University
  Press, 2000, pp. 256–75.
Mill, J. S., *Utilitarianism*, R. Crisp (ed.). Oxford: Oxford University
  Press, 1998.
Millgram, E., 'Practical reasoning: the current state of play', in E.
  Millgram (ed.), *Varieties of Practical Reasoning*. Cambridge:
  Cambridge University Press, 2001, pp. 1–26.
Moore, G. E., *Principia Ethica*, rev. edn, T. Baldwin (ed.). Cambridge:
  Cambridge University Press, 1993.
Nichols, S., *Sentimental Rules. On the Foundations of Moral Judgment*.
  Oxford: Oxford University Press, 2004.
Noddings, N., *Caring. A Feminine Approach to Ethics and Moral
  Education*. Berkeley: University of California Press, 1984.
Nussbaum, M. C., *Love's Knowledge: Essays on Philosophy and
  Literature*. Oxford: Oxford University Press, 1990.
—*The Fragility of Goodness. Luck and Ethics in Greek Tragedy and
  Philosophy*, rev. edn. Cambridge: Cambridge University Press,
  2001.
O'Neill, O., *Towards Justice and Virtue. A Constructive Account of
  Practical Reasoning*. Cambridge: Cambridge University Press, 1996.
—'Four models of practical reasoning', in O. O'Neill, *Bounds of Justice*.
  Cambridge: Cambridge University Press, 2000, pp. 11–28.
—'Practical principles and practical judgement', *Hastings Center Report*
  31 (2001), pp. 15–23.
—'Instituting principles: between duty and action', in M. Timmons (ed.),
  Kant's Metaphysics of Morals: Interpretative Essays. Oxford: Oxford
  University Press, 2002, pp. 331–47.
Parfit, D., *Reasons and Persons*. Oxford: Oxford University Press, 1986.
Parsons, T. and P. Woodruff, 'Worldly indeterminacy of identity',
  Proceedings of the Aristotelian Society 95 (1995), pp. 171–91.

Pietroski, P. M., 'Prima facie obligations, ceteris paribus laws in moral theory', *Ethics* 103 (1993), pp. 489–515.

Pietroski, P. M. and G. Rey, 'When others things aren't equal: saving ceteris paribus laws from vacuity', *British Journal of the Philosophy of Science* 46 (1995), pp. 81–110.

Prinz, J., *The Emotional Construction of Morals*. Oxford: Oxford University Press, 2007.

Rachels, J., 'Active and passive euthanasia', *The New England Journal of Medicine* 292 (1975), pp. 78–90.

Raz, J., *The Morality of Freedom*. Oxford: Oxford University Press, 1986.

—*Engaging Reason: On the Theory of Value and Action*. Oxford: Oxford University Press, 1999.

—'The truth in particularism', in B. Hooker and M. O. Little (eds), *Moral Particularism*. Oxford: Oxford University Press, 2000, pp. 48–78.

—'The trouble with particularism', *Mind* 115 (2006), pp. 99–120.

Richardson, H. S., 'Specifying norms as a way to resolve concrete ethical problems', *Philosophy and Public Affairs* 19 (1990), pp. 279–310.

Ridge, M., 'The many moral particularisms', *Canadian Journal of Philosophy* 35 (2005), pp. 83–106.

Roeser, S., 'A particularist epistemology: affectual intuitionism', *Acta Analytica* 21 (2006), pp. 33–44.

Rosch, E., 'Principles of categorization', in E. Rosch and B. B. Lloyd (eds), *Cognition and Categorization*. New Jersey: Lawrence Erlbaum, 1978, pp. 27–48.

Ross, W. D., *The Right and the Good*, P. Stratton-Lake (ed.). Oxford: Oxford University Press, 2002, first published 1930.

Russell, B., 'Vagueness', *Australasian Journal of Psychology and Philosophy* 1 (1923), pp. 84–92.

Sainsbury, R. Mark, 'Concepts without boundaries', in R. Keefe and P. Smith (eds), *Vagueness. A Reader*. Cambridge, MA: Harvard University Press, 1996, pp. 251–64.

Sandel, M., *Liberalism and the Limits of Justice*. Cambridge: Cambridge University Press, 1998.

Sartre, J.-P., *Existentialism is a Humanism*, J. Kulka (ed.), trans. C. Macomber. New Haven: Yale University Press, 2007.

Scanlon, T. M., *What We Owe to Each Other*. Cambridge, MA: Harvard University Press 2000, first published 1998.

Schauer, F., *Playing By The Rules. A Philosophical Examination of Rule-Based Decision-Making in Law and in Life*. Oxford: Oxford University Press, 1991.

Schiffer, S., 'Ceteris paribus laws', *Mind* 100 (1991), pp. 1–17.

Schnall, S., J. Haidt, G. L. Clore and A. H. Jordan, 'Disgust as embodied moral judgment', *Personality and Social Psychology Bulletin* 34 (2008), pp. 1096–109.

Schroeder, M., 'A matter of principle', *Nous* 43 (2009), pp. 568–80.

—*Slaves of the Passions*. Oxford: Oxford University Press, 2007.

Searle, J., 'Prima-facie obligations', in J. Searle, *Philosophical Subjects: Essays presented to P. F. Strawson*. Oxford: Oxford University Press, 1980, pp. 238–59.

Shafer-Landau, R., 'Moral rules', *Ethics* 107 (1997), pp. 584–611.

Shenon, P., 'Senators clash with nominee over torture and limits of law', *New York Times*, 19 October 2007.

Simon, H. A., *Models of Man. Social and Rational. Mathematical essays on rational human behavior in a social setting*. London: Wiley, 1957.

Singer, M. G., 'Actual consequence utilitarianism', *Mind* 86 (1977), pp. 67–77.

Sinnott-Armstrong, W., *Moral Dilemmas*. Oxford: Oxford University Press, 1988.

Slote, M., *Common-Sense Morality and Consequentialism*. London: Routledge, 1985.

Smith, B., *Particularism and the Space of Moral Reasons*. New York: Palgrave Macmillan, 2011.

—*The Moral Problem*. Oxford: Blackwell, 1994.

Strong, C., 'Specified principlism: What is it, and does it really resolve cases better than casuistry?', *Journal of Medicine and Philosophy* 25 (2000), pp. 323–41.

Sunstein, C. R., 'Moral heuristics', *Behavioral and Brain Sciences* 28 (2005), pp. 531–73.

Thomson, J. J., 'A defence of abortion', *Philosophy and Public Affairs* 1 (1971), pp. 47–66.

—'Killing, letting die, and the Trolley Problem', *The Monist* 59 (1976), pp. 204–17.

—'The Trolley Problem', in J. J. Thomson, *Rights, Restitution, and Risk. Essays in Moral Theory*. Cambridge, MA: Harvard University Press, 1986, pp. 94–114.

—*The Realm of Rights*. Cambridge, MA: Harvard University Press, 1990.

Tooley, M., 'Abortion and infanticide', *Philosophy and Public Affairs* 2 (1972), pp. 37–65.

Toulmin, S., 'The tyranny of principles', *The Hasting Center Report* 11 (1981), pp. 31–9.

Trammell, R., 'Saving life and taking life', *Journal of Philosophy* 72 (1975), pp. 131–7.

Tye, M., 'Vague objects', *Mind* 99 (1990), pp. 535–57.

Väyrynen, P., 'Usable moral principles', in M. N. Lance, M. Potrc and V. Strahovnik (eds), *Challenging Moral Particularism. Routledge Studies in Ethics and Moral Theory*. New York: Routledge, 2008, pp. 75–106.

—'Particularism and default reasons', *Ethical Theory and Moral Practice* 7 (2004), pp. 53–79.

—'Moral generalism: enjoy in moderation', *Ethics* 116 (2006), pp. 707–41.

—'Ethical theories and moral guidance', *Utilitas* 18 (2006), pp. 291–309.

—'A theory of hedged moral principles', in R. Shafer Landau (ed.), *Oxford Studies in Metaethics*, vol. 4. Oxford: Oxford University Press, 2009, pp. 91–132.

—'Moral particularism', in C. B. Miller (ed.), *Continuum Companion to Ethics*. London: Continuum, 2011, pp. 247–60.

Velleman, J. D., *The Possibility of Practical Reason*. Oxford: Clarendon Press, 2000.

—*Practical Reflection*. Stanford: Center for the Study of Language and Information, 2007.

Walzer, M., 'Political action: the problem of dirty hands', *Philosophy and Public Affairs* 2 (1973), pp. 160–80.

—*Spheres of Justice: A Defense of Pluralism and Equality*. New York: Basic Books, 1983.

Williams, B., 'Ethical consistency', *Proceeding of the Aristotelian Society, Supplementary Volumes* 39 (1965), pp. 103–24.

—*Ethics and the Limits of Philosophy*. London: Routledge, 1985.

—'Persons, character and morality', in B. Williams, *Moral Luck. Philosophical Papers 1973–1980*. Cambridge: Cambridge University Press, 1981, pp. 1–19.

Williamson, T. and P. Simons, 'Vagueness and ignorance', *Proceedings of the Aristotelian Society, Supplementary Volumes* 66 (1992), pp. 145–77.

Wong, D. B., *Natural Moralities. A Defense of Pluralistic Relativism*. Oxford: Oxford University, 2006.

INDEX